Supper Smoke

With A Dash of Sage

By
Ruby A. Seaman

authorHOUSE™

1663 LIBERTY DRIVE, SUITE 200
BLOOMINGTON, INDIANA 47403
(800) 839-8640
WWW.AUTHORHOUSE.COM

This book is a work of non-fiction. Unless otherwise noted, the author and the publisher make no explicit guarantees as to the accuracy of the information contained in this book and in some cases, names of people and places have been altered to protect their privacy.

© 2005 Ruby A. Seaman. All Rights Reserved.

No part of this book may be reproduced, stored in a retrieval system, or transmitted by any means without the written permission of the author.

First published by AuthorHouse 09/27/05

ISBN: 1-4208-7778-X (sc)
ISBN: 1-4208-7779-8 (dj)

Library of Congress Control Number: 2005907411

Printed in the United States of America
Bloomington, Indiana

This book is printed on acid-free paper.

The author wishes to acknowledge that most of the recipes in this book are not original, but have been collected from a variety of sources through many years.

She feels the success of this book is largely due to the generous sharing of the treasured recipes of family and friends, and wishes to heartily thank each one. Where mistakes have occurred in any way, she asks your pardon.

A special thank you is extended to Karen Seaman, who graciously took time from her busy schedule to create the beautiful artwork for the cover of this book.

The author wishes to gratefully acknowledge the skillful assistance and encouragement of Kris Schulte in the preparation of this book for publication.

The author wishes to acknowledge that most of the recipes in this book are not original, but have been collected from a variety of sources through many years.

She feels the success of this book is largely due to the generous sharing of the treasured recipes of family and friends, and wishes to heartily thank each one. Where mistakes have occurred in any way, she asks your pardon.

A special thank you is extended to Karen Seaman, who graciously took time from her busy schedule to create the beautiful artwork for the cover of this book.

The author wishes to gratefully acknowledge the skillful assistance and encouragement of Kris Schulte in the preparation of this book for publication.

Supper Smoke

A lonely wayfarer was he
Traversing alien land.
A goal had he, yet days ahead,
And dusk was nigh at hand.

All day he'd trod a solemn trail;
Each step entwined with thought.
And now, the sun had lately fled,
And dreads, the shadows wrought!

His feet burned hot for cooling wash.
His back grew numb with cold;
Head bowed, arms bent to thrust him on,
Lest courage loose its hold.

But then! O'er gentle rise he'd come,
And there, so humbly sheaved,
A gentle scene awakened him
To hungers, now perceived.

A light spilled from a little pane
Like treasures' hidden glow;
And supper smoke twined up the hill
And wreathed the scene below.

His soul hankered for simple folk
To sup with, and converse,
And to relax in such abode
And dwell on naught adverse.

A' weary, shod in crumbling boot,
And coat with damp earth soiled,
He turned to lift his burden up,
Such hopes within him foiled.

Yet HARK! That crudest door was flung
Awide! And spilling forth,
A tide of warmth now stemmed the chill;
The sight- a fortunes' worth!

And then, a manly, boisterous shout!
And gentler feet gave pause;
Stepped to his side, and bid him come
Where guarded home-fire was!

....

As travelers all, pray future eve;
All burdens cast aside,
We'll find a Golden Door flung wide,
And Joy and Warmth inside!

          R.A.S.

Introduction

I've wanted to write this book for ever so long. It's just that I haven't known how to begin.

Introduction? Acknowledgements? Dedication? Preface?

Well, I've been casting about for around two minutes, and I see that the introduction is done!

I may deal with acknowledgements later. Dedications? Got that.

As for the preface…I want so much to keep this book simple.

I'd rather tell a story

Once upon a time there lived a maiden by a cool, green river in North Idaho. She had quite a good time growing up. She, with her friends and siblings, jumped in and out of the cool, green river all summer, jumped in and out of the cold snows in winter, and between and among these, she read and slept; she worked, ate and grew.

Lots and lots of good things happened to her as she grew. Some bad things happened too. She forgot some of the good things, and remembered too many of the bad ones.

Did you know that this adds up to a bad word? Yes. The bad word is "bitter."

This bitter young maiden went out into the world and built herself a house of sticks. It wasn't a very good house at all, and sometimes it was really cold inside. There was hardly any food, and in the dark nights, and in the storms, it trembled and shook. But the young maiden didn't care, she said, because she was HAVING FUN. (Sometimes in the night, when the house shook, she cared A LOT. But she didn't tell anyone. Not even herself.)

She learned how to work hard, how to keep her little house of sticks neat and clean, and how to save money for the things she wanted. She did NOT learn to cook. She didn't care. She was HAVING FUN. She ate at her job, or otherwise she ate apples and potato chips and candy bars.

Then one fine day a handsome prince rode into her life on a shining steed. (Well, in truth it was a battered old Dodge.) The young prince smiled. Her heart went BUMP, BUMP, THUMP, and she smiled back. They fell in love, and one summer day, they married and lived happily ever after, or at least the rest of the summer.

One bright morning, after the honeymoon, the maiden arose, trotted to the kitchen, and began to make a breakfast for her shining prince. Soon he stood at her side and cautiously said, "Honey, you don't need to put oil in the pan to fry bacon."

"OH!"

The days, the weeks, and the months went by, and many things happened to the maiden and the prince. Many of them were good, and some were not. They began to see that they, together, were living in a house of sticks. And again, in the night it shook and trembled. (They didn't tell anyone. Not even themselves.) They didn't care, they said. They were HAVING FUN.

But now we shall hurry to the better part of this story. I can hardly wait to tell it.

GOD CARED

This is the most amazing thing about God. He can see way, WAY, down into our hearts. So far can He see that He knows more about us than we know ourselves. He sees the bitterness, the unanswered questions, and all the things that are stuffed way down DEEP. He cares enough to want to go way down to the bottom and clean us up.

He knows how.

But first, He must find a way to tell us this, because He will not, nor CAN He do this without our asking.

And you know what?

God reached down into that shaky little house of sticks, and He found a way to tell them.

They said, "YES, CLEAN US UP!"

And He did.

I am writing this little story over forty years later. It still brings tears to my eyes to remember how He came.

My handsome prince and I no longer live in a house of sticks. God has taken out the bitterness and un-answered questions. Our house no longer trembles and shakes, for God is the foundation. If the storms come (and they still do) or we awake in the night and are afraid, He comforts us. He stays awake all night, and He rides above the storms.

And now I want to end this story with the first recipe of the book. It is the very best one.

I will note here that all the ingredients are necessary, and it won't work to substitute, although the amounts may vary some.

Salvation

Ingredients:
1 house of sticks
¾ cup knowledge of God
1½ cups need
2 heaping cups sorry
2½ cups brokenness
4 cups prayer
2 cups faith
1 cup thanksgiving

Sift together the house of sticks, knowledge of God, need and the sorry.
Set aside.
In large mixing bowl combine brokenness and prayer. Beat well.
Add sifted ingredients alternately with faith and thanksgiving, blending well.
Bake in the arms of God.
Serve warm.

Dedication

In the first place, I wish to dedicate this book to God; to a God of love. Without His caring, our house of sticks would have long ago crumbled and blown away.

Next to my faithful husband Richard, who, having been a bachelor, did his best to teach me how to cook. He also bore long with me, and politely shoveled down one flop after another. Now he politely shovels down one new creation after another, while quietly longing for spuds and gravy.

And to these, our children…. and our joy:

To Tamara Anne, who challenges me to think.

To our son-in-law Dwight, who likes my bread pockets and divinity and who shares my love of coffee, and our daughter.

To Marla Sue, our traveler, who is thoughtful, and who knows my soul.

To Kirk Richard, who has always been a quiet rock for me.

To our daughter-in-law Karen, a wonderful cook, but mostly a very dear daughter.

And to these our grandchildren…. and our delight:

To Chad Douglas, who is thoughtful, and a knower of souls.

To Amber Jo, a whirlwind of brown eyes, determination, and spice.

To Brittany Anne who possesses treasures of the mind, and is a lover of creatures, both great and small.

To Jodi Rose, who is talkative and helpful.

To Jackie Nichole, who is able to dwell in solitary places.

To Callista Jo, who skips placidly and happily through her days.

To these my beloved, I dedicate this book. But not to these only, but to some young bride I may never know, who wakes up some morning to discover that she can't fry bacon! I wish to keep this book simple and plain, for such as these.

Have you heard of the bride of South Wooster?
She knew not a roast from a rooster!
Oh, how that gal tried!
But her dear husband cried.
"I wish you could cook like Mom used t'er!"

Albert

Martin and Amelia Amoth, my father's parents, came from Minnesota to North Dakota in about 1895. They established a homestead, built a sod house, and began pioneer life on the open prairie. The little family faced many hardships, but my father enjoyed a happy childhood. He was surrounded by a close-knit and loving family. They worked, laughed and played together. The winters were always long, lonely and severe, but Dad's eyes sparkled as he told us of how the prairie would suddenly come alive when the snow melted, and it seemed almost overnight that the wild flowers sprung up everywhere! And how the birds sang….especially the meadowlarks!

There was a little country school in the vicinity, which required a certain number of students in order to operate. One year they were lacking just one student of being enough. And so it was that little Albert began his formal schooling at the tender age of four! That first year though, his education centered primarily in the art of swatting flies. I suppose it was in the little schoolhouse that he acquired his life-long love of reading. Books were a luxury in pioneer homes and the Amoth family owned very few. Among these was one that little Albert read again and again. The title was "Indian Massacres and Savage Life!"

Dad left his carefree boyhood days behind at an early age, as his father began to suffer the early effects of multiple sclerosis. Together with his older brother Henry, they began to shoulder the responsibilities of the farm and the home.

In his youth my father began to feel a great need for a spiritual security. He searched diligently for that which would satisfy his soul, and when he found it, he grasped firmly to the hand of God. Together, they traveled a lifetime of mountains, hollows and deep valleys. At the end of his life, Dad was still holding fast to the hand of his God. There was a nurturing quality about Dad's faith that inspired one to seek it for one's self, and though he has been gone a number of years, his influence is still a vital part of my life.

He garnished our lives with the poetry he learned as a boy. One of my earliest memories was of sitting on his lap and listening to him reciting "The Highway Man." And there was "The Village Blacksmith," "Barefoot Boy," "The Schoolhouse," "The House Where I Was Born," and many, many more.

He loved to read to us and he read very well, peering at us from time to time to judge our reaction to the story. One of our favorites was a true story of a loyal little dog called "Greyfriar's Bobby." It was a sad tale, and Dad put his heart into the expression. A small cousin, who was a houseguest at the time, burst into tears of anguish and had to be led away and comforted!

The stories he read the most were those from the big old Bible storybook. His eyes would shine as he read to us of Daniel, the handwriting on the wall, the Red Sea parting, and many more. They came alive for us because he loved them. Wherever we go and whatever we do, those stories of truth will be a part of us.

In 1941, we settled on a wheat farm in the lovely Kootenai Valley of North Idaho. For recreation, my father strung a sturdy line across the river, anchoring it well on both sides. Then he baited the line with "trash" fish, and caught many a huge sturgeon. At times, this added a great deal of excitement to our lives, as well as delicious meals to our table.

As a young child, Dad taught me how to operate the boat he used to check his sturgeon lines. He also paid me a small sum for each trash fish I caught, so I warmed the fishing stool for hours!

The fish fed best in the evenings, so as the sun slipped behind the huge, blue-green mountains and shadowed the cottonwoods that guarded the cool river, I sat on the battered raft and cast in my line. Sometimes Dad, weary from a long day in the fields, would come down the path to join me. We never talked much, but rather sat in the comfort of a silent sharing; the gentle sounds of nature easing the cares of the day.

His sense of humor added a lot of spark to his life, and ours. He seemed to be able to see humor in almost any circumstance and he didn't hesitate to laugh at himself as heartily as everyone else!

He could sober up in a hurry though. His verbal instructions weren't so many, but his actions spoke volumes. Mom dealt with the minor issues of discipline, but in weightier matters, Dad took over. I can testify that his spankings were truly of a genuine sort, and wrought a most worthy work!

I can't recall him ever saying anything about respecting your fellow man, but he made friends with nearly everyone he met. From the smelly bachelor across the river to the refined atheist who lived on the mountainside, he seemed to find worth in them all. He always had time to visit, and Mom quietly went about serving many a simple meal to those he found too interesting, or too needy to turn away.

He was by no means a perfect man. He had many failings and shortcomings, but like a trusty old sailor, he sailed on. Sometimes life's currents were baffling, and he knew not how to go. A few of the storms were fierce enough to almost take him down, but he held to the hand of God, and sailed on. The sails he hurled the highest were humility, faith and courage, and they always brought him through. Toward the end of his sojourn, when his health failed him, his ship shuddered a little in the swells. Then one day he hurled a new sail as he quoted fervently from the book of Job; "Though

He slay me, yet will I trust Him!" And he then began to share with us the treasures he was finding in the Bible about the hereafter.

The old ship is crumbling out in a little cemetery, but the sailor is gone to a better shore. We put flowers there sometimes, but in time they fade away. The flowers we carry with us are blooming well, as we find courage from the example he left us. I believe his prayers of faith are still alive in God's hands and are availing for us.

I hope that I can learn to hurl the sails my father did. It takes humility to face yourself and to say, "I am sorry. I was wrong." It takes faith to reach out in the dark and take hold of the hand of God. And it takes courage to whisper "Tomorrow Lord, with your help I will try again."

Meadowlark Song

English words, Norwegian tone….
My Grandpa's voice remembers; low
But rich with fondness, tenderness,
The boyhood days of years ago.

The sun shone warm about his head
In spring, and touched a small pink toe
Tickled by prairie grass beneath,
In North Dakota years ago.

And flowers and flowers….sweet morning air
And laughter filled his lungs, and joy
Filled all his heart, still young, though years
Have passed since Grandpa was a boy.

His round white beard frames round blue eyes
Used to crinkling with his grin,
Now they are soft on looking back
Upon the little boy of then.

His ears are dulled, but still he hears
The song of those spring mornings when
The world was filled with meadowlarks;
Their songs were longer, sweeter then.

When years of time are long ago,
Where all is warmth and light around,
I want to see him standing there
Where flowers cover all the ground.

Where all the air is fresh and pure,
Where no one longs, is old, or sad,
Where bodies with the hearts are young,
And in God's presence all are glad.

And all about I want to hear,
Filling the air, and just as long
And sweet as when he was a boy,
The meadowlarks free, golden song,

And see his blue eyes growing round,
Then sparkling with a thousand grins,
And watch him, as a boy, throw back
His head, and laugh with joy again.

The Father's love encircles him,
And angels smile to hear that joy,
And, looking back, remember when
My Grandpa was a little boy.

       Tamara Seaman Koehn

Margaret

My mother, Margaret Klassen Toews, was born August 23, 1905, in Alberta, Canada.

Two years later, her mother Katherine, became very ill, and after eight weeks of severe suffering, she passed away on December 24th. She was thirty-two years old, and left a family of seven children.

My mother, then only two years old, has only one memory of her while she lived. She recalled she and her one-year-old sister playing around her, and sometimes on top of her, as she lay on the floor, trying to rest. The next memory was of the funeral day, and of her mother's coffin sitting in a large room. Family members were seated all around it. As a young child, she had no idea why they were there, or that her mother had died.

Her father Peter then gathered his young family and took them to Manitoba where he had friends and family. The children were placed in various of these homes to be cared for.

My mother and one older sister were fortunate in the care they received from the childless couple that took them in. They were so concerned for their welfare that they would wake them in the night, to feed them bread and jam!

Several years later, grandfather re-married, and with the exception of one, the children were brought together again. It must have seemed a tremendous challenge to this young woman whom Grandfather had chosen. She had left all of her family, and the well-established homes and rose gardens of Michigan, to assume the task of raising six children on the bare plains of Manitoba. Four more children were added, making a family of ten.

My grandfather was a carpenter by trade, but it was difficult to provide for such a large family. They moved to British Columbia, later to Alberta, and finally, with those children still at home, to a small town in California.

My mother had to leave her schooling at a young age, and seek employment as a maid in various homes. One of these was a very wealthy Jewish family in California. Their home seemed a mansion to my mother, and though they were good to her, yet as a maid she was expected to eat her meals alone in the kitchen. She was able to return home only on weekends, so she spent many lonely hours there. One of her tasks was to bake cookies. Only the perfectly round ones were served to the family. The rest were thrown away.

My mother possessed a generous, caring heart, and in later years, many neighbors and friends enjoyed her home-baked cookies. She was known as the "cookie lady" in our small town of Bonners Ferry. I doubt that hardly any of these cookies were perfectly round, but there was one ingredient that she never left out; that was love. She stirred it in generously.

When she was older, she found employment in other localities, including Michigan and North Dakota. While helping to cook for a threshing crew, she met a handsome young man called Albert. These are the words she used in describing him later. "Albert I was attracted to at once. He was the kind of Christian husband I wanted….humble, yet outgoing and friendly."

This feeling must have been mutual for I well remember the twinkle in Dad's eye when he recalled meeting Margaret!

They were married on a bitterly cold January day in 1930. All five of us children were born in North Dakota. Because of repeated crop failures due to the dust bowl years, they moved with their young family to Bonners Ferry, Idaho, in 1941. In 1945, we settled in the beautiful Kootenai Valley, where my father farmed for many years.

My first memory of my mother was as she endeavored to administer proper discipline. I was a transgressor, and I sped up and down the leafy raspberry rows, trying in vain to out run her!

I can't recall Mom ever saying anything about the virtue of sharing, but we observed it first hand, day after day, by her quiet example. It was never anything very big, perhaps a loaf of fresh bread, a dish of homemade cottage cheese, or fresh doughnuts, or sometimes an offering from her prolific garden. These little gifts seemed to go wherever Mom went, and if she couldn't get there, they were sent with us!

An incident that stands out in my mind was of a summer day when my sister and I decided to help ourselves to the neighbors' apple tree. No one would have thought twice about having a few, but we helped ourselves generously, and planned to hide them in our room to enjoy later. Mom found them though, and I can't ever remember a more severe lecture. We lost all pleasure in those apples, and I never again even considered taking something that was not mine.

I don't believe there was any influence on my life that was greater than my mother's prayers. Though we didn't often see her praying, nor did she speak of it much, somehow, without question, I knew I had a praying mother. I hardly dare think of where I'd be today, were it not for the prayers of my mother and father.

The days, the months, and the years wove in and out like threads of a tapestry. There were some most beautiful colors, but of course there were some very dark threads, too. There is one golden thread that seems woven through all the dark and bright years as a family. It was the knowledge of God's tender love for us all.

We children left home one by one, and then it was just she and Dad. They enjoyed some happy golden years together, along with the shadows, and then one fine spring day, Dad was gone, and Mom was alone.

One day Mom began to realize she was experiencing some strange symptoms in her knees and legs. A neurologist was suggested. In a flat, impersonal voice, he told us that our mother was suffering from Amyotrophic Lateral Sclerosis (Lou Gehrig's disease.)

We sat, stunned, as he explained the grim realities of this disease. There is a weakening and wasting away of all body muscle, and death usually occurs from heart failure, by choking, or starvation. There is no known cure, and he told us he thought she had about one year to live.

In the Bible, located in the book of Isaiah 45:3 are these words: "And I will give thee the treasures of darkness and the hidden riches of secret places, that thou mayest know that I, the Lord, which call thee by thy name, am the God of Israel."

It was during this dark and difficult year that we, as a family, began to learn of these treasures.

Mom had been a very active person all her life. Now she became steadily more helpless. For some time she had suffered severe hearing loss; now she could not speak, nor walk, nor finally, hardly could swallow.

We secured for her an erasable writing board and it was here that we discovered one of the treasures. We found that our quiet mother had a wonderful way of expressing herself in writing. I enjoyed some of the best visits of my life with Mom on that chalkboard. I learned to know her in a way I never had before. I treasure those visits now. They were all erased from the board, but made an indelible impression on my heart, for which I shall always be grateful.

Another treasure we began to enjoy was her sense of humor. During the cares and struggles of earlier life, we seldom saw her laugh. But now, helpless in the hands of her children, and her God, she was somehow able to surrender to the situation, and she sometimes laughed soundlessly at the foibles and complexities of her constant care. Oh, how happy we were to be able to laugh with her!

Of course, there was more than laughter. There was increasing physical distress and discomfort as well. Still, she could write to us, she could smile and she could pray. She told us that often songs of comfort would come to her, and though she could hardly make a sound, yet she could "sing" them in her mind.

During that last year, we became actively involved in her daily care, but especially in prayer for her. We earnestly beseeched the Lord to grant her peace of mind, leave her the strength of her hands so she could express herself….and over and over and over….we prayed "Please Lord, don't let her choke to death."

One morning my sister did all she could to make her comfortable, and at length, she seemed to be resting very peacefully. She roused then, and pointed to the ceiling. Unsure of what was meant, my sister took her hands and prayed with her, as we often did. Then she seemed to rest so very well…. so quietly she slept….on into the arms of her loving God.

And God shall wipe away all tears from their eyes; and there shall be no more death, neither sorrow, nor crying, neither shall there be any pain; for the former things are passed away.
Revelations 21:4

This is an old, old children's song our mother used to sing to us.

The New Moon

By Eliza L.C. Follen

Dear Mother, how pretty
The moon looks tonight!
She was never so lovely before;
Her two little horns
Are so sharp and so bright,
I hope they'll not grow any more.

If I were up there
With you and my friends,
I'd rock in it nicely, you'd see;
I'd sit in the middle
And hold up both ends
Oh, what a bright cradle t'would be!

I would call to the stars
To keep out of the way
Lest we should rock over their toes;
And there I would rock
Till the dawn of the day,
And see where the pretty moon goes.

And there we would stay
In the beautiful skies,
And through the bright clouds we would roam
We would see the sun set,
And see the sun rise,
And on the next rainbow come home.

Sequel

Oh Mother, how pretty
Your song was at night!
You were never so lovely as then.
You were small, but your arms
 Still reached 'round us all.
No matter how naughty we'd been.

If I were up there
Where you are tonight,
I'd hear your sweet singing once more
And we'd fly o'er the clouds
And swim in the stars,
And slide on a rainbow to shore.

And Mother, I'd tell you.
Yes, once more I would,
That way back on earth, thus and then.
"I'm sorry….so sorry I was a bad girl,
And I'll never be naughty again."

R.A.S.

To my own dearly loved sisters and brothers; Phyllis, Norman, Betty, and Victor, whom I wouldn't trade for any others the wide world over!

Do You Remember?

Do you remember, all of you…
The log house….silvered gray?
The cool and shadowed attic
Where we'd so often play?

Do you recall the weathered raft
….the Indian canoe?
The red-white rowboat, by the shore.
The rivers cool, green hue?

Oh, to lie up in the barn
Upon the scratchy hay,
The sunlight….streaming through the cracks
On a sleepy summer day!

And see the cows come slowly home
…. the evening shadows stealing.
The huge old mountains, changing blue
To lend an evening feeling.

Can you still see the icehouse
The sawdust….cool and wet?
The day we made the sawdust doll?
I never shall forget!

And one bright birthday morning
My heart brimmed o'er with glee
To spy—on top the cupboard high
A cart just made for me!

Remember still the kitchen stove
The warm and crackling heat
The wood box where we used to sit,
The kindling stacked so neat.

Would you like some dumpling soup
Or sturgeon, fried crisp brown?
A "grease cake", sugary and hot,
Or "boughten bread," from town?!

Or how about a wintry night
Around the "Ashley's" glow
Popcorn and apples, books and love
Ah….it seems so long ago….

And now, we each warm other hearths
And God will teach us how
To have….to hold….to learn and grow.
….We're making memories now.

We can't begin to stop the time,
Nor would we want to try;
For God has wisely made it so
Until the day we die.

Oh, loving Father, keep us all.
We treasure now each day….
Please grant us humble, grateful hearts.
Walk with us on our way.

Help us to treasure moments
As gifts of golden hue.
Guide us and keep us all our days,
And lead us home….to You.

R.A.S.

Introduction	ix
Dedication	xiii
Appetizers and Beverages	1
A Sampler of Salads	21
Soups and Stews and Brothy Brews	53
What's For Supper?	91
Bread and Beyond	173
Vegetables	231
Just Desserts	253
"Let them eat cake!"	273
Pie Baking	319
The Old Cookie Jar	347
Christmas	389

Appetizers and Beverages

Methuselah ate what he found on his plate
And never, as people do now,
Did he note the amount of the calorie count—
He ate because it was chow.
He wasn't disturbed as at dinner he sat
Destroying a roast duck or pie,
To think it was lacking in lime or in fat
Or a couple of vitamins shy.
He cheerfully chewed every species of food,
Untroubled by worries or fears
Lest his health might be hurt
By some fancy dessert,
And he lived over nine hundred years!

                Old Scrapbook
                Author Unknown

Appetizers

I believe in a plain, three-course meal,
No matter how hi-brows may feel,
And as for hors d'oeurves
They get on my nerves;
Let's keep this book simple and real.

****

This is the gospel of labour,
Ring it ye bells of the kirk!
The Lord of Love came down from above,
To live with the men who work;
This is the rose that He planted,
Here in the thorn-curst soil.
Heaven is blest with perfect rest,
But the blessing of Earth is toil.
   --Henry Van Dyke (1852-1933)

****

Work, and thou wilt bless the day
Ere the toil be done
They that work not, can not pray
Can not feel the sun.
God is living, working still....
   --William Cowper (1731-1800)

****

Even in the meanest sorts of labor, the soul of man is composed into a harmony the instant he sets himself to work.
   --Carlyle

****

No man is born into the world whose work is not born with him; there is always work, And tools to work withal, for those who will; And blessed are the horny hands of toil.
   --James Russell Lowell (1819-1891)

****

Work brings it's own relief;
He who most idle is has the most grief.
   --Eugene Fitch Ware (1841-1911)

Supper Smoke

Ham Ball

Ingredients:
1 (8 oz.) pkg. Cream cheese, softened
1/4 cup salad dressing
2 tbsp. parsley flakes
1 tsp. Minced onion
1/4 tsp. Dry mustard
1/4 tsp. Hot pepper sauce
2 cups ground ham
1/2 cup crushed nuts

Directions:
In mixing bowl, beat cream cheese and salad dressing until smooth. Stir in all remaining ingredients except crushed nuts. Chill. Form into a ball and roll in nuts. Chill again and serve with crackers.

Spinach Dip

Ingredients:
1 (8 oz.) container sour cream
8 oz. mayonnaise
1 box frozen, chopped spinach, thawed
1 can water chestnuts, drained and chopped
1 pkg. dry vegetable soup mix

Directions:
In mixing bowl, combine sour cream and mayonnaise. Open thawed box of spinach and squeeze dry. Add to mixture. Drain water chestnuts and chop. Add chestnuts and dry vegetable soup mix. Blend all together and chill.

Crab Dip

Ingredients:
16 oz. carton cottage cheese
16 oz. carton sour cream
1 cup mayonnaise
2 tsp. Prepared horseradish
1/8 tsp. Liquid smoke
3 tsp. Tabasco sauce
1/2 tsp onion salt
1/2 tsp. garlic salt
Salt and pepper to taste
1/2 to 1 pound imitation crab flakes

Directions:
Combine all ingredients in order given and chill to serve.

Picante Bean Dip

Ingredients:
3 (16) oz. cans refried beans
8 oz. Velveeta cheese, cubed
8 oz. picante sauce, medium
2 or 3 tbsp. bacon grease
Onion and garlic powder to taste

Directions:
Combine all ingredients and heat in crock-pot. Serve with tortilla chips.

Supper Smoke

Olive Cream Cheese Dip

Ingredients:
1 oz. pkg. cream cheese, softened
Mayonnaise
1 small can stuffed green olives, juice reserved
1 small can black olives

Directions:
In mixing bowl, combine cream cheese and enough mayonnaise to make spreading consistency. Add a little of the green olive juice and blend well. Chop the green and black olives and add. Chill and serve on crackers, or with chips.

Snappy Oyster Crackers

Ingredients:
1 12 to 16 oz. pkg. oyster crackers
1 pkg. Hidden Valley original buttermilk, dry dressing mix
1/2 to 1 tsp. dill weed
1/4 tsp. garlic powder
1/4 tsp. lemon pepper
3/4 cup salad oil

Directions:
Place crackers in large mixing bowl. In another bowl, combine remaining ingredients. Pour over crackers and stir well so all is absorbed. Spread on baking sheet and bake at 200 degrees for 15 to 20 minutes.

Honey Butter

Ingredients:
1 stick butter or margarine
1/2 cup powdered sugar
1 cup honey
1 tsp. cinnamon

Blend together until creamy.
A really tasty spread. Pooh would love it.

Beverages

Salinda's Easter Drink

Ingredients:
1 (6 oz.) pkg. green Jell-O
2 cups boiling water
2 cups pineapple juice
1 can frozen lemonade concentrate
1 large bottle of 7-Up

Directions:
In large container, dissolve Jell-O in boiling water. Add pineapple juice and lemonade concentrate. Mix well and refrigerate. When ready to serve, add 7-Up.

When one dines at Ed and Salinda's table, there is always a feast for the eyes as well as good taste. We have been privileged to enjoy these feasts many times.

But to be honest, I have feasted most of all, from telephone conversations with her. Her mind does not dig in the weeds of other's faults, but rather blooms with a vast variety of ideas and thoughts. I treasure her friendship.

Mexican Mocha

Ingredients:
2/3 cup sugar
2/3 cup brown sugar, packed
1/2 cup nonfat dry milk powder
3/4 cup baking cocoa
1/3 cup instant coffee granules
1 tsp. cinnamon
1/4 tsp. allspice
1 cup hot milk (for each serving)

Directions:
Combine all ingredients except milk. Store in an airtight container. For each serving, stir 3 Tbsp. dry mix into 1 cup hot milk.

Supper Smoke

Homemade Root Beer

Ingredients:
1 cup lukewarm water
1 tsp. yeast (1/2 tsp. if 90 degree weather)
5 pounds sugar
1 bottle Root Beer extract
5 gallons lukewarm water
6 one-gallon glass jugs

Directions:
In small bowl, dissolve yeast in warm water. In very large container (bathtub?...just kidding) pour in the sugar. Shake extract bottle well and add to sugar. Carefully pour in 5 gallons of lukewarm water. Add yeast mixture and stir well to blend. Pour immediately into jugs, leaving 2 inches of air space. Cap, or cork very tightly. (I put a double layer of saran wrap on jug top, and then screw on the cap as tight as I can.)

Place jugs on their sides in a warm, draft free place. Try to keep temperature evenly at about 70 to 80 degrees. Leave for three or four days, or until mixture begins to form little bubbles around the air space. Then place jugs, upright in a cool place, like a basement...but not as cool as the refrigerator. Let stand for 4 or 5 days. Refrigerate before serving.

Have you ever mused upon your childhood, and marveled at the simple things that wrought such pure delight? Every summer, Mom would brew at least one batch of Root Beer. We lived in a sagging, ugly, old log house, and dined on simple fare, and on faded oilcloth. But when Mom sent us to the "cellar" for the first jug of Root Beer....ahhhh....such pleasure was ours!

We poured out each portion into the thick "Sunday" glasses. The ice made the glasses frosty and cold, and when we took the first sip, we felt we were dining in a king's palace.

In later years, when our grown children returned home from far away places, we treasured each visit and tried to make every day a celebration. Once, in anticipation of a joyful holiday season, I decided to make a batch of Root Beer.

I'm not sure.... I know I carefully laid each fat jug on their sides, but I do believe the room must have been too hot. Let it suffice to say that we had an explosive Christmas season.

Appetizers and Beverages

Frothy Orange Drink

Ingredients:
1 (6oz.) can frozen orange juice concentrate, unthawed
1 cup water
1 cup milk
1/2 cup sugar
1 tsp. vanilla
8 to 10 ice cubes

Directions:
Combine all ingredients in blender and process until mixture is thick and slushy. Serve. Makes about 4 cups.

For a tropical touch, substitute Hawaiian's Own concentrate instead of orange juice, cut out the sugar, and add a banana.

Citrus Punch

Ingredients:
2 pkgs. Strawberry, tropical punch or cherry Kool-Aide, mixed with sugar and water as directed.
1 (12oz.) can frozen orange juice
1 (12oz.) can frozen grapefruit juice
1 large bottle grapefruit soda

Directions:
Combine all ingredients except grapefruit soda. Add that just before serving. Makes about 2 gallons.

    A number of years ago, our family enjoyed the acquaintance of a couple that had spent many years in mission work in Old Mexico. They regaled us with many fascinating accounts, and our youngest daughter Marla, was especially impressed. Her love affair with Mexico began when she decided to spend several years there herself. The mission work in which she was involved took her to various locations during that time, and she has enjoyed many travel adventures there since then.
    One of the latest of these was during a short trip through the lovely city of Guadalajara, known as the "City of Fountains." She and her two young nieces, Amber and Brittany, were in the midst of a cultural day, which

included a huge cathedral, the converted orphanage where many of the famous Orozco murals are displayed, and the largest market in Mexico. There, amid the gay throng, they discovered the licuado! Pronounced (lee QWA do.)

These frothy and frosty drinks are said to be like your first kiss! Years later, you still remember where you were.....Such a taste experience, coupled with the "hasta manana" mind set of the colorful natives, and the hot sunshine, is hard to put down on paper. You'll have to experience it yourself, and 'twould be best on Mexican soil! Here are two recipes. You can also experiment with many fruit combinations. Que sera sera.

Berry Licuado

Ingredients:
1 1/2 cups milk
1 cup fresh or frozen berries, such as blueberries, strawberries, or raspberries
1 ripe banana, sliced
2 tbsp. orange juice concentrate
3 tbsp sugar (optional)
1 cup ice

Directions:
Place all ingredients in blender or food processor, and blend 'til smooth. Serve cold. 2 servings.

Tango Mango Licuado

Ingredients:
1 1/2 cups milk
1 cup cubed, ripe mango
1 cup cubed, ripe papaya
1 tbsp. honey
1 cup ice cubes

Directions:
Place all ingredients in blender or food processor and blend 'til smooth. Serve cold. 2 servings.
If mango or papayas aren't available in your area, try pineapple and cantaloupe.

Colorful Orangeade Punch

Ingredients:
3 pkgs. Jell-O (choose Jell-O for color and flavor you desire)
6 cups boiling water
1 (6oz.) can frozen lemonade
1 (6oz.) can frozen orange juice
1 large (48oz.) can pineapple juice
3 cups sugar
1 gallon water
2 (28 oz.) bottles of ginger ale, or more

Directions:
In large container, dissolve Jell-O in boiling water. Add all remaining ingredients EXCEPT ginger ale. Mix well and freeze. When ready to serve, let mixture thaw until slushy. Add ginger ale and serve.

Ambrosia

Ingredients:
1 large can pineapple juice
1 (12oz.) can frozen orange juice
1 small can frozen lemonade
6 cups water
5 cups sugar
8 to 12 medium bananas, mashed
7-Up or lemon-lime soda

Directions:
In large container, combine all the ingredients and blend well. Cover and freeze for 12 to 24 hours. When ready to serve, fill tall drinking glass half full of fruit mixture and slowly fill glass with soda.

A blithesome brew!

Supper Smoke

Razzy Lemonade

Ingredients:
2 (12oz.) cans frozen lemonade concentrate, thawed
2 (10oz.) pkgs. frozen, sweetened raspberries, thawed
2 to 4 tbsp. sugar
1 large bottle club soda (or other soda of your choice)

Directions:
Combine lemonade concentrate, raspberries, and sugar in blender. Cover and blend. Strain blended mixture to remove seeds. In large container, combine raspberry mixture, soda and ice cubes.

Going on a long road trip, or a hearty hike? Take a reusable plastic soda or water bottle; fill 1/4 to 1/2 with water. Cap and freeze overnight Fill remainder in the morning and you have ice cold water for quite awhile.

Canned Tomato Juice

Ingredients:
Approximately 15 pounds ripe tomatoes
1 cup sugar
1/2 cup lemon juice
2 tsp. garlic salt
2 tsp. celery salt
1 tsp. pepper
7 tsp. salt

Directions:
Wash tomatoes and cut up in small chunks. Place in large kettles and add just enough water so tomatoes won't stick while cooking. Cook until tomatoes are soft. Run through food mill, reserving juice and discarding tomato pulp. Place in large cooking kettle and add all remaining ingredients. Stir well to blend. Pour into quart jars, seal, and process in water bath for 20 minutes.

It's a mess, but certainly worth the effort. This juice is delicious.

Appetizers and Beverages

Fireside Coffee

Ingredients:
2 cups instant cocoa mix
2 cups non-dairy creamer
1 cup instant coffee
1 1/2 cups powdered sugar
1/2 tsp. nutmeg
1/2 tsp. cinnamon

Directions:
Blend all ingredients thoroughly. Store in moisture proof container. To serve, spoon 3 or 4 heaping tsp. mix in coffee mug. Add hot water. A dollop of whipped cream makes this really special.

Cappuccino Mix

Ingredients:
1 1/2 cups powdered non-dairy creamer
1 cup instant chocolate drink mix
1 cup sugar
2/3 cup instant coffee granules
1/2 tsp, cinnamon
1/4 tsp. nutmeg
1 to 2 tsp. POWDERED vanilla*

Directions:
Combine all ingredients and blend well. To serve combine 3 tbsp. mix with 3/4 cup boiling water for each cup.

*I find powdered vanilla in our local health food store. The whole car smells lovely all the way home!

Supper Smoke

Tea Brew

1
Ingredients:
Boiling water
9 tea bags
1 cup sugar

Directions:
Bring water to boil in small kettle. Add tea bags and let steep. Pour over sugar and stir to dissolve. Add water to make 1 gallon.

#2
Ingredients:
6 cups boiling water
18 tea bags
2 1/4 cups sugar
1/3 cup lemon juice (family preference…you can skip this if you wish.)

Directions:
Bring water to boil. Add tea bags and let steep. Remove tea bags and pour over sugar. Stir to dissolve. Add lemon juice if preferred. Makes about 2 gallons.

#3
Ingredients:
6 cups boiling water
3/4 cup tea leaves
2 3/4 cups sugar

Directions:
Pour boiling water over tea leaves. Let stand at least 5 minutes. Strain over sugar and stir well to dissolve. Add water to make 2 or 3 gallons.

Note: if you need extra ice cubes for a special event, begin freezing them ahead, and store them in a brown paper bag in freezer. They won't stick together.

Appetizers and Beverages

Thumpin' Good Tea

Ingredients:
10 regular tea bags
1 cup sugar
Ice

Directions:
Place the tea bags in a pouring container. Pour ALMOST boiling water over the bags and let them steep as long as you want. Pour steeped tea over the sugar, being careful NOT TO SQUEEZE the tea bags. (This makes bitter tea.) Stir to dissolve sugar. Place ice in serving pitcher and pour brew OVER ICE, adding water to make 1 gallon.

Note: I was told of this method by a lively little teen named Micaela, who served it in her family home as part of a delicious Sunday dinner.

Grocery Shopping and Budgets

If you're not of age
You'd best turn the page
But if you've a firm chin
Stay right here! We'll begin!

I think I'll be right up front and admit it, even if it will sound strange to most of you.

I love to buy groceries, and I look forward to it every week!

I realize, of course, that there are "different strokes for different folks."

I'll admit that I hate to dust, and you may be crazy about it. So let's make a deal. I'll skip the dusting while I help you to enjoy grocery shopping! You may never learn to love it, but I'd like to help you to at least enjoy it more, and to become an intelligent shopper.

Back in the "dear, dead days beyond recall; when on the world the mists began to fall..." (in other words, shortly after Richard and I were married) we sat down together, all wide-eyed and bushy tailed, to "make out a budget."

Having very little money and no checking account or credit cards, this turned out to be quite simple. Richard worked at a local sawmill, and was paid the same amount weekly, which further simplified things. He laid his wallet on the table and we began.

We first estimated all our basic expenses. Then we simply labeled envelopes, such as **GROCERIES, RENT, GAS, UTILITIES,** etc. We divided the cash into these separate envelopes, and we were done. (A few minor adjustments in amounts were needed later.) It was as simple as that. The hard part came right afterward…. STICKING TO IT!

Well, okay Sweetie, this WAS pretty elementary. But before you roll your eyes and turn the page, let me quickly add one more fact about this simple little method.

IT WORKED

Though painful, it taught us some simple equations about life, work, and rewards that have stood us in good stead through many years. But let's just dwell on the grocery envelope now. You'll understand, of course, that this was a good many years ago, and the grocery envelope was crammed with the incredible sum of ten dollars! This seemed like quite a goodly sum to both of us.

Did you just now hear an imaginary thud? Well, that was me coming down to earth.

There were now two square meals to cook, besides a lunch bucket to fill. What to buy? How to stretch it to last the week? HOW TO COOK IT?

So began the trial and error method. This amounted to a good many errors and lots of trials. I pondered my way up and down unfamiliar grocery aisles, into my teeny closet kitchen, through my voluminous Betty Crocker cook book, and back down the grocery aisles again.

The grocery budget wavered, whined, and waned, but somewhere along the thorny way, it all became a challenge, and I began to enjoy it.

There were several things I learned that were, and still are, very helpful.

You must learn to make a grocery list. Keep this list in a handy place in your kitchen. Make a habit of writing down each item that is depleted, or run out.

Decide on the most convenient day of the week for shopping. Try to stay with that same day, within reason, of course.

Be sure to secure the grocery ads for your area so you are able to take advantage of the sales each week.

Before you shop, sit down with your accumulated list, the grocery ads, and your cook book(s.) I suggest that you shop in two stores, so if this is feasible for you, you will be making two lists, or one long one. Check the meats first, and taking into consideration what's on sale, make a tentative menu plan for the week. This will get easier as you learn of both your likes and dislikes, and what you enjoy cooking. When you

Appetizers and Beverages

have planned the main dishes for the week, you can fill in the rest of the meal plans in a more flexible way.

Now go through the ads, taking note of the specials. Keep in mind that they are not specials if they are an item you rarely use. If they are not perishable, and you will use them within a reasonable time, try to buy two sale items rather than just one. As a general rule refrain from more, remembering that your friendly grocer needs to make a living too. (Besides, hoarders begin to smell like old cheese.)

Try to divide your purchases fairly evenly between the two stores. It isn't fair to take advantage of only specials from one store on a regular basis. In time you will become familiar enough with both stores to note that some items will be consistently higher in one store, or the other.

You'll need to watch the sales carefully, as they can be tricky. A big splashy ad for saltine crackers at 3 boxes for $3.49 is no bargain if you can buy one box for $ .98.

Try to stick with the store brand, rather than the popular one that "mom always uses." Many times these store brands are as good, or better quality and less expensive. Of course, if you feel compelled to serve Sweetie ONLY the best brand name stuff, just because he has a cute lower lip, feel free to do that, remembering of course, that ultimately, Sweetie will have to work longer to fill up that grocery envelope.

So does this menu planning seem like a big pain? Maybe it won't work for you, but give it a good try before you decide. It is a wonderful help in keeping a check on your spending, and in a smoothly run kitchen, when you're not making hurried, last minute meal plans, you will avoid those quick trips to the store that add up so fast. If you can keep from going to the store more than once a week, you are certain to make your food dollars stretch further.

Keeping your grocery spending within a certain limit may be a new thought to some of you, but it is actually a very good practice. It promotes self-discipline, and you know how good THAT is for you, dearie!

And besides, a lot of the spendy extras are not always healthful choices anyway. A moderate, economical diet, prepared with simplicity, may not seem all that enticing when you're young, but just give this a thought or two. By so doing, you just may keep your Sweetie by your side for another ten years or so, on the other end of your life. Is it worth it?

How she loved the sweetheart she was given,
And she plied him with rich, country living.
But the truth seems so real

At the funeral meal.
(Will there be any French fries in heaven?)

I'll Remember

My parents, Albert and Margaret, began their married life on a bitterly cold January day near Langdon, North Dakota. For a little over a year, my grandmother Amelia shared her home with them. Then, with their first child Phyllis, they settled in a very basic, two story structure where the remainder of the family of five was born.

In 1941 we reluctantly left our North Dakota home, and began a new life in beautiful northern Idaho. I believe the old house remained empty much of the time after we left.

Over fifty years later, in the fall of 1992, the five children and some of our respective spouses accomplished something we had hardly thought possible. With busy schedules, various occupations, and from three different states, we gathered in north Idaho. With our old roots tugging us back, we rented a motor home and traveled together to North Dakota. What a wonderful time we had, and no words can express the feelings we experienced as we found and explored the old home once more!

Truly it was a dream come true, and we shall treasure that little island of time together all our days.

Appetizers and Beverages

I'll Remember

*I'll remember, I'll remember
The house where I was born,
I even saw the window "where the
Sun peeped in at morn."
We didn't come a day too soon,
Nor 'twas too long a day,
For soon....too soon, time's ruthless hand
Will crumble it away.*

*I'll remember, I'll remember
Those paths my father trod,
The vision of a prairie boy,
Bare feet upon the sod!
The wild, sweet smell of springtime;
The fields, awash with bloom,
The meadowlark's clear melody,
That vanquished winter's gloom.*

*I'll remember, I'll remember
The wheat fields, thick and high;
Their golden-headed stems so etched
Against Dakota sky.
I know 'twas but nostalgia
To view it....so forlorn,
But Oh! The joy it brought to see
The house where I was born!*

*R.A.S.
1992*

A Sampler of Salads

Let's dream up a ballad
Of a most toothsome salad,
Though we know we SHOULD balance our meals.
This one is not green
And it's mostly whipped cream,
Yet just think how ignoble we'll feel!

So we'll sing of greens too
Since they're so good for you.
Thus partaking, so virtuous we'll be.
And we'll chew, yea we will
'Till we've taken our fill
And we'll live 'til at least ninety-three!

Vickie's Seafood Pasta

I once read a delightful and true account of several young men traveling through the U.S. They fell on hard times and were in want of a solid meal. In passing a park, they took note of a large family reunion in progress. Perhaps it was their empty stomachs that gave them the bravado they needed to approach the crowd with happy smiles, handshakes, and first name introductions! They were enfolded in the group and enjoyed a fine meal and jovial small talk. They were soon on their way again, no doubt leaving behind a puzzled family, scratching their heads and comparing notes! This same scenario could easily take place during our annual Seaman picnic; a large congenial group, happy to share good times and good food.
This is another delicious recipe gleaned from one of these events. Thanks, cousin Vickie!

Ingredients:
1 small pkg. (no more than 10 to 12oz.) angel hair pasta
1 1/2 cups mayonnaise
1 cup buttermilk
1 pkg. Uncle Dan's Southern style dressing mix
1/2 cup chopped red onion
1 can (5oz.) water chestnuts, drained and coarsely chopped
1 cup frozen peas, cooked
2 to 3 cups imitation crab meat, chopped

Directions:
In boiling salted water, cook pasta. Drain, rinse and cool. In mixing bowl, combine mayonnaise, buttermilk and dry dressing mix. Set aside. To cooled pasta, add onion, water chestnuts, peas and crab. Add dressing mix, combining thoroughly.

*This salad tastes best when made ahead and refrigerated overnight.

Supper Smoke

Marjorie's Macaroni Salad

Ingredients:
2 cups uncooked macaroni
6 hard cooked eggs
1 carrot, shredded or chopped fine
1/2 cup chopped onion
1 or 2 tomatoes, chopped
1 or 2 dill pickles, chopped
1/2 cup black olives, sliced
1/2 cup frozen peas
8 oz. cheddar cheese, cubed
Mayonnaise, prepared mustard, pickle juice and seasoning salt.

Directions:
Cook macaroni in salted water, drain, rinse and chill. Boil eggs, cool and peel. In large mixing bowl, combine first nine ingredients. Salt and pepper to taste. In another bowl, combine the last four ingredients, starting with approximately 1 cup of mayonnaise and adding mustard, pickle juice and seasoning to taste. Mixture should be quite sloppy. Combine with macaroni mixture, chill and serve.

This recipe comes from my niece, who is one of the best cooks I know. As you can see, there is some guess work, especially when you make the dressing, but after you've made it a few times, you can adjust each of the above ingredients to suit your taste. It makes a very colorful and tasty salad, and I serve it over and over to summer guests.

Ila's Potato Salad

Ingredients:
4 to 6 large potatoes
8 eggs
1 small onion, minced
Salt, pepper, and parsley to taste
Dill pickles, chopped, optional
Approximately 1 cup mayonnaise
2 or 3 tbsp. prepared mustard

Directions:
In large kettle, cover potatoes with water and cook 'till done. Drain, cool and peel. Meanwhile boil eggs, cool and peel. Shred potatoes and eggs into large mixing bowl. Add onion. Season to taste with salt, pepper and parsley flakes. Add chopped dill pickle if you wish.

In another bowl, combine mayonnaise and mustard to taste. Pour over potato mixture and combine. Chill to serve.

This is a WELL USED recipe at our house, and I have received countless compliments regarding this dish. I always give credit to Ila, my favorite son-in-law's mother! She has a beautiful smile, snappy brown eyes, and the best potato salad recipe I've ever tried.

Supper Smoke

Hot Bean Salad

Ingredients:
3 slices bacon
1 cup green pepper, chopped
1/2 bunch green onions, chopped
1 can green beans, drained
1 can pinto beans, drained
1 can kidney beans, drained
1 can pork 'n beans
3/4 cup brown sugar
3/4 cup chili sauce

Directions:
In heavy skillet, fry bacon. Remove from pan and sauté green pepper and onion in bacon drippings. In large bowl, combine crumbled cooked bacon, onions and peppers and the four cans of beans; then brown sugar and chili sauce. Pour into greased casserole and bake for 30 minutes, or until mixture is bubbly.

Apple Medley

Ingredients:
1 cup sugar
1/4 tsp. salt
3 tbsp. flour
1 egg
1 1/2 cups pineapple juice
2 tbsp. vinegar
1 tsp. vanilla
2 to 3 tbsp. butter or margarine
Apple, pineapple, bananas, miniature marshmallow and (optional) chopped nuts and maraschino cherries.

Directions:
In saucepan, combine sugar, salt and flour. Add egg (beaten), pineapple juice, and vinegar. Bring to a boil and cook until thickened, stirring constantly. Add vanilla and butter. Set aside to cool.

Prepare fruits and marshmallows and pour cooled dressing over all. Let set for at least 1 hour before serving.

**Bananas store much longer if placed in a dark colored plastic or paper bag in the refrigerator.

Supper Smoke

Twenty-four Hour Salad

Ingredients:
3 egg yolks
1 tbsp. vinegar
2 tbsp. butter or margarine
2 tbsp. sugar
1 tsp. salt
1 cup whipping cream
1/2 cup sugar
1 can fruit cocktail, drained
1 can pineapple chunks or tidbits, drained
2 oranges, peeled, sectioned and cut small
2 cups miniature marshmallows

Directions:
In saucepan, beat eggs. Add vinegar, butter, sugar, and salt. Cook, stirring constantly, until mixture is thickened. Set aside to cool. Whip cream and add sugar. Combine with cooled dressing mix. In large bowl, combine all drained fruits, oranges and marshmallows. Fold in dressing mix. Chill and serve.

Five-Cup Fruit Salad

Ingredients:
1 can pineapple chunks, drained
1 can mandarin oranges, drained
1 cup coconut
1 cup miniature marshmallows
1 cup sour cream

Direction:
In large bowl, combine all ingredients and let stand, chilled, overnight.

This recipe comes from an elderly lady with whom I boarded years ago. She ran a tight ship and I was afraid of her, but she was a wonderful cook. After working my night shift, I'd creep up to my room and go to bed….until I heard her leave the house. Then I'd rush downstairs and raid the refrigerator!

A Sampler of Salads

Elaine's Creamy Cabbage

Ingredients:
1 head cabbage
1 (20 oz.) can pineapple tidbits, drained
1 1/2 cups miniature marshmallows
1 cup mayonnaise
2 tbsp. vinegar
1/4 cup sugar
1 cup whipping cream

Directions:
In large mixing bowl shred cabbage. Add pineapple and marshmallows. In separate bowl combine mayonnaise, vinegar and sugar. Set aside. Whip cream and fold into mayonnaise mixture. Stir into cabbage mixture and chill to serve.

Aunt Elaine raised a family, kept her hubby happy, and also worked as an obstetrical nurse for years. She has helped to deliver hundreds of babies, and found not a one under a cabbage.

Waldorf Coleslaw

Ingredients:
1 red apple, peeled, cored, and chopped
1 tsp. lemon juice
4 cups shredded cabbage
1 (20 oz.) can crushed pineapple, drained
1 cup red grapes
1/3 cup pecans
1 cup sour cream
1/2 tsp. salt
2 heaping tbsp. mayonnaise
4 tsp. sugar

Directions:
In small bowl, place chopped apples, tossing with lemon juice. Set aside. In large mixing bowl, combine cabbage, pineapple, grapes and pecans. Combine sour cream, salt, mayonnaise, and sugar and add to cabbage mixture. Add apples and combine all.

Supper Smoke

One More Cole Slaw!

Ingredients:
1/2 cup oil
1/2 cup vinegar
1 cup sugar
1 head cabbage
1 small onion, chopped
1 green pepper, chopped
Celery seed, salt, and pepper to taste

Directions:
In saucepan, combine oil, vinegar and sugar. Bring to a boil and stir until sugar is dissolved. Set aside to cool.

In large mixing bowl, shred cabbage. Add onion and green pepper. Season with celery seed, salt and pepper. Pour cooled dressing over all and chill overnight.

**When you're done chopping onion, sprinkle your hands with salt, rub together, and wash. No smelly hands!

The LAST Slaw Recipe!

Ingredients:
1 head cabbage (or about 8 cups, shredded)
1 medium carrot, shredded
1/3 cup sugar
1/2 tsp. salt
1/8 tsp. pepper
1/4 cup milk
1/2 cup mayonnaise
1/4 cup buttermilk
1 1/2 tbsp. vinegar
2 1/2 tbsp. lemon juice

Directions:
In large mixing bowl, shred cabbage and carrot. In another bowl, combine all remaining ingredients, stirring well to dissolve sugar. Pour over cabbage mixture and cover. Refrigerate at least 2 hours or more before serving.

Spring Rice Salad

Ingredients:
1 cup water
1/4 tsp. salt
1/2 cup rice
1 (15 oz.) can pineapple, drained and juice reserved
1 cup red grapes
1 cup green grapes
1/2 cup sugar
2 tbsp. flour
1 tsp. lemon juice
1 egg, beaten
1 cup whipping cream
1 tsp. vanilla
1 or 2 cups miniature colored marshmallows
4 bananas, cut in small chunks and dipped in lemon juice

Directions:
In saucepan, bring salted water to boil. Add rice and cover, cooking on low for 20 minutes. Set aside to cool. In large bowl combine drained pineapple, grapes, and cooled rice.

Add enough water to pineapple juice to make 1 cup. Combine with sugar, flour, lemon juice and beaten egg. Cook until thick and smooth, stirring constantly. Cool.

Whip cream, adding vanilla. Fold in marshmallows. Pour cooled juice mixture over rice and blend. Then add to whipped cream mixture. Refrigerate overnight, or several hours. Just before serving fold in bananas.

Supper Smoke

Rippin' Good Rice

Ingredients:
2 cups cooked and cooled rice
1 (8oz.) pkg. cream cheese, softened
2 or 3 tbsp. sugar
2 tbsp. mayonnaise
12 maraschino cherries, halved
1 can mandarin oranges, drained
1 (20 oz.) can pineapple, drained
1 (10 oz.) pkg. miniature marshmallows (optional)
1 cup whipping cream
1/4 cup sugar

Directions:
In large bowl, combine softened cream cheese, sugar, and mayonnaise. Stir until smooth. Add rice, cherries, oranges, pineapple and marshmallows. Whip cream, slowly adding sugar. Fold into rice mixture. Chill to serve.

**When cooking rice, add 1 tsp. lemon juice to each quart of water you use. This keeps the rice grains white and separate.

A Sampler of Salads

Graham Cracker Fluff

Ingredients:
6 tbsp. melted margarine or butter
6 tbsp. sugar
1 1/2 cups graham cracker crumbs (24 squares)
1 1/2 cups cold water
3 pkgs. Knox gelatin
6 egg yolks
1 1/2 cups sugar
2 1/4 cups milk
6 egg whites
3 tsp. vanilla
3 cups whipping cream OR 12 oz. Cool Whip

Directions:
Combine margarine, sugar and graham crumbs. Set aside. I large bowl; dissolve the gelatin in the cold water. Set aside to soften. In top of double boiler, beat the eggs; add sugar and milk. Cook over water until slightly thickened. Pour hot mixture over softened gelatin and stir until smooth. Chill until slightly thickened. In another bowl, beat egg whites until stiff. Fold into gelatin mixture. Whip cream and add vanilla. Fold this into mixture.

Spread half graham crumbs in bottom of large bowl or flat serving pan. Pour in fluff mixture and top with other half of crumbs. Chill.

Some folks feel this salad adds a special touch to a holiday meal. I feel it's a big pain and not worth the fuss. Good luck!

Supper Smoke

Layered Lettuce Salad

Ingredients:
8 slices bacon
4 eggs
1 head lettuce
1 1/2 cups frozen peas
1/2 cup green pepper, chopped
1 small red onion, chopped
2 cups mayonnaise
2 tbsp. lemon juice
2 tbsp. sugar
4 oz. grated cheddar cheese

Directions:
In skillet, fry bacon until crisp. Remove and blot with paper towels. Boil eggs and cool. In large salad bowl, or flat serving pan, break lettuce into small pieces. Spread frozen peas, then diced green pepper, then chopped onion, the eggs, peeled and chopped, and last, the bacon, crumbled.

In a separate bowl, combine mayonnaise, lemon juice and sugar and spread carefully over salad ingredients. Garnish with cheese Refrigerate 6 to 8 hours.

This is always a winner with our guests. It's a winner with me too, because it can all be done ahead, while you fuss with the rest of the meal. Try to shove it around the table 'til it's all gone though, because it goes totally wimpy by the next day.

Michelle's Garden Salad

Ingredients:
1 red pepper
1 green pepper
1 yellow pepper
2 or 3 green onions, chopped
1/2 to 1 cup black olives, sliced
2 tomatoes
1 small zucchini
1 small yellow squash
1/2 cup red wine vinegar
1/2 cup olive oil
1 pkg. ranch dressing, dry

Directions:
In large mixing bowl chop the peppers, add the onions and olives. Then chop the tomatoes and squash and add to all. In separate bowl combine vinegar, oil and ranch dressing. Pour over veggies and chill to blend flavors. Wonderfully good salad.

Besides cheerfully raising six children on her own, Michelle is one of those innovative cooks who can turn out a lovely meal without using a single recipe! I stand amazed, as I watch her whirl about her kitchen, weaving in and out through children and chatter, while I plod back to my orderly kitchen and my orderly recipes. Guess who has more fun?

Supper Smoke

Crunchy Crab Salad

Ingredients:
3 eggs
1/2 head lettuce
8 oz. imitation crab (or the real stuff if you're feeling fishy and affluent) SNIFF
2 or 3 green onions, chopped
1 tomato, chopped
1 small cucumber, chopped
1 cup salted peanuts
Salad dressing of your choice

Directions:
Boil eggs and set aside to cool. In large bowl break lettuce in small chunks. Add crab, also breaking in small chunks. Add onion, tomato, and cucumber. Add peeled and coarsely chopped eggs. Toss lightly. Just before serving, add salted peanuts. Serve with salad dressing of your choice

**If making a green salad for a crowd, try this. Wash the lettuce and put in a clean pillowcase. Rubber band it and throw it in your washing machine on a short spin cycle. Then store in the refrigerator where it stays crisp in the damp case, until you need it. (HEY WAIT! If you forget it, and throw in a load of underwear, I am not responsible!)

College Salad

Ingredients:
3 cups cauliflower florets
3 cups broccoli florets
1 cup cherry tomatoes, halved and seeded
OR
Thinly slice red pepper
1 red onion, chopped
1 cup black olives, sliced in half
1/2 envelope ranch-style dressing mix*
1/3 cup oil
1/8 cup vinegar
* You may substitute these for the dressing mix:
    1/4 tsp. garlic salt
    1/4 tsp onion salt
    1 tsp. dried parsley
    1/4 tsp. seasoning salt

Directions:
In large bowl, combine first five ingredients. Combine dressing ingredients in a jar. Cover and shake to blend. Pour over salad veggies and stir. Refrigerate at least three hours before serving, stirring occasionally.

**Cauliflower is only cabbage with a college education.

Broccoli Peanut Salad

Ingredients:
6 to 8 slices bacon
4 to 5 cups broccoli, cut small
1 small red onion, chopped
1 cup raisins
1 cup salted peanuts
1 cup salad dressing or mayonnaise
2 tsps. vinegar
2 tsps. sugar

Directions:
In skillet, fry bacon until crisp. Remove from pan and blot with paper towels. In large mixing bowl, combine broccoli, onion, and raisins. In separate bowl, combine salad dressing, vinegar, and sugar. Pour over broccoli mixture and let set several hours, or over night. Just before serving, add crumbled bacon and peanuts.

Jaws really swing when I serve this salad! People can't seem to get enough of it. It's just as well, 'cause the peanuts want to give up and go limp if held over 'til next day.

Crunchy Pea Salad

Ingredients:
1 (10 oz.) pkg. frozen peas
1 cup diced celery
1 cup coarsely chopped cauliflower
1/4 cup chopped green onion
1 cup chopped cashews
1/2 cup sour cream
1 cup prepared ranch dressing
4 to 6 strips crispy cooked bacon

Directions:
Combine the first five ingredients. In another bowl, combine sour cream and ranch dressing. Pour over vegetables. Just before serving, stir in the crumbled bacon. Chill to serve.

**I like to fry a whole package of bacon at once; layer pieces between paper towels and freeze. So handy to get out just what you need.

Jo's Salad

Ingredients:
1 quart small curd cottage cheese
2 avocados, peeled and cut up
1 green pepper, deseeded and chopped
Tomatoes, cut up
Garlic powder and pepper to taste
Mayonnaise

Directions:
Combine all together and chill. Enough for a crowd

Cousin Jo was truly a wonderful cook, one of the best who don't need recipes. So you have to do a bit of guessing here.

Supper Smoke

Ranch Dressing

Ingredients:
1/4 tsp. salt
1/4 tsp. onion powder
1/4 tsp garlic powder
1/4 tsp. pepper
1/4 tsp dried parsley
1 cup mayonnaise
1 cup buttermilk

Directions:
Combine all ingredients and chill well before serving.

Simple Salad Dressing

Ingredients:
1/3 cup milk
2 tbsp. mayonnaise
2 tbsp. vinegar
1/4 tsp. salt
1/2 cup sugar

Directions:
Combine all ingredients and chill well before serving.

This is so good over fresh lettuce from your garden (or someone else's!)

French Dressing

Ingredients:
3/4 cup oil
1/4 cup vinegar
1/3 cup catsup
1/2 tsp. garlic powder
1/2 tsp. salt
1/2 medium onion, chopped fine
1/2 cup sugar

Directions:
Place all ingredients in blender and blend well. Chill to serve.

Thousand Island Dressing

Ingredients:
1 cup mayonnaise
1/2 cup catsup
1/2 cup sweet pickles, chopped fine
1 tbsp. minced onion OR 1 tsp. onion salt
1 tsp. chili powder
1/4 tsp. garlic salt
1/8 tsp. pepper

Directions:
Mix well and chill before serving.

Phyllis's House Dressing

Ingredients:
1 cup mayonnaise
1/8 tsp. pepper
1/4 to 1/2 tsp. salt
1 tsp. dry mustard
1 1/2 tsp. salad seasoning mix
1/3 cup sugar
1/3 cup vinegar

Directions:
Combine all ingredients and stir briskly.

Phyllis is my own dearly beloved sister. She is also a wonderful cook. She has used this recipe for years and mixes it by taste. So….she says…."If it tastes good, you've got it right." "If it isn't quite right, add something!"

BEST Cole Slaw Dressing

Ingredients:
1/2 cup flour
1/2 cup sugar
2 tsp. salt
1/2 tsp. garlic salt
2 tsp. dry mustard
1/8 tsp. paprika
1 cup water
3/4 cup mild vinegar
2 eggs, slightly beaten
1 tbsp. butter or margarine
Mayonnaise

Directions:
In medium saucepan, combine the first six ingredients and blend well. Slowly add the water and vinegar. Cook over medium heat, stirring constantly, until mixture thickens and boils. Stir at least half the hot mixture into beaten eggs and then return to hot mixture. Bring to boil again, stirring constantly. Remove from heat and add the butter. Stir to blend. Chill. Mixture will be thick. Store in covered container in refrigerator. When ready for dressing blend this mixture half and half with mayonnaise.

Cole slaw is one of my favorite foods and I serve it to guests often. I've tried many cole slaw dressings, but I like this one by far the best. Stores well in cold place and since it is combined with equal amounts of mayonnaise, it makes lots.

South of the Border Dressing

Ingredients:
1/2 cup Miracle Whip
1/3 cup red wine vinegar
1/3 cup sugar
1/2 tsp oregano (rubbed between fingers to make finer)
1/4 tsp garlic powder
Salt and pepper (sprinkle to taste)
1/2 cup whipping cream

Directions:
Combine all ingredients in mixing bowl. Mixture will be runny. Beat with mixer so that cream will thicken the mixture. Serve with Mexican food.

This tasty recipe comes from my niece Marjorie, who got it from HER sister-in-laws and THEY put their heads together and figured out the recipe from a favorite Mexican restaurant and THEY may have got it from Spain and who knows, maybe Eve made it first. Anyway, it's really good.

Potato or Macaroni Salad Dressing

Ingredients:
1 cup cream
2/3 cup salad dressing
1 tbsp. vinegar
3 tsp. prepared mustard
2 tsp. salt
1/2 tsp. pepper

Combine all ingredients and use over cooked potatoes or macaroni, with additional salad ingredients.

Pineapple Cream Salad

Ingredients:
1 (20 oz.) can crushed pineapple
Water
1 (6 oz.) pkg. lemon Jell-O
1 cup whipping cream
1/4 cup sugar
1 cup cottage cheese, or more

Directions:
Drain pineapple, reserving juice. Add enough water to juice to make 2 2/3 cups liquid. In saucepan bring this liquid to boil. Add Jell-O, stirring well to dissolve. Chill until slightly thickened. Meanwhile, whip cream, gradually adding sugar. Fold into Jell-O mixture. Stir in cottage cheese and pineapple. Chill in serving bowl at least 3 hours, or overnight.

**Cottage cheese, sour cream, etc. will keep much longer if you store it upside down in the refrigerator.

Cherry Cola Salad

Ingredients:
1/2 cup water
1/2 cup sugar
1 can cherry pie filling
1 (6 oz.) box cherry Jell-O
1 can crushed pineapple with juice
1 tbsp. lemon juice
1 can cola

Directions:
In large saucepan, combine water and sugar and bring to a boil. Add cherry Jell-O, stirring to dissolve, and bring to boil again. Add pineapple, lemon juice and cola. Chill to serve.

Supper Smoke

Martha Mae's Pineapple Delight

Ingredients:
3/4 cup sugar
2 tbsp. cornstarch
1/8 tsp. salt
1 3/4 cups pineapple juice
                OR
1 (15 oz.) can crushed pineapple, undrained
3 or 4 oranges, peeled and cut in chunks
1 can pineapple chunks, drained
3 or 4 bananas, cut in chunks and dipped in lemon juice
Nuts, coconut, raisins or miniature marshmallows may be added.

Directions:
In saucepan, combine sugar, cornstarch and salt. Add pineapple juice OR crushed pineapple and cook until it comes to a boil and thickens. Cool. In large mixing bowl, combine fruits and pour cooled dressing over all.

Martha Mae has been like an older sister to me for many years. We have enjoyed placing our feet beneath her table innumerable times, including many holiday meals. This is one of the recipes she has shared with me, and I love it so much that I always hope there's some left over for the next day!

Orange/Kiwi Delight
(Variation of Pineapple Delight)

Ingredients:
3/4 cup sugar
2 tbsp. cornstarch
1/8 tsp. salt
1 3/4 cups orange juice
3 or 4 oranges
3 or 4 bananas
4 or 5 kiwi
Maraschino cherries

Directions:
In a saucepan, combine sugar, cornstarch and salt. Add orange juice and cook until thickened. Cool. In large mixing bowl, combine oranges, peeled and cut in chunks, bananas, peeled and dipped in lemon juice, and kiwi, peeled and sliced. Pour dressing over all, mix and serve, using maraschino cherries as garnish.

Very pretty salad, and tasty!

Apricot Pineapple Salad

Ingredients:
1 (6 oz.) pkg. orange Jell-O
1 quart or 1 can apricots
1 can pineapple chunks
1 cup whipping cream and sugar to taste

Directions:
Drain apricots and pineapple, reserving juice. Puree apricots in blender, adding a little juice to make very thick liquid. Dissolve Jell-O in 2 cups boiling water. Stir well to dissolve. Add apricot puree, and enough pineapple juice to make 2 cups. Stir and partially set. Add pineapple chunks. Pour into serving bowl and let set until firm. Whip 1 cup whipping cream adding sugar to taste. Spread over Jell-O and serve.

Supper Smoke

Camella's Cherry Jell-O

Ingredients:
1 large box cherry Jell-O
2 cups boiling water
1 cup cold water
1 can cherry pie filling

Directions:
In large mixing bowl combine Jell-O and boiling water and stir well. Add cold water and cherry pie filling.

Richard and I enjoyed this salad in a lovely Southern home, graced with warm hospitality. Hubby declared later that it was the best Jell-O salad he had ever eaten, so I proceeded to write for the recipe! Hope your hubby thinks so, too. Thank you, Camella.

Citrus Crush Salad

Ingredients:
1 can crushed pineapple
1 can grapefruit sections
1 (6 oz.) pkg. lime Jell-O
2 cups boiling water
1 tbsp. vinegar
1/4 tsp. salt
Shredded cheddar cheese (optional)

Directions:
Drain pineapple and grapefruit, reserving juice. In large mixing bowl, combine lime Jell-O and boiling water, stirring well. Add enough water to reserved juice to make 2 cups. Add this juice, the vinegar and salt, stirring well. Chill until partially set. Add drained fruit; pour into serving bowl and chill to serve. Garnish with shredded cheddar cheese if you wish.

A Sampler of Salads

Frosted Lemon Jell-O

Ingredients:
1 (6 oz.) pkg. lemon Jell-O
2 cups boiling water
1 can lemon-lime soda
1 (20 oz.) can crushed pineapple
1 small can mandarin oranges
2 cups green grapes, halved
1/2 cup sugar
2 tbsp flour
1 egg
1 tbsp. butter or margarine
1 cup whipping cream

Directions:
In large bowl, dissolve Jell-O in boiling water. Slowly stir in soda and refrigerate until partially set. Meanwhile, drain pineapple and mandarins, reserving juice. Stir pineapple, oranges, and grapes into Jell-O. Pour into lightly oiled 9 by 13 inch pan and chill to set. In a saucepan, combine sugar, flour, egg and butter. Stir in reserved fruit juices, (not to exceed 3/4 cup.) Cook until thickened, stirring constantly. Cool. Whip cream and fold into thickened mixture. Spread over Jell-O and chill.

Creamy Orange Salad

Ingredients:
1 (20 oz.) can crushed pineapple, drained WELL
1 (3 oz.) pkg. orange Jell-O
2 cups cream style cottage cheese
1 (8 oz.) tub Cool Whip

Directions:
In large mixing bowl, combine well-drained pineapple and dry orange Jell-O. Stir well to dissolve Jell-O. Add cottage cheese and Cool Whip. Chill to serve.

This comes from a lady who worked with me in the school hot lunch program years ago. As near as I can remember, we had sense enough not to serve it to children, who are almost all hostile to cottage cheese in any form. Green Jell-O is lovely, too.

Supper Smoke

Red Mold Salad

Ingredients:
3 small pkgs. red Jell-O
3 cups boiling water
1 (20 oz.) can crushed pineapple with juice
1 small can frozen lemonade
Whipping cream

Directions:
In large bowl, dissolve Jell-O in boiling water. Chill until partially set. Stir in pineapple and lemonade, undiluted. Pour into lightly oiled Jell-O mold and chill until firm. Unmold on serving plate and garnish with whipped cream.

Tasty salad and pretty enough for the in-laws.

Bavarian Peach Mold

Ingredients:
1 (16 oz.) can sliced peaches
1 (6 oz.) pkg. peach, apricot, or orange Jell-O
1/2 cup sugar
2 cups boiling water
1 tsp. almond extract
1 (8 oz.) carton whipped topping

Directions:
Drain peaches, reserving juice to 2/3 cup. Chop drained peaches and set aside. In another bowl, dissolve Jell-O and sugar in boiling water. Stir in reserved juice. Chill until slightly thickened. Stir in extract and whipped topping. Fold in peaches. Pour into lightly oiled 6-cup mold. Chill firm. Unmold and serve.

**Try adding 1 tsp. of white vinegar to any flavor Jell-O as you make it. Peps it up, and Jell-O stiffens better.

A Cradle of Prayer

Long ago, by a great, wide stream,
A mother wrestled with tears;
Her bleeding heart was aching so,
As she gave to God her fears.

She found a rest, and her faith grew strong,
As she worked by the river's flow;
She prepared an ark, both sound and sure,
And quietly watched it go.

And many an aching heart, since then,
Has found a comfort sweet,
In preparing a careful ark of prayer,
Down low, at the Savior's feet.

Not in spite of it, but because of love,
"Babes" rock on the rivers wide,
Safe in a cradle pitched with faith,
While Mother stands aside.

And many a lost and wandering one,
Has found the harbor home,
When Mother staunched her anxious fears,
And trusted to God alone.

How often a young one, leaving home,
For a distant, unknown land,
Has felt the shove of a trusting heart,
And the strength of God's own hand.

Oh Mother! Fashion an ark of prayer,
Like those of the saints of old,
Though washed with the tears of your loving heart,
They're watched by an angel fold.

Though the streams are wide, and the currents strong,
And they drift far from our view,
They're safer far in God's own plan,
And He will see them through.

Supper Smoke

Now rise from the dreary riverside;
Look homeward, with faith anew.
Trust in the Lord with all thine heart;
He has a song for you.

R.A.S.

The Lord is my strength and my shield; my heart trusted in him, and I am helped; therefore my heart greatly rejoiceth; and with my song will I praise him.

Psalms 28:7

Soups and Stews and Brothy Brews

Come hither, good friends,
Such a damp, cold day!
We'll quaff our stew
And our troubles away!

Soup Hints

If concerned about low-fat meals and have time, cook chicken, beef, etc. for soups the day before and refrigerate. Next day you can easily skim off the fat.

Soup too salty? Add a raw peeled potato, cut in fourths, let it simmer 15 minutes and remove.

You can stretch stew by serving over hot rice.

Try serving chili over baked potatoes, sprinkled with grated cheese. Spoon over breakfast eggs for huevo rancheros, over hot dogs with chopped onion and cheese, or heated in a tortilla with shredded cabbage.

If your soup seems too thin, sprinkle instant potato flakes in, 1 tbsp. at a time, cooking to thicken.

Be sure and don't waste the very inside of the celery bunch. Those pale green leaves have lots of flavor!

If you can't serve cream soup right away, keep it hot over warm water in another kettle, or it will scorch.

Don't discard vegetable juices that are drained off before serving. They are full of flavor and vitamins. Refrigerate or freeze and throw it in your next soup.

Any meats that are browned before adding to soup will give a richer flavor and better color.

Vegetables added to soups will lend a better flavor if they are first sautéed in butter or margarine.

Canned chicken broth is much more expensive than broth made from bouillon cubes, and the flavor difference is slight. However, if you need to be concerned about sodium intake, then canned broth is better.

If soup seems too greasy, drop in a lettuce leaf to absorb excess grease. Remove before serving.

Supper Smoke

North Idaho Moose Stew

Ingredients:
1 large moose, chopped (reserving ears and tail for moose juice)
1 (10 lb.) bag of yellow onions, peeled and chopped
50 lbs. carrots, shredded
5 1/2 cases canned tomatoes (reserving cases for other use)
30 clumps celery, chopped fine
50 cloves of garlic, peeled and minced
25 lbs. rutabagas cut in chunks
100 lbs. Idaho Russet potatoes, peeled and chopped
3 boxes Snortin's Salt
2 large cans pepper
*1 gallon fresh, or frozen, huckleberries, sautéed in bear grease

Directions:
Combine first eight ingredients, and add as many gallons of Kootenai River as will cover all ingredients. Bring to a boil and simmer 1 week. Add salt, pepper and sautéed huckleberries and simmer 6 days. Skim hair and taste. If lacking in flavor, throw in one leather hippie hat and allow to simmer another day.

*This may seem strange, but is actually the ingredient that will add the subtle taste difference. Don't leave it out.

French Onion Beef Stew

Ingredients:
3 lbs. stew beef, cut in cubes
4 medium potatoes, peeled and quartered
2 medium onions, quartered
1/2 tsp. pepper
2 tbsp. quick cook tapioca
1 3/4 cup water
6 carrots, pared and diced
4 stalks celery, diced
1 tbsp. sugar
1 tbsp. salt
1 (10 oz.) can tomato soup
1 (4 oz.) can mushrooms, undrained

Directions:
Place all ingredients, except mushrooms, in 4-quart casserole. Cover and bake at 300 degrees for 4 hours. Just before serving, add mushrooms.

Note: This is a favorite recipe of Richard's Uncle Howard Seaman, who pioneered close to the tiny town of Fernwood, Idaho. His wife Elizabeth taught school there.

Richard and his siblings were known in the neighborhood as the "Seaman Demons" and they thought things would work their way when Aunt Elizabeth became their teacher. She was a small woman with a huge determination and she soon had the "the Seaman Demons" whipped into shape!

Who knows, perhaps this stew was one of her strengths. At any rate, I owe her a debt of gratitude!

Supper Smoke

Big Old Brown Beef Stew

Ingredients:
1 to 2 lbs. stew meat
Kitchen Bouquet
1/2 cup flour
1/4 tsp. garlic salt
1/2 tsp. salt
1/2 tsp pepper
1 quart water
4 or 5 potatoes, cubed
2 or 3 carrots, diced
4 ribs celery, chopped
1 medium onion, chopped
2 cloves garlic, minced
1/2 green pepper, chopped
3 beef bouillon cubes
1 tbsp. Worcestershire sauce
2 cans diced tomatoes
salt and pepper to taste
2 or 3 tbsp. cornstarch

Directions:
In a plastic bag, toss the stew meat and Kitchen Bouquet. In a small bowl combine the flour, salt, pepper, and garlic salt. Add to bag and toss 'til meat is well coated. In heavy stew kettle, brown beef in small amount of oil. Pour the water over the meat, cover and simmer for 2 hours. Add the potatoes, carrots, celery, onion, garlic, green pepper, Worcestershire sauce and tomatoes. Cover and simmer 2 or 3 hours more. If stew is too thick for your liking, add more water. Season with salt and pepper to taste. If you like thick stew you may thicken with cornstarch mixed with a little water. Add to bubbling stew and stir until thickened.

Note: You can't hurry stews. Try to shove 'em along too fast and they'll get tough on ya. Just like a lot of husbands.

Clam Chowder

Ingredients:
5 medium potatoes cut up small
2 stalks celery, including some chopped leaves
1 onion, chopped
1 carrot, grated
salt and pepper
4 potatoes, grated
2 or 3 cans minced or chopped clams, undrained
1/4 tsp. thyme
cream or top milk
2 or 3 slices cooked, crumbled bacon
2 or 3 tbsp. butter

Directions:
In soup kettle, place the 5 cut-up potatoes, celery, onion, and carrot. Add water to cover, and begin cooking. Add salt and pepper to taste. While these are cooking, add the grated potatoes, the clams and thyme. Continue cooking until the cut-up potatoes are done. Add cream or top milk, bacon and butter. Simmer to blend flavors, but do not boil.

My good friend Salinda shared this recipe years ago. I've made it so many times since that I'm not sure it is even the original recipe. We love it.

Supper Smoke

Salmon Chowder

Ingredients:
6 large potatoes, peeled and cut up
2 medium carrots, peeled and chopped small
1 medium onion, diced
4 stalks celery, chopped
1 (14.5 oz.) can chicken broth
1 (14.5 oz.) can salmon, boned
4 tbsp. margarine or butter
4 tbsp. flour
1 tsp. salt
1/2 tsp. pepper
1/8 tsp. cumin
1 cup evaporated, canned milk
3 to 4 cups milk
Cooked and crumbled bacon, optional

Directions:
In large soup kettle, place potatoes, carrots, onion, and celery. Adding water to cover, cook until vegetables are tender. Mash with shortening cutter until only small pieces remain. Add chicken broth and de-boned salmon. Cook slowly. Meanwhile, melt margarine or butter in medium saucepan. Add flour and seasonings. Stir to a boil. Slowly add canned milk and regular milk, stirring constantly. Bring to a boil and continue stirring until thickened. Add to vegetable/salmon mixture. Re-heat, but do not boil. Add cooked and crumbled bacon just before serving.

Pious Potato Soup

Ingredients:
1/3 cup butter or margarine
2 stalks celery, chopped
3/4 to 1 cup chopped onion
2 cans chicken broth
2 1/3 cups potato flakes
1 1/2 cup milk
1 cup cubed cheddar cheese
1 tsp. garlic salt
1/4 tsp. chili powder
1/2 cup sour cream

Directions: In a large saucepan sauté the onion and celery in melted butter. Stir in broth. Bring to a boil, remove from heat and sprinkle in potato flakes, stirring until smooth. Return to heat and continue to stir and cook until thickened. Add cheese, garlic salt and chili powder. Stir until cheese is melted. Slowly add milk. Heat through and then add sour cream. Don't allow to boil.

Supper Smoke

Po' Boy Potato Soup

Ingredients:
3 slices bacon
1/2 large onion, chopped
2 or 3 stalks celery, chopped
6 potatoes, or more, cubed
1 tsp. salt
1/4 tsp. pepper
1 can undiluted cream of mushroom soup
2 or 3 cups milk
1 tsp. crumbled parsley

Directions:
In heavy soup kettle, brown the bacon. Remove bacon and crumble and reserve. In bacon drippings, sauté the onion and celery. Peel and cut up potatoes and add to kettle. Barely cover with water and cook until potatoes are done. Mash, or leave in chunks, as you prefer. Add salt and pepper, mushroom soup and milk. Heat through, but do not boil. Add crumbled bacon and parsley. Heat again.

Note: In a hurry? Just use a bag of home-style hash browns instead of potatoes from scratch.

Soups and Stews and Brothy Brews

Chompy Cheese Chowder

Ingredients:
3 cups water
3 or 4 medium potatoes, cubed
1 cup celery, chopped
1/2 cup carrots, chopped fine
1/2 cup onion, chopped
2 tsp. salt
1/4 tsp pepper
1/4 tsp. thyme
2 cups cubed ham
    OR
1 lb. hamburger, cooked
    OR
1 lb. Kielbasa cut in slices
1/2 cup margarine or butter
1/2 cup flour
1 qt. milk
1 cup Velveeta, or cheddar cheese, shredded

Directions:
In large soup kettle combine the water, potatoes, celery, carrots, onion, salt, pepper and thyme and cook until tender. Add the meat, cover and simmer to blend flavors. In a separate saucepan, melt the margarine. Stir in the flour and cook 'til it bubbles. Slowly add the milk, stirring as you add, and bring to a boil. Boil 1 minute. Add the cheese and stir to melt. Slowly stir into potato mixture. Simmer, but do not boil.

Supper Smoke

Chipper Chili

Ingredients:
2 lbs. small red beans
3 lbs. hamburger
4 or 5 onions
Salt
Pepper
1 (46 oz.) can tomato juice
4 to 6 tbsp. chili powder
1 1/2 tsp. cumin
6 beef bouillon cubes
2 or 3 cloves garlic, chopped
1 tsp. pepper

Directions:
In large soup kettle, cover beans with water and soak 8 hours or overnight. Drain, add water to amply cover and cook beans until soft. Meanwhile, in a large skillet brown the hamburger, adding the chopped onion as it cooks. Add the hamburger/onion mixture to the cooked beans, then the tomato juice, chili powder, cumin, bouillon cubes, garlic and salt and pepper to taste. Simmer to blend flavors.

Hear tell of a lady of means,
Who yearned for a pottage of beans.
She soaked twenty pounds;
Then she cooked them in mounds.
She used WHOLE HOG SEASONING, it seems.

Lima Bean Stew

Ingredients:
1 lb. pkg. small lima beans (dry)
3 (14 1/2 oz.) cans chicken broth
1/2 lb. pork sausage
1 large onion, chopped
3 celery ribs, chopped
1 small red pepper, diced
3 medium carrots, chopped
3 medium potatoes, diced
1/2 tsp. marjoram
1 tsp. salt, or to taste
1/2 tsp. pepper
1/2 tsp. oregano
1 cup cream OR canned milk

Directions:
Cover beans with water and cook until soft. Drain. Add broth. Meanwhile, in heavy skillet fry sausage along with the onion, celery, red pepper, and carrots until sausage is done and vegetables are soft. Add to bean and broth. Add potatoes and seasonings. Cook until potatoes are done. Add cream or canned milk and re-heat, but do not boil.

Supper Smoke

Vegetable Bean Soup

Ingredients:
1 lb. dry navy beans (2 cups)
2 1/2 quarts water
1 meaty ham bone OR 2 smoked pork hocks
1 bay leaf
4 cloves garlic, chopped
2 medium carrots, cubed small
1/2 large onion, chopped
5 celery ribs, chopped
2 tsp. salt
1/2 tsp. pepper
1/8 tsp. paprika
2 (15 oz.) cans tomatoes
1 or 2 tbsp. Worcestershire sauce
Chicken broth

Directions:
Rinse beans and cover with the water. Bring to a boil and cook for 2 minutes. Remove from heat and let stand for 2 hours. Add ham, bay leaf and garlic. Cover and simmer 1 1/2 to 2 hours, or until beans are almost tender. Add carrots, onion, celery, salt, pepper, paprika, tomatoes, and Worcestershire sauce. Simmer one hour more. If you prefer a soup with more liquid, add chicken broth or 2 chicken bouillon cubes and 2 cups water.

Split Pea Soup

Ingredients:
1 pkg. split peas (green or yellow)
4 cups chicken broth
2 cups water
3 tbsp. margarine or butter
1 small onion, chopped
2 carrots, diced
3 celery stalks, diced
1 cup, or more, diced ham
1 bay leaf
1/4 tsp. garlic powder
1 tsp. celery salt
Salt and pepper to taste
Milk or cream

Directions:
In a large kettle soak the peas in the chicken broth. When peas have swelled add the water. Simmer. Meanwhile, in a heavy skillet melt the margarine or butter. Sauté the onion, carrots, celery and ham. Add to simmering peas the bay leaf, garlic powder, celery salt and salt and pepper to taste. Add sautéed vegetables, cover and continue cooking until peas are soft. Add milk or cream 'til of serving consistency.

Supper Smoke

A Tad Tony Minestrone

Ingredients:
1 lb. Italian sausage
1 tbsp. vegetable oil
1 cup onion, diced
2 carrots, diced
1 clove garlic, minced
2 tsp. basil, crumbled
2 small zucchini, sliced
1 pint canned tomatoes
6 beef bouillon cubes
3 cups water
1/4 tsp. pepper
2 cans Great Northern beans, undrained
Chopped parsley
1 or 2 tbsp. Worcestershire sauce

Directions:
Slice sausage and brown in large soup kettle. Add onions, carrots, garlic and basil and cook 5 minutes. Add zucchini, tomatoes, bouillon cubes, water, pepper and Worcestershire sauce. Simmer 1 hour. Add beans and simmer 20 minutes more. Garnish with parsley.

Cheese 'N Chicken Chowder

Ingredients:
2 tbsp. butter or margarine
1 cup chopped celery
1 cup chopped green pepper
1 cup chopped onion
1/4 cup oatmeal, (dry)
4 cups chicken broth
1 3/4 cup milk
Salt to taste
1/8 tsp. cayenne pepper
1 tsp. parsley, crushed
1 cup grated cheese

Directions:
In large stew kettle, melt butter or margarine. Sauté celery, green pepper and onion until almost soft. Sprinkle oatmeal over all and stir for about 2 minutes. Gradually add chicken broth, stirring until blended. Bring to a boil, lower heat, cover and simmer 15 or 20 minutes. Add milk and seasonings to taste. Add cheese and stir to melt. Re-heat, but do not boil.

Note: For a heartier meal, cooked chicken may be added. This is a favorite at our house.

Chicken Barley Soup

Ingredients:
1 fryer (3 to 4 lbs.) cut up
Water to cover
3 cups carrots, diced
2 cups celery, diced
2 cups barley, cooked
1 cup chopped onion
2 cans stewed tomatoes, chopped
1 (8 oz.) can tomato sauce
6 to 8 chicken bouillon cubes
2 bay leaves
1 tsp. poultry seasoning
1 tsp. pepper
1/2 tsp. sage

Directions:
Cover chicken with water and cook slowly until done. Strain broth and reserve. Debone and cut up chicken. While chicken is cooking, cook the barley, drain and reserve. In large soup kettle, combine the chicken broth, chicken, carrots, celery, and onion. Bring to a boil, lower heat and add the bouillon cubes, tomatoes, tomato sauce, the cooked barley and the seasonings. Cover and simmer 1/2 to 1 hour to blend flavors, adding water if necessary. Remove bay leaves and serve.

Soups and Stews and Brothy Brews

Southern Chicken Gumbo

Ingredients:
4 tbsp. butter or bacon grease
4 tbsp. flour
1 clove garlic, minced
1/4 cup chopped onion
1/4 cup chopped celery
1/2 green pepper, chopped
4 cups chicken broth
1 can sliced tomatoes, undrained
1 (16 oz.) can okra
1 cup fresh or frozen corn
2 bay leaves
1 tsp. salt
Dash of pepper
1 tsp. thyme
1 tsp. oregano
1/4 tsp. Tabasco sauce
2 cups cooked chicken
1 cup sliced, smoked sausage
1 tbsp. dried parsley
1 tbsp. gumbo file
Hot rice

Directions:
Melt butter or grease in heavy soup kettle. Blend in flour and stir continually until flour is brown. Add next four ingredients and cook 'til soft. Stir in broth and next nine ingredients. Heat to a boil and simmer 15 minutes. Stir in meat and parsley. At this point, refrigerate mixture overnight to blend flavors. Next day heat mixture, take out a small amount of liquid to blend with file and return to pot. Stir until combined. Serve over hot rice.

WHEW! Is it worth it? If you want to make like a Southerner, it is!

Supper Smoke

Hissy Chicken Soup

Ingredients:
1 to 1 1/2 cups brown rice, cooked
5 to 6 cups chicken broth
1 large can stewed tomatoes
1 medium onion, chopped
1 medium carrot, peeled and grated
1 cup celery, chopped
1/2 tsp. garlic salt
1/4 tsp. pepper
1 bay leaf
2 to 3 cups chicken, cooked and cubed
2 tbsp. butter or margarine

Directions:
Heat oven to 350 degrees. Spread cooked rice in greased baking pan and bake 30 minutes. Meanwhile, in large soup kettle combine all remaining ingredients except chicken and butter. Bring to a boil, lower heat and simmer 15 to 20 minutes. Add chicken and simmer 20 minutes more. Just before serving soup, melt butter in heavy skillet. Cook and stir rice over medium heat until it begins to turn a very light brown. Be careful not to scorch…5 to 10 minutes. Ladle soup into individual serving bowls and while rice is still hot, spoon several tablespoons into each bowl. It will hiss and sizzle, and makes a very flavorful soup. It's FUN and well worth the trouble.

Mexican Turkey Bean Soup

Ingredients:
2 cans stewed tomatoes
2 cans chicken broth
1 (4 oz.) can green chilies, chopped
2 medium onions, chopped
1 tsp. oregano, crushed
1/2 tsp cumin
1 tsp. garlic salt
1/2 tsp. pepper
1 tsp. chili powder
2 to 4 cups turkey or chicken, cooked and cubed
1 or 2 cans kidney or chili beans
Cheese

Directions:
In a large kettle, combine the tomatoes, broth, chilies, onion, and seasonings. Bring to a boil; reduce heat, and simmer, covered, to blend flavors, about 30 minutes. Add turkey or chicken, and beans and continue simmering until well heated through. Serve with shredded cheese.

Note: This soup is a tasty way to get rid of the remains of Tom Turkey lurking in your refrigerator after the holidays.

Supper Smoke

Hamburger Dumpling Soup

Ingredients:
1/2 lb. hamburger
1 large can stewed tomatoes
4 cups water
3 to 5 beef bouillon cubes
3 stalks celery, chopped
1 carrot, grated
1 tsp. dry onion flakes
1/2 tsp. garlic powder
1/2 tsp. onion powder
1/4 tsp. cumin
1/2 tsp. chili powder
1 egg, beaten
1/2 tsp. salt
1/2 tsp. baking powder
1/2 cup flour

Directions:
Fry hamburger, drain and set aside. In soup kettle, combine next 10 ingredients. Cover and simmer about 20 minutes. Add hamburger and continue to simmer. Combine salt, baking powder and flour. Add beaten egg and mix until crumbly. To gently boiling soup add small spoonfuls of dumpling mixture, cover, lower heat and simmer 10 to 15 minutes more.

Pedacitos de Masa Stew

Ingredients:
1 lb. hamburger
1/2 medium onion, chopped
3 cloves garlic, minced
1 large can stewed tomatoes
3 cups water
1 chicken bouillon cube
1 can kidney, or chili beans
2 tbsp. taco seasoning mix
1/4 tsp. garlic salt
1 tsp. seasoning salt
Chili powder to taste

Dumplings
1/2 cup corn meal
1/2 cup flour
1 tsp. baking powder
1 tsp. sugar
1/2 tsp. salt
1 egg, beaten
1/2 cup buttermilk

Directions:
Brown hamburger along with the onion and garlic. Drain and set aside. In a large stew kettle (10 to 12 inches diameter) combine the hamburger mixture, tomatoes, water, bouillon and beans. Bring to a boil and reduce to a simmer. Add the seasonings and simmer 20 to 30 minutes to blend flavors. Meanwhile, in small bowl, combine the corn meal, flour, baking powder, sugar and salt. Make a well in center. In another bowl combine the beaten egg and buttermilk. Pour in flour well and mix only until liquid is dissolved. Drop by spoonfuls into simmering stew. Cover and simmer about 20 minutes. DON'T PEEK.

Humungous Hamburger Hullabaloo

Ingredients:
2 lbs. hamburger
1 onion, chopped
12 potatoes, cubed
4 carrots, diced
1/2 green pepper, diced
1/2 head cabbage, shredded
1 can green beans, undrained
1 can peas, undrained
1 large can tomato sauce
1 can pork 'n beans
1 pkg. dry onion soup mix
1/2 tsp. Accent
2 or 3 bay leaves
2 tsp. chili powder
2 or 3 whole peppers
Salt and pepper to taste

Directions:
In large soup kettle, brown hamburger with the chopped onion. Add all the remaining ingredients and enough water to cover well. Bring to a boil, reduce heat and simmer 1 or 2 hours, adding water if necessary.

Note: This makes enough soup to feed everyone in sight and a few around the corner.

Taco Soup

Ingredients:
2 lb. ground beef
1 tsp. garlic powder
1 tsp. onion salt
1 tsp. pepper
1 onion, chopped
3 (4 oz.) cans chopped green chilies
1 can pinto beans, drained
1 can white beans, drained
1 can dark kidney beans, drained
2 quarts canned tomatoes
1 pkg. taco seasoning mix
1 pkg. Ranch dressing mix
2 cups water
Shredded cheese

Directions:
In heavy skillet or stew kettle, brown hamburger, seasoning with the garlic powder, onion salt, and pepper. Add the chopped onion and continue to cook until hamburger is done. Add all the rest of the ingredients except the cheese. Bring to a boil, lower heat and simmer to blend flavors. Serve with shredded cheese as garnish.

Supper Smoke

Picante Tortilla Soup

Ingredients:
1 medium onion, chopped
2 or 3 cloves garlic, minced
2 tbsp. vegetable oil
3 cans stewed tomatoes
1 (10 oz.) can condensed beef broth
1 (10 oz.) can condensed chicken broth
1 (10 oz.) can tomato soup
2 cups water
5 chicken bouillon cubes
2 beef bouillon cubes
1 cup picante sauce
1 tbsp. Worcestershire sauce
1 tsp. cumin
1 tsp. chili powder
2 cans red beans
1 can garbanzo beans

Directions:
In heavy stew kettle sauté onion and garlic in oil. Add all the remaining ingredients and bring to a boil. Reduce heat and simmer 1 to 2 hours. Serve with shredded cheese.

Note: For a heartier soup, you may add 1 pound cooked hamburger.

Hamburger Stew

Ingredients:
1 lb. hamburger
1 whole carrot, unpeeled
2 small onions, whole
4 potatoes, cubed
3 stalks celery, chopped
2 or 3 carrots, peeled and chopped
1 bay leaf
1 tbsp. Kitchen Bouquet
1 (8 oz.) can tomato sauce
2 beef bouillon cubes
2 strips bacon
Salt and pepper to taste

Directions:
In a stew kettle, place the whole carrot and the onions. Cover with water and cook until they are soft. Carefully remove, squeezing juice from the onions. Discard vegetables, but reserve the broth. Meanwhile brown and drain the hamburger. To the vegetable broth add the hamburger, potatoes, celery, carrots, bay leaf, Kitchen Bouquet, tomato sauce, bouillon cubes, and the two strips of bacon. Cover and simmer 'til potatoes and carrots are soft. Remove bacon and discard. Add salt and pepper to taste and continue to simmer for 20 minutes. Additional water may be added during cooking time.

Supper Smoke

Meatball Stew

Ingredients:
1 egg, beaten
1 tsp. salt
1 tsp. Italian seasoning
1/4 tsp. pepper
2 cloves garlic, minced
1 small onion, chopped
1 cup soft bread crumbs
1/2 lb. pork sausage
1 lb. ground beef
2 cans condensed beef broth
1 can cream of chicken OR golden mushroom soup
1 can tomato soup
4 to 6 cups water
1 medium onion, chopped
3 to 4 medium potatoes, cut small
2 to 3 celery stalks, chopped
3 medium carrots, chopped
2 tbsp. parsley flakes

Directions:
Combine egg, seasonings, garlic, onion, crumbs, pork sausage and ground beef. Form into small balls and brown in small amount of oil. Set aside. In large soup kettle, add all remaining ingredients and bring to a boil. Cook for 15 minutes, then add meatballs and simmer for 1 to 2 hours.

Have you read of the maiden of Crete?
She used stew pots for soaking her feet.
"A receipt! Oh, Please do," cried her friends
                not a few,
"For that wonderfully flavorful stew!"
                (Would you?)

Cream of Broccoli Soup

Ingredients:
1 tbsp. butter or margarine, melted
1 small onion, chopped
1 stalk celery, chopped
2 cups water
2 chicken bouillon cubes
2 tbsp. uncooked rice
2 (10 oz.) pkg. chopped broccoli
1/2 cup cream

Directions:
In soup kettle, sauté onion and celery in melted butter. Add the water, bouillon cubes and rice. Bring to a boil, lower heat and simmer 15 to 20 minutes. Add chopped broccoli and continue to simmer until broccoli is broken up and heated through. Just before serving add cream. Reheat, but do not boil.

Supper Smoke

Cream of Cabbage Soup

Ingredients:
1/4 cup butter or margarine
3 stalks celery, chopped
1/2 cup onion, chopped
1 carrot, grated
1 to 2 cups cabbage, diced
4 cups chicken broth, divided
6 tbsp. flour
1/4 tsp. pepper
1 tsp. salt
1/2 tsp. thyme
2 tbsp. parsley, crushed
1 to 2 cups cubed ham, sliced kielbasa, or smokies
 2 or more cups cream or milk

Directions:
In large soup kettle melt margarine. Sauté celery, onion and carrot until tender. Add diced cabbage. Cover and simmer on low heat. In a saucepan, combine 1 cup broth with flour, mixing 'til smooth. Add slowly to simmering vegetables. Then add 3 more cups broth, the seasonings and the meat. Simmer to blend flavors, 20 to 30 minutes. Just before serving, add cream or milk. Reheat, but do not boil.

Soups and Stews and Brothy Brews

Cauliflower Bacon Chowder

Ingredients:
1/4 lb. bacon, cooked and crumbled
4 cups water
6 chicken bouillon cubes
1 medium head of cauliflower
3 stalks celery, chopped
1 medium onion, chopped
1 tbsp. lemon juice
2 tbsp. margarine or butter
1/4 cup flour
1 1/2 cups milk
1/8 tsp. pepper

Directions:
In large soup kettle combine water and bouillon cubes. Bring to boil and dissolve bouillon. Remove 2 cups of broth and set aside. To remaining broth add cauliflower, celery, onion and lemon juice. Heat to boiling, reduce heat, cover and simmer 15 to 20 minutes or until vegetables are broken up, or tender. Do not drain. With pastry cutter or small mixer, break up vegetables into small pieces. In a saucepan, melt margarine, add flour and bring to a bubble. Slowly add reserved broth. Add milk and continue cooking until thickened. Pour over vegetables and add pepper and bacon. Reheat, but do not boil.

Note: Cauliflower is nothing but cabbage with a college education. – Mark Twain

Supper Smoke

Toothsome Tomato Soup

Ingredients:
2 tbsp. butter or margarine
2 tbsp. flour
1/4 tsp. onion powder
Dash of pepper
1 tbsp. dry onion flakes
1/2 to 1 tsp. chili powder
2 cubes chicken bouillon
1 (16 oz.) can tomato sauce
2 cups water
2 cups milk
1 cup cooked brown rice

Directions:
In soup kettle, melt butter. Stir in flour, onion powder, pepper, onion flakes and chili powder. Place over heat and bring to a bubble while stirring constantly. Remove from heat and add bouillon cubes and slowly stir in tomato sauce and water. Return to heat and bring to a boil, stirring to thicken. Add milk and cooked rice, blending well. Reheat, but do not boil.

You really should have a crack at this. It is so basic, but very tasty. If you use skim milk, you have a very low fat meal.

Soups and Stews and Brothy Brews

E.E.A.O.W.! Diet Vegetable Soup
(EAT, EAT, all one wants!)

Ingredients:
Cooking spray
5 medium carrots cut thin
3 stalks celery, chopped
3 large onions, chopped
2 cloves garlic, minced
1 small head boc choy cabbage, shredded
2 medium sweet potatoes, yams OR parsnips
1 to 2 cups chopped broccoli
2 (28 oz.) cans tomatoes, chopped
2 to 3 pints water
3 bouillon cubes
1 tbsp. dried parsley
1 tsp. salt
1/2 tsp. pepper
1 pkg. dry mushroom gravy mix

Directions:
Spray large soup kettle with cooking spray. Add all vegetables, stirring as you add. Add tomatoes, water, bouillon, seasonings, and gravy mix. Bring to a boil, reduce heat and simmer until vegetables are soft.

Note: I tell you, (and I kid you not)
          If you eat only soup in this pot
          You'll either be thin clear up to your chin
          Or you cheated somewhere, and got caught.

Supper Smoke

Low Fat Bean/Rice Soup

Ingredients:
1 pkg. mushroom gravy mix, cooked as directed
2 cups water
2 chicken bouillon cubes
2 cups tomato juice
1 can non-fat refried beans
2 cups brown rice, cooked
Hot sauce to taste

Directions:
To cooked mushroom gravy, add water, bouillon and tomato juice. Bring to boil, cover and simmer 'til bouillon is dissolved, 10 or 15 minutes. Add beans, rice and hot sauce to taste. Add more water if you prefer. Simmer until ready to serve.

Note: Take it or leave it. At least it swats down the hunger pangs.

The Music of Life

When we reach heaven, I feel assured that there will be music. We will be greeted with grand and glorious anthems, such as we have never dreamed to hear on earth. I believe there will be numberless compositions, arrangements, chords and melodies, all to the Glory of God. Surely we will each become a part of making this music real.

It seems to me there will be one vital chord, perhaps the most beautiful of all, which will echo and resound through every part of heaven. It is a chord that every true child of God has already heard on earth. It is the chord of thanksgiving.

We heard it first on a cold, dark mountain. We had traveled many a weary mile, and the burden we carried had become so heavy. As we stumbled along, darkness closed in about us, and we knew we were lost. Wild and fierce beasts stalked us from the shadows, and even the brave little fire we tried to kindle could not banish the fears, nor the creeping cold. The night wore on, without rest, until at last we heard a call! Could it be? YES! Someone was searching for us! Someone with a light!

We answered that call, and plunged toward it. When our seeking Savior found us, and He shone His light upon us, all fear and shadows fell away. The heavy burden was taken from us, and it was then that a warm and joyous fire was kindled within, and we heard that first clear chord of thanksgiving ring out in our heart! Every child of God will carry it with him here, and on into heaven.

He will also begin to learn that the music of life is not tuned to circumstance, possessions, or events; but the music comes from that flame that is glowing within his own soul. Every person views his own circumstances through the reflection of what is burning within.

If he nurtures this flame, he can be assured that he will never find himself in real poverty, nor any poor or dismal dwelling. For the light of this flame, mingled with cords of thanksgiving, shed a glow on the meanest of scenes, and are blessed by God.

Yet we are all so human. Our feet shuffle through the dust of this earth, and from time to time, we find that our flame has diminished to a tiny flicker, and the music seems gone from our lives.

Thankfulness is vital to a child of God. We simply cannot prosper without it. How then, to re-kindle the flame, and again hear the music?

We must face ourselves honestly, but how? We cannot hope to re-kindle the flame of thanksgiving until we are willing to see ourselves in God's light. It has been said that no man is a failure until he begins to blame others for his mistakes. It could also be said that no man can be truly thankful until

Supper Smoke

he ceases to blame circumstances for the lack of music in his own heart. We must search for the root cause within, and for this search, we need the help of God.

As a child of God moves along life's pathway, he learns that his Father is one in whom he can place his total trust. He begins to see that worry is a heavy load, and not suited for a child of God. It is a well-disguised need to be in control. When one lets go of that need to control, and yields to God's plan for his life, then he is given a precious gift of trust. This allows God to work His wonders through us…to keep His promises to us…and to fan the flames of thanksgiving.

It is so important that we believe in God's plan for our lives. Each of us is a unique individual, planned and formed by the Master's hand. There are no two on earth just the same. He who has formed us with care, also delights in us, and longs to bring us to Glory. Once we have surrendered to God's plan for us, the music of our lives WILL come. The flame within will glow quietly, and so steadily that no adverse wind can stifle it.

Yes, there are steep mountains to climb, and we need not think we shall escape the dark valleys, but nevertheless, the child of God never travels alone. Even should he stumble and fall, there is a steady, caring hand to help him up and along.

The child of God, led by his Father, and warmed by this steady flame, will find the music of life in the very mundane affairs and duties. He will not require many possessions, or outstanding experiences; for the flame of his heart will light the simplest scenes and the ordinary events of life. He will be a steady light for others. It has been said that people are like stained glass windows. They glow and sparkle when it is bright and sunny, but when it grows dark, their beauty is revealed only if there is a light inside.

He will find pleasure in the music he hears from those about him. He will look upon all men in the light of God's love, as God sees him, enhanced by the warm treasures he carries in his own heart.

A life of thanksgiving does not mean we will never seek to better our circumstances, nor look for God-given pleasures where we may find them. But if, in our going and seeking, we find that impatience, restlessness, and discontent have become our companions, we would do well to step aside and re-kindle the flame.

The thankful one will not be found trying to avoid hard work, or the menial and monotonous chores of everyday living. He will have learned that there are hidden gifts in work that must be done, whether we like it or not. Forming a habit of completing the job, and doing it well, will result in temperance, strength of character and a contentment the idle man will never know.

The thankful one loves to share. Thanksgiving and sharing are inseparable. It has been said that the grace of stewardship is progressive, the more one is thankful, the more one gives, and the more one gives, the more he receives, thus creating a beautiful circle of blessing. He will share much more than his material goods. So it will be also, in the returns he receives. God's gifts are chosen precisely for each individual need, and they are always larger and better than our own.

How good it is to hold to our Father's hand as we look into the future! We can view it as an enticing book we have not yet read. We will know that, as we turn each new page of our lives, that it will not be events or circumstances, but our own thoughts, reflected in the flame of God's love, that will bring music to each day, and will determine the story as the chapters unfold.

R.A.S.

What's For Supper?

Our children grew on humble fare
Quite happy too, because
They thought hamburger and wieners
Were the only meat there was!

Waikiki Supper

We awoke on the twelfth floor of a hotel in Honolulu. We had recovered from a long overseas flight, and, in my case, airsickness as well. Now we were ready for a brighter day. Our daughter and her friend, and Richard and I departed in opposite directions, agreeing to check the hotel lobby for messages as to where we should meet later. But later came and went, and no messages. We waited. Still none. We loaded all our luggage in the rental car and checked out of our room, since we were to leave on an evening flight. A very wealthy, but kindly old dowager approached us, revealing that she had seen the girls earlier and one of them and looked "very pale." Richard began to pace the streets. At last we spotted them, rushing down the street toward the hotel, looking hale, hearty and excited. They'd had a wonderful day, and were now thrilled about a catamaran cruise they had done, and were anxious to join us in another one! Hubby was cross, tired and hungry and by then no longer interested in adventure. But SOMEHOW he was persuaded, with the provision that we find something to eat first. We found an establishment where we could purchase food "to go" and then, clutching our sack suppers, we tore through the sands of Waikiki beach toward the LAST catamaran going out that evening! Maybe they saw the sand flying as we came, because they waited, and YES, they would take us out on the sunset cruise! We waded out and climbed aboard and soon began our belated supper, since we were starved by then. The two very congenial natives took us out about 1/2 mile all the while regaling us with native lore of the Islands. Then they cut the motor, hoisted the sail, and we were adrift. Silence descended, as well as evening shadows, and as we rode the swells, we watched the lights began to twinkle along the harbor, and the sunset to glorify the evening sky. It was one of the most thrilling events of my life, and to think we almost missed it!

The Hawaiian supper we enjoyed? Yes, I want to give you that recipe. I want to tell you that…when adventure calls…GRAB A BIG MAC AND GO!!

Supper Smoke

Bread Pockets

Ingredients:
    Filling: 1 lb. hamburger
                1 medium onion, chopped
                1 tsp. salt
                1/4 tsp. pepper
                1 (15 1/2 oz.) can barbeque beans
                1 tsp. to 2 tbsp. chili powder, depending on taste
                Tomato sauce

    Bread: 1 1/2 cups warm water
                2 pkg. dry yeast
                1/3 cup sugar
                1 tsp. salt
                3 cups flour

1 to 1 1/2 lb. cheddar cheese, shredded
1/3 cup butter or margarine, melted
Corn meal

Directions:
Filling: Fry hamburger with the chopped onion and salt and pepper. Drain. To the hamburger mixture add the beans, chili powder and enough tomato sauce to make a slightly sloppy mixture. Cover and simmer 15 or 20 minutes. Cool.

Bread: In large mixing bowl, sprinkle the yeast over the warm water. Sprinkle a small part of the sugar over yeast mixture to hasten dissolving. When dissolved, add the rest of the sugar, the salt and the flour all at once, stirring to make a stiff dough. Turn out on floured surface and knead to soft and elastic, adding more flour if necessary. Shape into round ball and place in greased bowl. Cover and let rise.

Grease two large baking sheets. Have the cooled hamburger mixture, the shredded cheese, the melted butter and the corn meal ready. Now punch down the dough and divide into 10 balls. Flour a board and roll each ball into 7-inch diameter. Place 1/2 cup meat mixture on one side of a dough round. Place about 1/3 cup shredded cheese on top. Flop other half of dough over meat mixture, crimping edges to form a half circle. Place on greased baking sheet, brush with melted butter and sprinkle with corn meal. Continue with dough rounds, placing five finished rounds on each baking sheet. Let rise until slightly puffy. Bake at 350 degrees for 10 to 15 minutes.

NOTE: I devised this recipe years ago and it's always been a family favorite. I think I could almost make them with my eyes shut. I've found them especially suited to "take out" meals for new mothers, sick, suffering or WHATEVER. Wrap them individually in foil for easy re-heating and add a salad and a dessert and you have a meal that an all-thumbs husband can easily serve up.

Helen's Meat Loaf

Ingredients:
3 eggs, slightly beaten
1 (8 oz.) can tomato sauce
3 tsp. salt
1 tsp. pepper
1/2 tsp. cumin
1 medium onion, chopped OR 1 pkg. onion soup mix
Green pepper to taste
2 1/4 cups crushed saltine crackers (44 squares!)
3 lbs. hamburger

Directions:
In large mixing bowl combine all ingredients in order given. Place in large baking pan, rounding the top. Bake at 325 degrees for 1 1/2 hours.

NOTE: I secured this recipe from my dear sister-in-law Helen, who turned out delicious fare with an easy and nonchalant hand. Helen "threw things together" with wonderful results, so it wasn't easy to nail her down to a recipe. I have blessed her over and over and over for this one; an all-time favorite.

Supper Smoke

Mini-Meatloaves

Ingredients:
1 cup ketchup
1/4 cup brown sugar
1 tsp. dry mustard
2 eggs, beaten
3 tsp. Worcestershire sauce
2 cups crushed corn flakes
2 tsp. onion powder
1/2 tsp. chili powder
1/2 tsp. garlic powder
1/4 tsp. pepper
2 pounds ground beef

Directions:
In large mixing bowl, combine ketchup, brown sugar, and dry mustard. Reserve 1/2 cup. Add remaining ingredients and divide into greased, larger muffin tins. Brush reserved sauce over each. Bake at 375 degrees for 20 minutes.

These are nice to freeze, individually wrapped.

Poor Man Steak

Ingredients:
1 cup cold water
1 cup cracker crumbs
1 tsp. salt
1/2 tsp. garlic salt
1/2 tsp. pepper
3 lbs. hamburger

1 cup water
1 can tomato soup
1 can cream of mushroom soup
1 can water
1 tbsp. Kitchen Bouquet
1 large onion, sliced

Directions:
In a mixing bowl, combine the first six ingredients. Press firmly into a greased 9 by 13 inch pan. Chill. Cut the chilled meat mixture in squares or oblongs; dip each in flour and fry in small amount of cooking oil, until golden brown. Reserve drippings and arrange meat in greased casserole. To the meat drippings add the water, stirring and heating to dissolve meat bits. Add the soups, the additional water, and the Kitchen Bouquet. Stir to blend well. Layer sliced onion over meat pieces. Pour soup mixture over all. Cover and bake at 350 degrees for 1 hour.

Note: Ever since my friend Ruth gave me her variation of this old favorite, it has been a winner. Guests always polish it all off, sometimes politely leaving one lone piece swimming around in the gravy.

Supper Smoke

Seaman Supper Steak

Ingredients:
Meat Mixture:
- 1 egg, slightly beaten
- 1/2 cup bottled barbeque sauce
- 1/2 tsp. salt
- 1/2 tsp. garlic powder
- 1/2 tsp. pepper
- 1 tbsp. parsley, dried
- 1 tsp. chili powder
- 1 1/2 tsp. baking powder
- 1/4 cup dried onion flakes
- 1/2 cup cracker crumbs
- 1 1/2 lbs. hamburger

Coating mix:
- 1/2 cup flour
- 2 tsp. salt
- 1 tsp. pepper
- 1 tsp. paprika
- 2 tsp. garlic powder
- 1/2 tsp. oregano
- 1/4 tsp. thyme

1/4 cup cooking oil
1 1/2 to 2 cups water
1 can cream of mushroom soup

Directions:
Combine meat ingredients and set aside. Combine dipping mix ingredients. In dipping mix, shape and pat 6 oblong patties. In heavy pan, brown patties in hot oil, reserving drippings. Arrange patties in baking pan. Add enough oil to drippings to make 1/4 cup. Add 1/4 cup of dipping mix, heating and stirring to a bubble. Slowly add water, boil. Add cream of mushroom soup. Pour over patties.

Cover and bake at 350 degrees for 30 to 45 minutes.

Rice and Mushroom Casserole

Ingredients:
1 cup raw regular rice
1 stick margarine (1/2 cup)
1 can onion soup
3/4 cup water
1 jar or small can sliced mushrooms, undrained

Directions:
Place dry rice in a greased two-quart casserole. Melt margarine and add the soup, water and mushrooms. Pour over rice. Cover and bake at 325 degrees for 1 1/2 hours.

Meatball Stroganoff

Ingredients:
1 egg
1/2 tsp. salt
1/4 tsp. pepper
1/2 cup finely chopped onion
1 slice bread, crumbled
1 lb. hamburger
1 can cream of mushroom soup
1/2 cup sour cream
1/3 cup water
Noodles

Directions:
In a mixing bowl, combine egg, salt and pepper, onion, bread and hamburger. Form into small meatballs and brown in cooking oil. Set aside. In saucepan, combine soup, sour cream, and water. Add meatballs, cover and simmer 15 to 20 minutes. Serve over cooked noodles.

> I've never met a meatball
> I couldn't call "success."
> Now doesn't that just beat all?
> And make up for all the mess?

Supper Smoke

Mushroom Meatball Supreme

Ingredients:
4 slices bread
1 cup milk
1 tsp. salt
1/4 tsp. pepper
1 tsp. baking powder
1 lb. hamburger
3 tbsp. oil
1 can cream of mushroom or golden mushroom soup
1/2 cup milk

Directions:
In a large mixing bowl, combine bread and milk and beat to whipped cream consistency. Add the seasonings and hamburger. Form into balls and brown in hot oil. Place in baking dish. Combine soup and milk. Pour over meatballs, cover, and bake at 350 degrees for 1 hour.

Note: Old time favorite. Three Seaman children grew up on this.

Turkey Meatballs

Ingredients:
3 tbsp. oil
1 onion, chopped
1 green pepper, chopped
2 cloves garlic, minced
2 cans tomatoes
2 tbsp. tomato paste
2 tsp. oregano
pinch of sugar
1 tsp. salt
1/4 tsp. pepper
1/4 cup parsley, chopped
1 egg, slightly beaten
1 medium onion, chopped
2 cloves garlic, minced
1 tsp. basil
1 tsp. oregano
2 tsp. salt
1/2 tsp. pepper
2 slices dry bread, crumbled
2 lbs. ground turkey

Directions:
Tomato sauce: In heavy saucepan, sauté the onion, green pepper and garlic in the oil. Add the next seven ingredients and simmer 20 to 30 minutes. Meanwhile, in large bowl, beat the egg. Add all the rest of the ingredients and form into small balls. Brown in oil and add to tomato sauce. Simmer 20 to 30 minutes. Serve with rice or noodles.

Supper Smoke

Tamale Balls

Ingredients:
Meatballs:
- 1/2 cup tomato juice
- 3/4 cup corn meal
- 2 tsp. cumin
- 2 tsp. chili powder
- 1/2 tsp. salt
- 2 cloves garlic, minced
- 1/4 tsp. cayenne pepper
- 1/2 lb. ground beef
- 1/2 ground pork or sausage

Sauce:
- 3 1/2 cups tomato juice
- 2 tsp. cumin
- 2 tsp. chili powder
- 1/2 tsp. salt

Directions:
Meatballs: Combine all ingredients in large bowl and set aside.

Sauce: In large stew kettle, combine all ingredients and bring to a boil. Lower heat and form small balls from meat mixture, adding to sauce. Cover and simmer for 45 minutes.

OR

Form meatballs and place in greased baking pan. Pour sauce over all, cover and bake at 300 degrees for 1 hour.

OR

Forget the sauce part. Rather stir up a batch of your favorite biscuit dough. Roll out and cut in squares. Put raw meatball on each square, wrap each separately and bake on a cookie sheet for about 35 minutes.

Sweet & Sour Meatballs

Ingredients:
2 eggs, beaten
1 tbsp. soy sauce
2/3 cup cracker crumbs
1/2 cup minced celery
1 clove garlic, minced
1/3 cup minced onion
1 tsp. salt
1 1/2 lbs. hamburger
Cooking oil

1 can pineapple tidbits, drained and juice reserved
1 cup chicken broth
1/2 cup vinegar
2 tbsp. soy sauce
1 cup brown sugar
3 tbsp. cornstarch
2/3 cup chopped green pepper

Directions:
Meatballs: Combine first 8 ingredients, form in small balls and brown in hot cooking oil. Set aside.

Sauce: Set drained pineapple aside. Combine juice, broth, vinegar, soy sauce, brown sugar and corn starch. Blend well and cook over medium heat until thickened, about 1 minute. Add pineapple tidbits and green pepper. Combine sauce and meatballs in heavy saucepan and simmer for 20 to 30 minutes. Serve over hot cooked rice.

Supper Smoke

Barbeque Meatballs

Ingredients:
3/4 cup oatmeal, uncooked
1 cup milk
1 1/2 tsp. salt
1/2 tsp. pepper
1 small onion, chopped
1 1/2 lbs. hamburger

2 tbsp brown sugar
1 tbsp. cornstarch
1/2 tsp. chili powder
1/2 tsp. garlic salt
1/4 tsp. onion salt
1 cup catsup
1/2 cup water
2 tbsp. vinegar
1 tbsp Worcestershire sauce
1 tsp. liquid smoke

Directions:
Meatballs: Combine all 6 ingredients in order given. Shape into balls and brown in cooking oil. Place in baking dish.

Sauce: In a saucepan combine dry ingredients and mix well. Add next five ingredients. Cook until sauce has thickened. Pour over meatballs, cover, and bake at 350 degrees for 1 hour.

** When storing tomatoey leftovers in plastic containers, spray inside of container with cooking spray to prevent staining.

Company Beans and Meatballs

Ingredients:
2 eggs, slightly beaten
1 1/3 cup milk
1 pkg. onion soup mix
2 tsp. salt
1 tsp. pepper
2 tbsp. parsley leaves, crushed
1 1/2 cups dry bread crumbs
3 lbs. hamburger

2 large cans pork and beans
1 (8 oz.) tomato sauce
1/2 cup chopped onion
1 tsp. salt
1/2 tsp. pepper
1 tsp. dry mustard
Brown sugar to taste

Directions:
Meatballs: Combine all ingredients in order given. Shape in balls and brown in oil. Set aside.

Beans: Combine all ingredients in order given. Arrange meatballs in large greased baking pan. Pour bean mixture over all. Cover and bake at 300 degrees for 1 1/2 to 2 hours.

Note: This recipe brings "tongue in cheek" memories. I worked it out as a young bride about the same time I learned to run a can opener, and while we struggled with a thrifty food budget. I served it to guests many times, and bless their hearts, they cheerfully ate it. I include it because it's actually kind of good, especially for picnics.

Supper Smoke

Meat and Taters

Ingredients:
1 lb. ground beef
1/2 cup sour cream
1/2 cup crushed soda crackers
1 small can mushroom pieces and liquid
1/2 cup chopped onion
1/2 tsp. salt
1/8 tsp pepper
4 cups thinly sliced potatoes
1 medium onion
1 tsp. salt
3/4 cup grated cheese

Directions:
Combine the first seven ingredients and set aside. Grease bottom and sides of 2 quart baking dish. Arrange the potato slices, onion, seasonings and cheese. Place hamburger mixture on top. Cover and bake at 350 degrees for 1 to 1 1/2 hours.

Big Dinner Casserole

Ingredients:
1 egg, beaten
1 cup sour cream or buttermilk
1 cup crushed soda crackers
1 (4 oz.) can sliced mushrooms, drained
1 cup chopped onion
2 tsp. salt
1/2 tsp. pepper
1/2 cumin
2 lbs. hamburger
1/4 cup margarine or butter
1/4 cup flour
1 tsp. salt
1/2 tsp. dry mustard
1 1/2 cups milk
1 1/2 cups shredded cheddar cheese
6 or 7 potatoes, peeled and cut in 1/4 inch slices
1/2 to 1 cup chopped onion
3 stalks celery, chopped
5 medium carrots, sliced
Salt and pepper

Directions:
In large mixing bowl, combine first nine ingredients and set aside. In saucepan, melt margarine. Add flour, salt and dry mustard and heat 'till bubbly, stirring constantly. Remove from heat and add milk. Heat to boiling and add cheese. Set aside. In greased large roasting pan, layer the potatoes, onion, celery and carrots, seasoning with salt and pepper. Pour milk mixture over vegetables. Arrange meat mixture over all. Cover tightly and bake at 300 degrees for 3 hours. Serves 10.

Supper Smoke

Corn Bread Pie

Ingredients:
1 pound hamburger
1 large onion, chopped
1 can tomato soup
1 1/2 cups water
1 tsp. salt
3/4 tsp. pepper
1 tbsp. chili powder
1 can corn, drained
1/2 cup chopped green pepper
3/4 cup corn meal
1 tbsp. sugar
1 tbsp. flour
1 1/2 tsp. baking powder
1 egg, well beaten
1/2 cup milk
1 tbsp. oil

Directions:
Brown the hamburger and onion in skillet. Drain. Add the soup, water, seasonings, corn and green pepper. Simmer 15 minutes to blend flavors. Pour mixture into greased casserole. Make a batter of the following seven ingredients. Pour over meat mixture and bake at 350 degrees for 25 or 30 minutes.

Hamburger-Garden-Steamy-Creamy

Ingredients:
1/2 to 1 lb. hamburger
1 cup chopped onion
1/2 tsp. garlic powder
1/2 tsp. salt
1/4 tsp pepper
1 cup beef broth
Carrots, cauliflower, celery, potatoes, and broccoli
1/4 cup margarine or butter, melted
1/4 cup flour
1/2 tsp. salt
1/8 tsp. pepper
1 cup, or more, milk
1 cup, or more, grated cheddar cheese

Directions:
In heavy skillet, cook hamburger with chopped onion and seasonings. Drain. Add beef broth and begin to simmer. Begin to add chopped vegetable, starting with the hardest. Cover and steam on low heat. While veggies are steaming, make a white sauce. In saucepan, melt butter. Add flour and seasonings and bring to a bubble. Slowly add milk, stirring constantly and cooking until thickened. Add cheese and stir until melted. Serve over vegetable meat mix.

Note: This recipe comes from my daughter-in-law, Karen. She and son Kirk raise a bountiful harvest of veggies each summer, and they all rise up on leafy stalks and shout rudely to be steamed, fried, roasted, canned, and frozen. Occasionally I go there and throw open my trunk and come home laden with offerings.
Note-Note: When choosing a daughter-in-law, try to find a generous gardener.

Supper Smoke

Mountain Macaroni
A fine recipe from the Swiss Alps

Esther's Guesthouse snuggles on a cliff side beneath the mighty Jungfrau, and yet high above the Lauterbrunnen Valley. We found it in the tiny Alpine village of Gimmelwald, Switzerland, and we settled right in. There are shelves at the bottom of the winding stairway where all the guests are to leave their shoes. On the wall in our cozy room there is a sign that says BITTE NICHT AUF DEN BETTEN HERUMSPRINNEN (Please don't jump on the bed.)

Weary from travel, Richard and I found a restful peace that we shall never forget. It was as though we had stepped back in time one hundred years or so.

On the far edge of Gimmelwald we found a bench and a kitty who bade us a hearty welcome. The view of the Jungfrau from this vantage is so breath taking that we felt a hushed reverence, such as one would feel in a cathedral, just before the service begins.

Esther graciously submitted this recipe for my cookbook. It is delicious.

Ingredients:
2 to 3 cups coarsely chopped onions (yes, CUPS!)
4 tbsp. butter, melted…sorry, margarine won't do here
Salt and Pepper
2 medium potatoes, peeled and cubed
2 cups dry macaroni
1 cup cream
2 cups shredded cheese, such as Parmesan, Gouda, Swiss or cheddar

Directions:
Heat oven to 425 degrees. Place chopped onion in greased 2-quart casserole dish. Sprinkle with salt and pepper. Drizzle butter over all. Bake for 30 minutes, or until golden brown, stirring occasionally. While onions are baking, peel and cube potatoes. Bring to a boil in salted water. Add macaroni and cook until both are just tender. Meanwhile slowly heat, but do not boil the cream. Add shredded cheese and stir to blend. When onions are done, drain potatoes/macaroni mixture. Take casserole from oven and remove onions. Pour hot potatoes/macaroni mixture in

What's For Supper?

casserole. Spread onions over top. Pour cream/cheese mixture over all. Serve at once.

> Esther's Guesthouse
> Esther von Allmen
> Gimmelwald, Switzerland

Champion Cheesy Casserole

Ingredients:
2 cups noodles, uncooked
1 pound hamburger
1 tbsp diced onion
1 tbsp salt
1 1/2 cups cottage cheese
1 can cream of mushroom soup
1 cup milk
1 egg
1 cup grated cheese

Directions:
In boiling salted water, cook noodles until only partially done. Drain and set aside. Cook hamburger, onion and salt together. Drain. Add cottage cheese and set aside. In greased casserole, layer noodles and hamburger mixture, starting and ending with noodles. Blend together soup and milk and pour over casserole ingredients. Beat egg and pour over top. Sprinkle with grated cheese. Bake at 350 degrees for 1 hour.

**You can keep cheese from molding much longer if you store it in a cloth wrung out in vinegar.

Supper Smoke

Carole's Spaghetti Sauce

Ingredients:
2 (3 oz.) pkgs. Lawry's original style spaghetti seasonings
2 (15 oz.) cans tomato sauce
5 cups water
4 tbsp. butter

3 (4 oz.) cans mushrooms, drained
1 (quart) jar Prego mushroom spaghetti sauce
3 lbs. hamburger, cooked and drained

Directions:
In large cooking pot, blend the first four ingredients. Bring to a boil, lower heat and simmer for 30 minutes, stirring occasionally. Add the next 3 ingredients and simmer all together for 30 minutes. Serve over spaghetti noodles.

Carole and I have been good friends for over 40 years. We live in the same town and always say we're going to "get together," but somehow we seldom do. Now at least we've done it in a cookbook! Carole worked this recipe out herself and we love it. Thanks Carole…let's get together, okay?!

Spaghetti Casserole

Ingredients:
12 to 16 oz. pkg. spaghetti
Salt and pepper
2 cups shredded cheddar cheese
1 pound hamburger*
Seasoning to taste
1 tbsp. margarine or butter
1 cup chopped onion
1 cup chopped green pepper
1 pint canned tomatoes
1 (8oz.) can tomato sauce
1 (4oz.) can mushrooms, drained
1 cup chopped olives
1 can cream of mushroom soup
1/4 cup parmesan cheese
2 tsp. oregano

Directions:
Cook and drain spaghetti. Season with salt and pepper. Arrange in greased 9 by 13 inch baking pan. Sprinkle with cheese. In large skillet, fry hamburger, seasoning to taste. Drain and arrange over cheese. In a large saucepan, melt the margarine or butter. Sauté the onion and peppers. Add all the rest of ingredients. Simmer to blend flavors. Pour over spaghetti mixture and bake at 350 degrees for 30 to 45 minutes.

*Research tells us that by rinsing 80% pan-fried ground beef with hot water can reduce the fat content by 50%.

Supper Smoke

Meatball Spaghetti Sauce

Ingredients;
1 medium onion, chopped
1 clove garlic, minced
2 tbsp. salad oil
2 1/2 cans, or 2 cups, canned tomatoes
2 (6oz.) cans tomato paste
1 cup water
1 tbsp. sugar
1 1/2 tsp. salt
1/2 tsp. pepper
1 1/2 tsp. oregano
1 bay leaf

4 slices bread
1 lb. ground beef
2 eggs
1/2 cup parmesan cheese
2 tbsp. chopped parsley
1 clove garlic, minced
1 tsp. crushed oregano
1 tsp. salt
1/4 tsp. pepper

Directions:
Sauce: In large kettle, sauté onion and garlic in oil. Add remaining ingredients and simmer for 30 minutes or more, uncovered. Remove bay leaf.

Meatballs: Soak bread in water 2 or 3 minutes. Squeeze water out with hands. Mix with all remaining ingredients, form in balls and brown in oil. Add to simmering sauce and simmer 30 minutes more. Serve over spaghetti.

Mexican Pizza

Ingredients:
1 pkg. flour tortillas
2 cans pinto beans, drained
1 small onion, chopped
3 cloves garlic, minced
1 tsp. chili powder
1/2 tsp. garlic salt
1/2 to 1 tsp. cumin
Hot sauce to taste
1 chicken bouillon cube
1/2 cup water
Cheddar cheese
Shredded lettuce, chopped tomato, chopped olives and sour cream

Directions:
Sauté chopped onion and garlic in small amount of oil. Add drained and mashed pinto beans and seasonings. IF DRY, add the bouillon cube, dissolved in water. Simmer to blend flavors. Spread bean mixture on flour tortilla, generously sprinkle with cheese and top with another tortilla. Fry on each side in hot oil. Place each on a serving plate and cut in fourths. Serve with chopped lettuce, tomato, chopped olives and sour cream.

Supper Smoke

Mezetti

Ingredients:
1 lb. ground beef
1 cup chopped onion
1/4 cup chopped green pepper
2 tbsp. chili powder
2 tsp. garlic salt
1 (8oz.) pkg. egg noodles
1 can cream of mushroom soup, undiluted
1 can tomato soup, undiluted
1 cup water
1 cup grated cheese
Butter
Breadcrumbs
Garlic salt

Directions:
Brown the ground beef, adding the onion, green pepper, and seasonings as you brown the meat. Arrange in greased casserole. Arrange noodles (uncooked) over meat mixture. Combine soups and water and pour over noodles. Sprinkle on the grated cheese. Combine the breadcrumbs with melted butter and season with garlic salt. Spread on top. Cover and bake at 350 degrees for 45 minutes, removing the cover the last few minutes to crisp the crumbs.
Serves 6.

Ah…Bless that dear benignant soul
Who first dished out this casserole!

Vegetable pizza

Ingredients:
2 cans buttermilk biscuits
1 (8oz.) pkg. cream cheese
1/2 cup butter
1/4 cup salad dressing
1/4 cup sour cream
1/2 tsp. onion powder
1 tsp. garlic powder
1/2 tsp. dill weed
1 tsp. sugar
Most, or all, of the following vegetables: chopped carrots, onion, broccoli, cauliflower, celery, cucumber, tomato.

Directions:
Roll out or press biscuits in greased pizza pan. Bake until done. Combine next 8 ingredients and spread on baked, cooled crust. Chop vegetables and arrange on top.

Pizza Burgers

Ingredients:
1 lb. sausage or hamburger
1 medium onion, diced
1 small green pepper, diced
5 oz. pepperoni, cut in small pieces
1 tsp. salt
1/4 tsp. oregano
1/2 tsp. garlic powder
1 (14oz.) can pizza sauce (equals 2 cups)
8 oz. mozzarella cheese
5 English muffins

Directions:
In a skillet, fry and drain the sausage or hamburger. Add the next seven ingredients and simmer to blend flavors. Cool. Separate the muffins, making 10 mini-crusts. Butter each muffin and spoon on filling. Sprinkle on the cheese. Bake at 350 degrees for 10 to 15 minutes.

Supper Smoke

Pop-Over Pizza

Ingredients:
1 lb. hamburger
1 large onion, chopped
1 (1 1/2 oz.) spaghetti sauce mix
1 large can tomato sauce
1/2 cup water
1 (8oz.) pkg. mozzarella cheese, sliced
2 eggs
1 cup milk
1 tbsp. vegetable oil
1 cup flour
1/2 tsp. salt
1/2 cup grated Parmesan cheese

Directions:
Brown hamburger and chopped onion. Drain. Stir in sauce mix, tomato sauce and water. Simmer 10 minutes. Pour into greased 9 by 13 inch pan. Top with cheese slices. Beat eggs, milk, and oil until foamy. Add flour and salt and beat until smooth. Pour batter over meat mixture, spreading to cover completely. Sprinkle with Parmesan cheese. Bake at 400 degrees for 30 minutes, or until golden brown and puffed.

Burrito Supreme

Ingredients:
4 cups cooked beans (or two cans, drained)
1/2 cup chopped onion
Salt, pepper and hot sauce to taste
1 dozen small flour tortillas
Grated cheese
2 lbs. hamburger
1 onion, chopped
1 tsp. garlic powder
1/4 tsp. cumin
1 (4oz.) can green chilies
1 can cream of mushroom soup
2 cubes chicken bouillon, dissolved in water
Salt and pepper to taste
Lettuce, tomato, grated cheese and olives

Directions:
Drain and mash the beans. Cook together with the onion and seasonings. Spread on tortillas, and add cheese. Roll up and place in greased baking pan.

Meanwhile, fry hamburger with the onion. Drain. Add the seasonings, the green chilies, soup and bouillon. Simmer to blend flavors. Mixture should be sloppy. Pour over burritos and bake at 350 degrees until heated through, around 30 minutes. Serve with chopped lettuce, tomatoes, grated cheese and olives.

Supper Smoke

Beef 'N Bean Tacos

Ingredients:
1 lb. ground beef
2 garlic cloves, minced
1 tsp. cumin
1 can bean with bacon soup
1/2 cup water
12 taco shells
Shredded cheese and lettuce

Directions:
Fry hamburger and garlic in small amount of oil. Drain. Add cumin, soup and water. Cover and cook until thoroughly heated. Serve in taco shells with cheese and lettuce.

A bride, in a strict "budget faze,"
Fixed hamburger three hundred ways.
"Let's eat out" hubby pleaded.
"There's a change badly needed!"
So they did…. and had burgers and fries.

Karen's Burritos

Ingredients:
2 lbs. hamburger
1 medium onion, chopped
1 (4oz.) can chopped green chilies
1 (15oz.) can pork and beans, undrained
1 (8oz.) can tomato sauce (or more)
1/2 tsp. chili powder, or to taste
1/2 tsp garlic salt
1/4 tsp. pepper
1 lb. cheese, shredded
2 dozen flour tortillas

Directions:
Fry the hamburger in skillet, adding chopped onion. Drain. Add the chilies, beans, tomato sauce and seasonings. Simmer to blend flavors. Cool slightly and spread over tortillas. Sprinkle with cheese. Roll up, wrap in foil and bake.

Note: The pork and beans sound strange, I know, but it's the best burrito recipe I've tried.

Paco's Hamburgers

Our daughter Marla had fallen in love with Mexico, and we were enjoying our first visit to her there. A kaleidoscope of sound, color, and scent delighted us, from every curb and corner of Chihuahua City. When the mauve shadows of evening began to cool the air, we sauntered down to Paco's hamburger stand. There, amid the roar and dash of the nearby street sounds, we relished the best hamburgers you'll find anywhere! They are topped with Paco's own Salsa Verde and the shy smiles of his sweet little wife and children. We ended the meal with a deliciously soothing hot drink.

Paco has generously shared these recipes, and should you ever find yourself in Chihuahua City, be sure to seek out Paco at suppertime!

Ingredients:
Hamburger buns
Bacon, fried
Cheese slices
2 pounds ground beef
3 garlic cloves, medium size, smashed
1 1/2 cups oatmeal
1 tsp. seasoning salt
Salt and pepper to taste
2 tbsp. dry chicken bouillon
2 slices dry bread, crumbled in fine pieces
1/4 cup milk
Lettuce, tomato, onion and Salsa Verde

Directions:
In large bowl combine the hamburger, seasonings and breadcrumbs, mixing well. If mixture seems too stiff, add the milk. Form patties and place between waxed paper. Place waxed paper covered patties in tortilla press to flatten. Using a small amount of cooking oil fry patties in large frying pan or griddle. When cooked on one side, flip, and place cheese slice over meat to melt. In another skillet with small amount of oil, toast buns and spread with mayonnaise and mustard. Place cooked patty with cheese on toasted bun, top with slice of fried bacon and lettuce, tomato and onion to taste. Add generous amount of Salsa Verde.

Salsa Verde

Ingredients:
1 or 2 green chilies
1 clove garlic
1 pound tomatillos
1 thick slice onion
1/8 tsp. cumin
Salt and cilantro to taste

Directions:
Wash chilies and remove stems. Place chilies, garlic, tomatillos, and onion in kettle with enough water to cover. Cook until chilies are soft. Cool. Drain, reserving juice. Blend in blender with small amount of cooking juice. Add cumin, salt and cilantro to taste.

Café Con Leche

Ingredients:
1/2 cup milk
1/4 tsp. Nescafe (instant coffee)
2 tsp. sugar
1/2 cup milk

Directions:
Heat 1/2 cup milk to boiling. Add Nescafe and sugar, blending well. Add 1/2 cup cold milk and serve.

Supper Smoke

Spicy Rice

Ingredients:
3 cups water
1 tsp. salt
1 1/2 cups dry rice
2 lbs. hamburger
1 large onion, chopped
1 large green pepper, chopped
1 can diced tomatoes
1 can green chilies, undrained
1 cup beef broth
1 tbsp. Worcestershire sauce
1 to 2 tbsp. chili powder
2 tsp. salt
1/4 tsp. hot pepper sauce
2 cups sour cream
2 cups shredded cheese
Corn chips

Directions:
In large saucepan, bring salted water to boil. Add rice, cover and lower heat to simmer. Cook 20 minutes. In skillet, fry hamburger with onion. Drain. Add next 8 ingredients and simmer 10 minutes. Add rice, sour cream, and cheese. Cook, stirring constantly until cheese is melted. Serve over corn chips. May garnish with shredded lettuce and chopped tomatoes.

Serves 10 to 12 generously

Mexican Rice

Ingredients:
2 cups uncooked rice
1/4 cup oil
6 cups water
1/2 cup onion, chopped
5 to 6 chicken bouillon cubes
1 tbsp. or less, Accent
2 or 3 bay leaves
1/2 tsp salt
1/4 tsp. pepper
1 tsp. garlic powder
1/2 to 3/4 lb. mozzarella cheese
1 (4oz.) can green chilies

Directions:
Fry rice in the oil until browned, stirring constantly. Set aside. To the water, add all the seasonings, bring to a boil and simmer 20 minutes. In a greased 9 by 12 inch pan, arrange half of the browned rice. Then add the cheese, then the green chilies. Cover with the remaining rice. Pour seasoned water over all. Cover and bake at 350 degrees for 1 hour.

Supper Smoke

The Enchilada Casserole

Ingredients:
2 lbs. hamburger
1 medium onion, chopped
Salt and pepper to taste
1 cube margarine
3/4 cup flour
2 to 3 tbsp. chili powder
1 tsp. salt
1/2 tsp. pepper
1 quart tomato juice
1/3 to 1/2 lb. cheddar cheese, shredded
12 corn tortillas

Directions:
Fry together the hamburger, onion, salt and pepper. Drain and set aside. In large saucepan, melt the margarine. Stir in the flour, chili powder and salt and pepper. Slowly add the tomato juice, stirring to blend. Heat to boiling and stir until thickened. In large greased baking pan, pour enough tomato mixture to cover bottom. Then dip four tortillas in sauce and lay on bottom, then a layer of hamburger, then cheese. Repeat layering two more times. Pour remainder of sauce over all, sprinkle with cheese, cover and bake in slow oven 250 to 300 degrees for 1 1/2 hours.

Note: I have tried numerous enchilada casseroles, but we are always happiest with this one. It is one of hubby's favorite dishes.

Laredo Casserole

Ingredients:
1 lb. hamburger
1 tsp. salt
1/2 tsp. pepper
2 tsp. chili powder, or to taste
1/4 cup water
1 pkg. corn tortilla chips
1 can cream of chicken soup
1/2 cup water
1 medium can tomatoes
1 small can green chili peppers
1 bunch, or less, green onions, chopped
1 can chili beans
3/4 lb. sharp cheddar cheese

Directions:
Brown hamburger with salt and pepper. Drain. Add chili powder and water, cooking 'til dry. In a greased 9 by 13 inch baking pan, spread part of chips. Combine soup, water, tomatoes, peppers and onions. Spread half over chips. Spread chili beans next, then other half of tomato/soup mixture. Top with another layer of chips and then cheese. Bake at 300 degrees for 1 hour.

Beef and Potato Nacho Casserole

Ingredients:
2 lbs. ground beef
3/4 cup chopped onion, divided
1 pkg. taco seasoning mix
3/4 cup water
1 (8oz.) can tomato sauce
1 (16oz) can red kidney beans, drained
1 (4oz.) can chopped green chilies
1 (24oz.) pkg. frozen hash brown potatoes, thawed
1 can nacho cheese soup, undiluted
1/2 cup milk
1/4 cup chopped green pepper
1/4 tsp. sugar
1 tsp. Worcestershire sauce
Paprika

Directions:
Brown beef with onion in skillet. Drain. Stir in taco seasoning, water and tomato sauce. Bring to a boil and simmer 1 minute. Spread mixture in bottom of greased 9 by 13 inch pan. Top with chilies, beans and potatoes. In mixing bowl combine soup, milk, green pepper, remaining onion, sugar and Worcestershire sauce. Pour over potatoes. Sprinkle with paprika. Cover with foil and bake at 350 degrees for 1 hour. Remove foil and bake another 15 minutes.

Sunday Dinner Roast

Ingredients:
Beef roast (a cheaper cut is fine)
Browning sauce, such as Kitchen Bouquet
1 pkg. dry onion soup mix
1 can undiluted cream of mushroom soup
Potatoes, peeled and halved
Carrots, peeled and cut in large chunks
1 to 2 cups water

Directions:
Brush beef roast on all sides with browning sauce. Place in large roasting pan. Sprinkle dry onion soup mix on top. Carefully spread mushroom soup over roast, arrange potatoes and carrots round sides. Add water, cover tightly and bake at 275 to 300 degrees for 3 to 4 hours, depending on size of roast.

I love to fix this Sunday morning, clean up the kitchen, and go to church. One can add a salad and bread and VOILLA, dinner is served. And you're not left staring at a pile of dirty dishes while hubby stretches out on the daveno! As my sister Betty Jo once wrote…
'Though sin abounds
And God grants wishes
The Mother…
She must do the dishes!'

Leftover Sunday

Ingredients:
3 potatoes, cubed small
1 large carrot, chopped
2 or 3 ribs celery, chopped
2 small onions, chopped
Salt
3 cups leftover beef gravy
2 cups leftover beef roast, cubed

1 3/4 cups flour
1 tsp. salt
1/2 cup shredded cheddar cheese
1/2 cup oil
4 tbsp. ice water
1 egg, beaten

Directions:
In large saucepan, place the first four ingredients, salt and barely cover with water. Cook until tender-crisp. Drain and save water. Add gravy and beef roast, and enough reserved water to make a thick stew-like consistency. Heat and pour into a large 12 inch quiche pan.

Make a crust by combining the flour, salt, and cheddar cheese. Stir in oil with fork until flour is blended evenly. Sprinkle ice water, one tbsp. at a time, over flour mixture until dough is moist and clings together. Form in round ball and place on large sheet of wax paper. Cover with another sheet and then roll out carefully into a 14-inch circle. Peel off top layer of paper and carefully flop over onto filling, then peel bottom paper off. Trim edges and crimp. Cut air holes and brush with egg. Bake at 425 degrees for 25 to 30 minutes. (You may have to loosely cover with foil during last of baking time, to prevent over-browning.)

Beautiful pie, and BETTER than Sunday dinner!

Steak 'N Gravy

Ingredients:
1 or 2 tbsp. browning sauce, such as Kitchen Bouquet
1 lb. round steak, cut in small pieces

3 tbsp. flour
1 tsp. cumin
1 tsp. garlic powder
1/2 tsp. salt
1/4 tsp. pepper

1 (8oz.) can tomato sauce
1 cup water
1 (8oz.) can mushrooms WITH juice
1/2 large onion, chopped

Directions:
In a mixing bowl toss steak and browning sauce together. Combine next five dry ingredients and toss with meat. Arrange in roasting pan. Combine tomato sauce, water, mushrooms and onion. Pour over meat, cover and bake at 250 degrees for 4 hours OR cook in crock pot on medium for about 8 hours. Serve over rice or noodles.

Supper Smoke

Round Steak Bake

Ingredients:
1/2 cup flour
1 tsp. salt
1/2 tsp. pepper
1/2 tsp. paprika
2 or 3 lbs. round steak, cut in pieces

1 large green pepper
1 large onion, chopped
1 (8oz.) can mushrooms, chopped
1 (13oz.) small bottle catsup
1 cup water

Directions:
Combine first four dry ingredients. Toss with steak pieces and pound as much flour into meat as possible with meat tenderizer. Brown in hot oil and arrange pieces in baking dish. Combine green pepper, onion, mushrooms (undrained), catsup and water. Pour over steak pieces, cover and bake at 300 degrees for 2 1/2 hours.

The following scene, and the recipe, comes from a most fascinating journey we were privileged to enjoy. We were visiting close friends who were serving as missionaries on the Philippine island of Leyte.

On this Sunday we had made an arduous jaunt to the neighboring island of Samar, where we were to enjoy a fellowship meeting in a small fishing village. This little village seemed beautiful to me, with it's many little nipa huts built on stilts. (For when the tides come in.) Huge coconut palms shaded the area, and the ground was packed hard from the soles of many feet. After a very moving worship service in the little nipa church, the native members proceeded to serve a lunch. We had been told that this village depends almost entirely upon the sea for their livelihood, and they were very poor. Nonetheless, with the help of the missionaries, they provided a wonderful feast. It included rice, mussels, pork adobo, crab, sweet potato, cooked banana, lansonies, and other delights. Little dogs rushed about gleaning the crumbs, and a small lizard whisked up my skirt in hopes of some tidbit. The termites were proceeding to ignore the Sabbath as tiny showers of sawdust filtered down on our food for garnish.

I went for a stroll after the meal and noticed three small girls launching a large banca and setting off gaily down the little river. Fishing nets hung from the hut walls and one large net was spread out for mending. A huge pig settled down and spread her "buffet" for her little ones.

I felt that I was treading through the pages of National Geographic, those magazines that my parents had always provided in our home. In reality, my father traveled very little, but in his mind, he traversed many a strange and exotic land, and delighted in reading of them.

I felt so close to him that day, and so grateful, since it was the small inheritance he left us, which had made this experience possible for us. I want to believe that in the exotic land that awaits him, he will be discovering fascinating visas, and the souls of his feet will tread through endless passages of delight.

Pork Adobo

Ingredients:
1 to 2 lbs. pork, cut in chunks
1/2 to 1 onion, chopped
2 or 3 large garlic cloves, minced
Several small black peppers, crushed
3 bay leaves
1 or 2 tbsp. brown sugar
1/2 cup soy sauce
1/8 to 1/4 cup white vinegar (coconut vinegar if it can be found)
Salt to taste
Cornstarch

Directions:
Place all ingredients in heavy kettle and add water, just enough to cover meat. Cook 2 or 3 hours. If it seems too sweet, add a little vinegar. If too sour, add salt and water. Some folks thicken this just a little with cornstarch.
Serve over hot rice.

Supper Smoke

Company Chicken Mushroom Casserole

Ingredients:
6 slices bacon, cooked and crumbled, reserve bacon grease
3/4 cup chopped onion
1/2 cup chopped celery
1/4 cup chopped green pepper
1 (4oz.) can mushrooms slices, with juice
1 can cream of celery soup
1 cup sour cream
Salt and pepper to taste
3 cups chicken, cooked and cut up
1/2 to 3/4 cups cheddar cheese, grated
2 eggs
1/2 cup milk
2 cups Bisquick

Directions:
Fry bacon, reserving drippings, and set aside. In drippings, sauté onion, celery and green pepper. Add mushrooms, bacon, soup, sour cream, seasoning, and chicken. Pour in greased casserole. Sprinkle on cheese. Combine eggs, milk and Bisquick and spread over all. Bake at 350 degrees for 30 to 35 minutes.

Carol's Chicken Casserole

Ingredients:
3/4 cup uncooked long-grain rice
1 can cream of mushroom soup
2/3 cup canned milk
1 UNDRAINED (4oz.) can mushroom pieces
1 pkg. dry onion soup mix
6 to 8 chicken thighs, or breasts, skinned and seasoned (salt and pepper)

Directions:
Grease 9 by 13 inch baking pan and sprinkle rice evenly on bottom. In mixing bowl, combine mushroom soup, canned milk, undrained mushroom pieces, and onion soup mix. Reserve about 1/2 cup of mixture.

Pour soup mixture over rice. Layer chicken on rice/soup mixture. Pour reserved soup mixture over each chicken piece. Cover and bake at 325 degrees for 1 hour. Uncover and bake 15 minutes more.

Carol and Richard's brother Bill, were married in 1957, and she industriously began helping Bill to complete his education. In time he became a prestigious professor of psychology of U.C.L.A., teaching at Berkeley. In delivering dissertations they frequently traveled to Europe, and at one time, included Richard's mother Edith, in an extended tour, including her beloved Ireland.

Their lovely old home nestled in the hills above Oakland, and was filled with their beloved animals and antiques. Our eldest daughter recalls a fairy-tale night as a small child, gazing from her bed and over the twinkling lights of the city.

I remember a swift ride in Bill's Jaguar, and the delicious breakfast Carol served in her sunny kitchen. The entrée was eggs scrambled with mushrooms, and there was also a marvelous cheese bread toast.

I also remember Ivan their infamous rapscallion of a dog whom they rescued from the street life of New York City. I once found him curled serenely upon my snowy white bedspread. I firmly bid him descend. He replied, in guttural tones that he would not. I left my own bedroom a chastened woman!

Supper Smoke

Chicken Rice Casserole

Ingredients:
1 chicken, cooked and de-boned (about 4 cups)
1/4 cup margarine or butter, melted
1 1/2 cups uncooked rice
Salt and pepper
1 pkg. onion soup mix, dry
1 can cream of chicken soup
3 cans water
1 pkg. Stove Top dressing

Directions:
In a large baking pan, spread melted butter or margarine. Evenly spread dry rice. Arrange chicken pieces over rice, seasoning to taste. Combine soups and water. Pour over all. Cover and bake 1 hour at 350 degrees. While baking, prepare Stove Top dressing as directed. Remove casserole and top with dressing. Return to oven and bake, uncovered for 30 minutes.

Fried Chicken Casserole

Ingredients:
One 3 lbs. chicken, cut up and skin removed
1/4 cup butter or margarine
1 can cream of chicken soup
1/4 to 1/2 cup chopped onion
1 tsp. salt
1/2 tsp. pepper
1 tbsp. chopped parsley
1/2 tsp. celery salt
1/2 tsp. thyme
1 1/2 cups water
1 1/3 cups minute rice

Directions:
Melt margarine or butter in skillet. Brown chicken. Remove and set aside. Stir into the drippings: the chicken soup, onion, salt and pepper, parsley, celery salt, thyme and water. Stir and bring to a boil. In a shallow greased casserole, spread the minute rice. Pour all but 1/3 of the soup mixture over rice. Top with browned chicken pieces. Pour remaining soup mixture over chicken. Bake, covered, at 375 degrees for 30 to 45 minutes.

Supper Smoke

Mediterranean Meal

Rudyard Kipling once said that "the first condition of understanding a foreign country is to smell it."

When you prepare this meal, and as the aroma wafts throughout your kitchen, then imagine a few more pungent odors such as fresh fish and tobacco smoke. Seat yourself at a dimly lit street table, and pretend to absorb the mellow mood of a Mediterranean evening.

Ingredients:
1 1/2 cups water
2 tea bags
2 chicken bouillon cubes
2 or 3 boneless, skinless chicken breasts
2 tbsp. olive oil
3 to 4 cloves garlic, sliced
2 cans (14 1/2oz.) tomatoes
1/2 cup chopped onion
1/2 cup chopped green pepper
1 tsp. basil
1 tsp. oregano
1/2 tsp. garlic salt
1/2 tsp. pepper
1 tsp. sugar
1 bay leaf
1 cup sliced olives
1 tbsp. cornstarch
Rice

Directions:
At least one hour prior to rest of recipe preparation, prepare marinade by bringing water to boil. Add tea bags and bouillon cubes. Cool while cutting up chicken breasts in small pieces. Remove tea bags and pour marinade in zip-lock bag. Add chicken pieces, close and set aside, flipping occasionally. Assemble and prepare rest of ingredients. In heavy stew pot brown marinated chicken in olive oil on medium high heat, several minutes on each side. Add sliced garlic and cook and stir 1 minute more. Add tomatoes, chopped onion and green pepper and all seasonings. Bring to a boil, reduce heat, cover, and simmer for 20-25 minutes. Uncover and stir in olives. Combine cornstarch with small

amount of water and add to mixture, stirring and cooking until mixture thickens and boils.

Serve over hot rice (I like to add 1 chicken bouillon cube to unsalted water when cooking rice for this dish.)

Chicken or Turkey Enchilada Casserole

Ingredients:
2 cups pinto beans, dry
Salt and pepper
2 to 3 tsp. chili powder
1 can cream of chicken soup
1 can cream of mushroom soup
2 (8oz.) cans tomato sauce
1 pkg. dry taco-seasoning mix
1 small onion, chopped
1 pkg. corn tortillas (12)
3 to 4 cups cooked chicken or turkey
Shredded cheddar cheese

Directions:
Soak dry kidney beans 6 to 8 hours. Cook until soft. Drain and mash slightly. Season with salt and pepper to taste and chili powder. Set aside. Combine the soups, tomato sauce, taco seasoning and chopped onion. In a greased casserole dish layer sauce mixture, broken tortillas, beans and cheese. Repeat layers 1 or 2 times. Cover with foil and bake at 250 degrees for 2 1/2 hours.

Supper Smoke

Chicken Biscuit Pie

Ingredients:
5 to 6 pieces of chicken
2 celery stalks, chopped
1/2 medium onion, chopped
1 small carrot, grated
2 tsp. salt
1/2 tsp. pepper
2 chicken bouillon cubes
4 tbsp. flour
1/2 tbsp. dry parsley

Directions:
In a medium saucepan combine chicken celery, onion, carrot, salt and pepper. Cover with water and cook 20 to 30 minutes, or until chicken is done. Remove chicken, debone and cut in chunks. Strain broth. Broth should equal 2 cups. Add water if necessary. Add bouillon cubes and flour. Cook until it boils and thickens, stirring constantly. Add chicken pieces and parsley. Pour into greased 9 by 13 inch pan and top with biscuits. Bake at 375 degrees for about 1/2 hour or until biscuits are golden brown and broth is bubbly.

Biscuits:

Ingredients:
2 cups flour
4 tsp. baking powder
1/2 tsp. salt
1/2 cup shortening
2/3 cup milk (approximately)

Directions:
In mixing bowl, combine the first three ingredients. Work the shortening into flour mixture with your hands until crumbly-not too fine. Add milk, stir, and lightly work into a ball. Place on floured board. Knead about 18 times. Pat down lightly to 1/2 inch thickness. Cut and place on chicken mixture.

Stewed Chicken

Ingredients:
1 pkg. dry onion soup mix
2 cans cream of chicken soup
1 can water
One 3 lb. chicken, cut up

Directions:
In a mixing bowl combine onion soup mix, soups, and water. Arrange chicken in roasting pan. Pour soup mixture over all. Cover and bake at 300 degrees for 2 hours. Remove chicken pieces, bone, and return to gravy. Serve over rice or hot biscuits.

Chicken Hash brown Casserole

Ingredients:
1 pkg. frozen hash browns
1/4 cup margarine or butter, melted
2 to 3 cups cooked chicken
1 can cream of chicken soup
1/2 cup chicken broth
8 oz. sour cream
1/2 tsp. salt
1/2 cup chopped onion
12 oz. shredded cheddar cheese
1/4 cup margarine or butter, melted
2 cups crushed corn flakes

Directions:
Layer potatoes in greased 9 by 13 inch baking pan. Drizzle melted margarine over potatoes. Arrange chicken over potatoes. Combine next 6 ingredients and pour over chicken. Combine corn flake crumbs and margarine and sprinkle over all. Cover and bake for 45 minutes at 375 degrees. Uncover and bake 15 minutes more.

Supper Smoke

Oven Barbeque Chicken

Ingredients:
3 to 4 lbs. fryer, skinned and cut up
1 1/2 cup flour
2 tsp. salt

1/4 cup margarine
1 cup water
1/4 cup catsup
1/4 cup vinegar
1 capful liquid smoke
1/4 cup Worcestershire sauce

1/3 cup brown sugar
2 tbsp. cornstarch
1 tsp. dry mustard
2 tsp. chili powder
1 tsp. paprika
1 tsp. garlic salt
1/2 tsp. celery salt

Directions:
In a sack, combine flour and salt. Add chicken pieces and shake to coat. Set aside. In a saucepan combine the next six ingredients. Combine the seven dry ingredients and add to the liquids. Cook until thickened, stirring constantly. Preheat oven to 400 degrees. Line large, flat baking pan with foil and coat with cooking spray. Arrange floured chicken pieces on foil and spread with half the barbeque sauce. Bake, uncovered for 25 minutes. Remove from oven and turn pieces, coating with remaining sauce. Bake 30 minutes more.

Note: Summer falls on a Tuesday in Idaho. We go to a lot of trouble to do picnics on the other days.

Chad's Grilled Chicken

Ingredients:
1 bottle clear Italian dressing
1 pkg. chicken fajita mix, dry
Chicken breasts

Directions:
In mixing bowl, combine the Italian dressing and the fajita mix. Pour into large zip-lock bag. Place chicken breasts in the bag, close and place in a shallow pan. Marinate for 7 to 8 hours, turning frequently. Drain and grill.

Over half of our family live in South Texas, so we have enjoyed many visits there. Summer evenings hold a soft and exquisite aura. The departed sun leaves behind a huge sky, draped in lavender hues and sparkling with fireflies. On such an evening we arrived to find grandson Chad grilling this chicken for us. What a lovely meal we had!

Crispy Baked Chicken

Ingredients:
1 stick margarine or butter, melted
1 egg, beaten
1/2 cup milk
1 cup flour
1 tsp. salt
1 tsp. garlic salt
1 tsp. baking powder
2 tsp. paprika
1 cup crushed corn flakes or rice crispies
1 fryer chicken, cut up

Directions:
Pour melted butter in large, shallow baking pan. In small bowl beat egg and combine with milk
In another bowl combine all the rest of ingredients except chicken. Dip each chicken piece in milk mixture, then in seasoning mix. Arrange each piece in baking pan. Bake at 400 degrees for 30 minutes. Turn pieces, lower heat to 350 degrees and bake 30 minutes more. Add more butter if needed.

Supper Smoke

Fry and Bake Chicken

Ingredients:
1 to 1 1/2 cups flour
2 tsp. chili powder
2 tsp. salt
1 tsp. pepper
1 1/2 tsp. garlic salt
1 1/2 tsp. thyme
Buttermilk
1/4 cup margarine
1/4 cup oil
1 fryer chicken

Directions:
Combine all dry ingredients, place in plastic sack. Cut up chicken. Melt margarine and oil in heavy skillet. Dip chicken in buttermilk, then shake in seasoning sack, doing 3 or 4 pieces at a time. Brown in skillet, 10 to 15 minutes on each side. Place in greased baking dish. Cover tightly and bake at 200 degrees for 1 hour.

Apricot-Onion Chicken

Ingredients:
3 tbsp. cooking oil
3 garlic cloves, minced
4 to 6 chicken breasts, skinned
1/2 cup apricot jam
1/4 cup barbeque sauce
1/4 cup water
2 tbsp. dry onion soup mix

Directions:
In skillet, sauté minced garlic in oil. Brown chicken in the same oil. Place chicken in greased flat casserole. Combine remaining ingredients and pour over chicken. Cover and bake at 375 degrees for 20 minutes. Uncover and bake 10 or 15 minutes more.

Greek Chicken Roast

Who would expect to find a succulent chicken recipe on a night freighter between Italy and Greece? Yet it was there that we made the delightful acquaintance of a freighter employee and his wife, Thonassis and Kathy Kafkias. We found ourselves charmingly entertained with drinks, Greek mythologies, culture lessons, and even a midnight tour of the ship! Thonassis and Kathy were enthused about sharing this favorite recipe. We love it too.

Ingredients:
1/4 cup olive oil
3/4 tsp. salt
1/8 tsp. pepper
1 tsp. oregano
1 chicken, cut up (do not skin chicken)
8 potatoes, peeled and quartered
4 carrots, peeled and cut in chunks
1 1/2 to 2 cups water
Salt and pepper
4 or more garlic cloves
1/3 to 1/2 cup lemon juice

Directions:
Combine olive oil, salt, pepper and oregano and place in large ziplock bag. Add cut up chicken, close bag, and set aside. Turn the bag frequently while preparing vegetables. Arrange quartered potatoes and carrot chunks in greased 9 by 13 inch pan. Add water, enough to be about 1/2 inch deep in bottom of pan. Season vegetables with salt and pepper. Remove chicken from bag and carefully insert thick slices of garlic under skin of chicken here and there. Arrange on top of vegetables. Bake, <u>uncovered</u>, at 375 degrees for 1 1/2 hours. Remove from oven and carefully turn each chicken piece. Pour lemon juice over each piece. Return to oven and bake 30 minutes more.

Supper Smoke

Chicken or Pork Chop Coating

Ingredients:
2 1/2 cups fine whole wheat bread crumbs
2 tbsp. dry onion soup mix
1/2 tsp. salt
1/2 tsp. pepper
1/2 tsp. garlic powder
1/2 tsp onion powder
1 tbsp dried parsley flakes
1/2 tsp. dry oregano flakes
Buttermilk

Directions:
Combine all ingredients, except buttermilk. Dip each piece of meat in buttermilk, then in coating mixture. Arrange in shallow roasting pan. Bake uncovered at 325 degrees for 1 hour and 20 minutes.

**If you're in a hurry, throw a bag of dry seasoned dressing mix in your blender and give it a whirl. You might add a little seasoning of your choice, but not much. Fine coating for chicken or pork chops.

Easy Thanksgiving Day

Ingredients:
1 turkey, any size
2 cans chicken broth
4 to 6 cups water
Lemon pepper
Salt and pepper
Dressing mix (or your own)

Directions: THE DAY BEFORE, (or even a week before, if this suits you better) place thawed turkey in large roasting pan. Add chicken broth and the water, depending on turkey size. Cover tightly and bake for required time. IF TURKEY IS FROZEN, bake at 200 degrees for at least 8 hours.

Remove turkey and cool. Strain the broth and reserve. Remove meat from bones of cooled turkey, and in large roasting pan, layer meat, white on one side and dark on the other, seasoning each piece as you layer them. (Save small bits and pieces for turkey soup later.) Now pour enough of strained broth over layered meat so it just peeps up between the slices, but NOT COVERED. You may now cover and freeze for turkey day, OR if this IS turkey day, then mix up your favorite dressing, place on top, cover tightly, and bake at 300 degrees for about 3 hours, depending on turkey size (You'll have to bake it longer if it's frozen.)

Note: If you dread the hassle of last minute stuff on turkey day THIS IS THE RECIPE FOR YOU. Many of my friends and I are sold on it. However, if you are a traditionalist, run around and sweat, I can't help you.

Note, Note: If you use an oven thermometer bake 'til 180 degrees.

Supper Smoke

Boneless Turkey Roast, Barbequed

Ingredients:
1 boneless turkey roast
2/3 cup soy sauce
1/4 cup oil
2 tbsp. molasses
2 tsp. garlic powder
2 tsp. ginger
2 tsp. dry mustard

Directions:
Thaw turkey roast and slice in fairly thick slices. In large bowl, combine the next six ingredients. In shallow pan, arrange turkey slices and pour marinade over all. Marinade for 2 or 3 hours, turning occasionally, Meanwhile heat briquettes or light the grill and barbeque the slices, testing for doneness with fork. It doesn't take long. Place in roaster pan, cover and keep warm until ready to serve

Note: This recipe came from my friend Marlyn, under whose table our legs have been thrust innumerable times, always to our great advantage. This recipe will give you a taste of our pleasure, but you are denied the full meal deal without her hubby Roy's good humor mixed in!

Karen's Stromboli

Ingredients:
1 1/3 cups warm water
1 tbsp. dry yeast
1/4 cup oil
1/2 tsp. salt
4 to 5 cups flour
3 tbsp. prepared mustard
12 to 15 slices American cheese
12 to 15 slices pepperoni
1/4 to 1/2 lb. sliced ham
Mozzarella cheese
1 lb. hamburger or sausage, browned
(Karen sometimes adds cooked, crumbled bacon)
Egg white and oregano

Directions:
Dissolve yeast in warm water. Add next three ingredients to make a dough. Cover and chill for at least one hour or overnight. Roll dough into two large rectangles. Layer remaining ingredients, except egg white and oregano, in the center third of each rectangle. Fold one third over meat mixture, then other third, sealing edges. Carefully place on greased baking pans. Brush tops with beaten egg whites and sprinkle with oregano. Bake at 350 degrees for about 20 minutes.

When we dine at our son and daughter-in-laws, and I see that she has created another stromboli, I feel like clicking my heels for joy! Instead, I slide into my place at the table, smiling like a cat full of cream. Of all the things Karen cooks, this is my favorite!

Corned Beef 'N Cabbage

(A Seaman household "MUST" on St. Patrick's Day)

Ingredients:
1 pkg. corned beef with seasonings
Carrots
Potatoes
1 head cabbage
Mayonnaise, mustard, and prepared horseradish

Directions:
Remove corned beef from pkg. and reserve seasoning mix. In large kettle, cover beef with water, bring to a boil, and boil gently from 1 ½ to 2 hours. Remove from heat and drain. Add fresh water to kettle as well as seasoning pkg. Return to stove and cook until corned beef is almost done. Add sliced carrots, peeled and quartered potatoes, and 1 head of cabbage, cut up in 6 slices. Add pepper to taste. Cover and simmer all together until vegetables are tender.

Just before serving, blend together a mixture of mayonnaise, horseradish and mustard. This is to serve over the corned beef, if you wish.

This recipe comes from Richard's cousin Peg, who, along with her sister Jo, spent more time babysitting Richard and his brothers than she cares to tell about. After long years have passed, it seems miraculous that all seems forgiven and they regard each other as nigh unto brother and sister: After Peg married, and moved out, she took in the boys for one whole summer. There were a few required chores, and all the rest of the golden days were spent in the St. Joe River! Richard tells me it is the happiest time of his whole childhood.

Cajun Red Beans and Rice

Ingredients:
1 lb. red beans
1/2 lb. ham, ham bone, or pork hocks
1 bunch green onions, chopped
1 cup chopped bell pepper
3 cups chopped onion
1 cup chopped fresh parsley
2 or 3 cloves garlic, chopped
1 (8oz.) can tomato sauce
1 tbsp. salt
1 tsp. black pepper
1/4 tsp oregano
1 tsp. red pepper
1/4 tsp. thyme
2 or 3 dashes Tabasco sauce
1 lb. smoked sausage
Serve over hot rice

Directions:
Soak beans overnight. Drain and cover with 2 quarts water. Add ham and cook for 45 minutes to 1 hour. Add all vegetables, seasonings and tomato sauce and cook slowly for one hour. Add more water if needed. Add sausage, cut in thin slices. Cook 45 minutes. Cool. Reheat, bringing to a boil and then simmer 30 to 40 minutes.

This recipe comes from Laura, down in the land of bluebonnets, fire ants, and our grandchildren! Thanks Laura. If you feel that life is passing you by, cook up a pot of this. It's sure to light your fire and set you going again! It's GOOD, but HOT!

Supper Smoke

Porky Pig Pie

Ingredients:
1/3 cup oil
1/3 cup soy sauce
3/4 tsp. garlic salt
3/4 to 1 lb. boneless pork chops or sirloin, cubed
1/4 cup flour
1 tsp salt
1 tsp garlic powder
1/2 tsp paprika
1/8 tsp. allspice
1/4 cup cooking oil

1 cup carrots, cubed
1 cup celery, chopped
3/4 cup onion, chopped
2 cups potatoes, cubed
2 cups water

1/4 tsp chili powder
1 tsp. dried parsley

1 3/4 cup flour
1 tsp. salt
1/2 cup oil
1/2 cup cheddar cheese, shredded
4 tbsp. ice water
1 egg, beaten

Directions:
Combine oil, soy sauce and garlic salt. Pour over cubed meat and marinate 6 to 8 hours or overnight. Combine the flour, salt, garlic powder, paprika and allspice. Add the marinated pork and shake well, reserving any leftover coating mixture.

In heavy skillet, heat cooking oil and brown the floured meat. While meat is browning, prepare vegetables. Starting with carrots, add each prepared vegetable to pan, stirring often. Slowly add 2 cups water, any remaining coating mixture and the chili powder and parsley. Bring to a boil and cook for 10 minutes, or until potato cubes are almost done.

Transfer to a large baking pie pan. To make crust, combine the flour, salt and oil. Sprinkle ice water over flour mixture, 2 tbsp. at a time, stirring to form a ball. Turn out on large sheet of wax paper. Top with another sheet and roll out to large circle. Peel off top layer of paper and carefully turn over onto meat mixture, crimp edges and cut slits, or designs in crust. Brush crust with beaten egg. Bake at 425 degrees for 25 to 30 minutes. You may have to cover this lightly the last part of baking time, so crust doesn't get too brown.

This is some trouble, I'll admit, but pretty impressive when served hot out of the oven with a big green salad to go with it. A real hungry hubby pleaser.

Haggis

This recipe comes from Dundee, Scotland and is a famous national dish. I'll confess that we haven't tried it, but 'tis nought ta' say yee canna'!

Ingredients:
1 cooking bag, made from a sheep's stomach*
1 heart, liver and the lungs from a sheep, (called pluck)
2 small onions
2 teacupfuls toasted oatmeal
8 oz. shredded suet
1 tsp. salt
1/2 tsp. black pepper

Directions:
Scrape and clean bag in cold, then warm water. Soak in salt water overnight. Wash, pluck and boil for two hours, with windpipe draining over side of pot. Retain one pint of stock. Cut off windpipe and remove surplus gristle. Chop or mince heart and lungs. Grate best part of liver (only about half.) Parboil and chop onions and mix all together with oatmeal, suet, salt and pepper, and reserved stock to moisten. Pack mixture into bag, allowing space for swelling. Boil for three hours, pricking regularly all over.
*If sheep's stomach not available, steam in greased basin, covered with greaseproof paper and cloth for four to five hours.

Supper Smoke

> Farewell to the Highlands, farewell to the North
> The birthplace of valour, the country of worth!
> Wherever I wander, wherever I rove,
> The hills of the Highlands forever I love.
> Chorus:
> My heart's in the Highlands, my heart is not here
> My heart's in the Highlands a-chasing the deer.
>
> From My Heart's in the Highlands
> Robert Burns
> (1759-1796)

Corn, Cheese and Wieners

Ingredients:
1/4 cup butter or margarine
1/4 cup flour
1/2 tsp. salt
1/4 tsp. pepper
2 cups milk
2 cups grated cheese
1 (15oz.) can cream style corn
1 (16oz.) pkg. wieners

Directions:
In saucepan melt margarine or butter. Add flour, salt and pepper and bring to a bubble over medium heat. Slowly stir in the milk and cook until mixture comes to a boil and thickens, stirring constantly. Remove from heat and add grated cheese, stirring to melt. Add cream style corn and blend. In a greased 9 by 13 inch pan arrange wieners in a single layer. Pour corn mixture over them and bake, uncovered at 350 degrees for 20-30 minutes, or until wieners have swelled and mixture is bubbly.

I'm not surprised if your nose is turned up. Mine was too, when I first learned of this strange concoction! Hubby and all his siblings grew up on it and I doubt any of them know where the recipe originated. Our children love it and I've made it so many times I could do it in the dark. And I've learned to like it myself!
If you can't lick 'em,
Then join 'em!

It seems to go really well with crispy fried potatoes.

Supper Smoke

Marjorie's Verenicka Casserole

Ingredients:
13 lasagna noodles
1 (16oz.) pkg. DRY cottage cheese
3 eggs
1 tsp. salt
1/8 tsp. pepper
1 cup medium or sharp cheddar cheese, shredded
1/2 cup margarine or butter
1/2 cup flour
1/2 tsp. salt
1/2 tsp. pepper
1 (32oz.) container sour cream
4 cups chopped ham
2 cups milk (about)

Directions:
In boiling salted water, cook lasagna noodles. Drain and set aside. Combine cottage cheese, eggs, salt and pepper and cheese. In a deep 9 by 12 inch baking pan (greased) layer 3 cooked noodles, then cheese mixture, then noodles, continuing until the last layer of 4 noodles, continuing until the last layer of 4 noodles. Cover with foil and bake at 350 degrees for 20 to 30 minutes.

While baking, melt margarine or butter in large saucepan. Add flour and salt and pepper and bring to a bubble. Remove from heat and slowly add 1 cup of the milk and all of the sour cream. Return to heat, stirring constantly and cook until mixture thickens, adding more milk to make a gravy. Heat ham chunks in boiling water and drain. Add to gravy. Pour over baked cheese mixture and keep warm in low heat oven until ready to serve.

Note: A whoppin' good casserole from our niece who is one whoppin' good cook!

Spam Sham

Ingredients:
1/2 cup corn flake crumbs
2 tbsp. brown sugar
1/8 tsp. ground cloves

1 (12oz.) can Spam
2 tbsp. prepared mustard
1 can pineapple slices, drained
1/4 cup margarine or butter, melted

Directions:
In mixing bowl, combine first 3 ingredients and set aside. On greased cookie sheet, place 8 pineapple slices. Pour melted butter over these. Slice canned Spam in 8 slices. Spread each slice with mustard, then coat with corn flake crumbs. Lay each slice on a buttered pineapple slice. Bake at 350 degrees for 20 minutes.

Note: I have fixed this simple main dish for years, always resulting in happy supper faces.

Supper Smoke

Sausage Zucchini Bake

Ingredients:
4 cups sliced zucchini
1 lb. bulk pork sausage
1 1/2 cups dry breadcrumbs, divided
3/4 cup Parmesan cheese, divided
1 cup milk
1 tbsp. parsley flakes
1/2 tsp. salt
1/2 tsp. oregano
2 eggs
1/4 cup margarine or butter, melted

Directions:
Cook zucchini in boiling, salted water until just tender; don't over cook. Drain. In skillet cook sausage until crumbly and brown. Drain. In large mixing bowl, combine zucchini, sausage, 3/4 cup of the breadcrumbs, 1/2 cup of the Parmesan cheese, the milk and seasonings. Beat eggs slightly and fold into zucchini mixture. Turn into greased casserole. Melt margarine and combine with remaining 3/4 breadcrumbs and 1/4 cup remaining cheese. Sprinkle over top and bake, uncovered at 325 degrees for 30 minutes or until set.

This is a wonderfully flavorful way to use up those zucchini that sneak to your back porch like illegitimate children. Cousin Charlene generously shared this recipe.

Supper Sausage Casserole

Ingredients:
1 lb. pork sausage
1/2 cup finely chopped green pepper
1/2 cup chopped onion
1 cup chopped celery
2 1/4 cup boiling water
1 pkg. chicken noodle soup mix, dry
1/2 cup rice, uncooked
1/4 tsp. salt
1/8 tsp. pepper

Directions:
Brown sausage; drain. Add green pepper, onion, and celery and sauté until vegetables are crispy. Set aside. In boiling water, add soup mix, rice and seasonings. Combine with sausage mixture and place in greased casserole. Cover and bake at 350 degrees for 20 minutes.

Supper Smoke

Breakfast Sausage Casserole

Ingredients:
4 cups cubed day old bread
2 cups shredded cheddar cheese
10 eggs, slightly beaten
4 cups milk
1 tsp. dry mustard
1 tsp. salt
1/4 tsp. onion powder
1/4 tsp. pepper
1 lb. pork sausage, cooked and drained
1/2 cup sliced mushrooms
1/4 cup chopped pimento, optional

Directions:
Place bread in greased 9 by 13 inch casserole. Sprinkle with cheese. Combine the next six ingredients and pour over bread mixture. Sprinkle crumbled sausage, mushrooms and pimento over all. Cover and chill overnight. Bake at 325 degrees, uncovered for 1 hour. Cover loosely with foil if it browns too fast.

I like to use this when we have overnight guests. It goes well with muffins and fruit.

Little Quiche

Ingredients:
1/4 lb. pork sausage, cooked and drained
        OR
2 slices cooked ham
        OR
4 to 6 slices bacon, cooked and drained
2 eggs, beaten
2/3 cup milk
1/2 tsp. salt
1/4 tsp. pepper
1/2 tsp. dry mustard
2 slices bread, crusts removed
1 green onion, chopped
2 tbsp. shredded cheddar cheese

Directions:
In a small bowl, beat eggs. Add milk and seasonings and blend. In a greased individual casserole, cube the bread and arrange on bottom. Arrange meat and onion over bread cubes. Pour egg mixture over all. Sprinkle with cheese. Bake, uncovered, for 30 minutes at 350 degrees. Let set a few minutes before serving.

Note: If you've a hungry hubby, you'll have to let him eat the whole thing, with a green salad thrown in besides. However, if you are two old couch potatoes, you can share it.

Supper Smoke

Ham or Bacon Quiche

Ingredients:
1 9-inch pie shell, unbaked
1 cup coarsely shredded cheese
1 pkg. (3oz.) thinly sliced ham, cut in strips
              OR
4 to 6 slices bacon, cooked and crumbled
1 cup coarsely shredded cheese
2 green onions, with tops, sliced thin
4 eggs, slightly beaten
1 1/4 cups half and half
1/2 tsp. salt
Dash of pepper
Parsley or paprika

Directions:
Sprinkle cheese in bottom of pie shell. Add ham or bacon, and sliced onion. Beat eggs and combine with half and half and seasonings. Bake at 350 degrees for 1 hour.

Taco Quiche

Ingredients:
1 lb. hamburger
1/4 cup chopped onion
1/4 cup chopped green pepper
1 envelope taco-seasoning mix
1 cup shredded cheese
1/2 cup biscuit mix
2 eggs, beaten
1 cup milk

Directions:
In large skillet, brown hamburger, adding onion and green pepper. Drain. Add taco-seasoning mix. Spread in 9-inch greased pan. Sprinkle with cheese.

In mixing bowl combine biscuit mix, eggs and milk. Pour over hamburger cheese mixture and bake at 400 degrees for 20 to 25 minutes.

Supper Smoke

Baked Eggs

Ingredients:
1/4 cup margarine or butter
1/4 cup flour
1/8 tsp. pepper
1 tsp. salt
1 tsp. prepared mustard
2 cups milk
1 1/3 cups grated cheese
8 eggs
6 to 8 slices bacon, cooked and crumbled

Directions:
In medium saucepan, melt margarine or butter. Add flour and seasonings and bring to a bubble. Remove from heat and slowly add milk. Return to heat and bring to a boil and stir until thickened. Add cheese and continue stirring until cheese is melted. Grease 4 individual baking dishes or 8 by 8 inch pan. Pour half of white sauce in pan. Carefully break eggs into sauce and then pour remaining sauce over top. Sprinkle with crumbled bacon. Bake at 325 degrees for 20 minutes.

Note: Who says you can't have breakfast for supper? Make a batch of muffins, pour out the juice and coffee and Hubby'll be so happy he may even render a rooster crow or two.

Deviled Tuna Bake

Ingredients:
2 tbsp. butter or margarine
2 tbsp. flour
1 tsp. dry mustard
1/2 tsp. salt
1 1/2 cups milk
1/4 tsp. bottled red pepper seasoning
1 tbsp. lemon juice
1 can tuna, drained
3/4 cup saltine cracker crumbs (18 squares)
3 hard-cooked eggs

Directions:
In saucepan, melt butter or margarine. Remove from heat and blend in flour, mustard and salt. Slowly add milk. Return to heat and cook until thickened. Remove from heat and add pepper seasoning, lemon juice, tuna, and 1/2 cup of the crackers. Chop eggs and add. Pour into shallow 8-inch greased baking dish. Sprinkle with remaining crumbs. Bake at 350 degrees for 20 minutes.

My personal opinion about this casserole is this. The only thing going for it is it's fast and cheap! However, I have made it umpteen times and will make it umpteen and one times more, because for some strange reason, Hubby loves it! Maybe you will too.

Yummy Sandwich Filling

Ingredients:
2 cups shredded ham or Spam
1/2 cup chopped celery
1/3 cup chopped radish
1/2 cup chopped black olives
1 cup shredded cheese
3/4 to 1 cup Ranch Style dressing

Supper Smoke

Ham Barbeque Sandwiches

Ingredients:
3/4 cup brown sugar
1/3 cup horseradish sauce
1/4 cup lemon juice
5 lbs. rolled ham, butcher cut in
Wafer thin slices

Directions:
In mixing bowl, combine brown sugar, horseradish sauce, and lemon juice, stirring to dissolve sugar. In a large flat pan, layer the meat slices and the sauce until all meat is layered. Store in refrigerator overnight, or up to 20 hours. Bake in the sauce for one hour at 350 degrees, or 2 1/2 hours at 250 degrees. Serve on hamburger buns with pickles and mayonnaise, or condiments of your choice.

These sandwiches were served at a recent wedding reception to the great pleasure of the guests! The mother of the bride graciously shared the recipe with me, and here it is! Thanks Carolyn. May all your daughters marry well and live happily ever after.

Roast Beef Sandwich Spread

Ingredients:
1 cup chopped roast beef
1 tbsp. minced onion
2 dill pickles, chopped
1 small carrot, grated
1/2 to 1 cup shredded cheese
Salt and pepper to taste
1 tbsp. mustard
Mayonnaise to taste

Frankfurter Filling

Ingredients:
6 cooked frankfurters, ground or shredded
2 dill pickles, ground or shredded
1/3 cup finely chopped celery
1/4 cup chopped onion
1/4 cup catsup, or to taste
1 tbsp prepared mustard
3/4 to 1 cup mayonnaise

Heard the tale of young Maude Macaroni?
Who deigned to disguise some baloney?
She served it au gratin,
And cried "They've been gotten!"
(Does she know that we call her Miss Phony?)

Egg Salad Filling

Ingredients:
10 hard-boiled eggs, chopped or shredded
2 tbsp. finely chopped onion
6 to 10 strips of bacon, cooked and crumbled
1/2 tsp. pepper
2 tbsp. prepared mustard
1 cup mayonnaise, or to taste

Directions:
Combine all ingredients. Should make 8 to 10 sandwiches.

**Easy egg peeling: Drain water off hard cooked eggs; shake the eggs together in the pan until shells are cracked. Pour cold water over them and let sit a few minutes, and then peel.

Supper Smoke

Lo-Fat Gravy

Ingredients:
2 cans non-fat chicken broth
2 tsp. chicken bouillon
1/2 tsp. onion powder
1/4 cup cornstarch OR 1/3 to 1/2 cup flour
1/8 tsp. pepper
1/4 tsp. Accent
1/4 tsp. garlic powder
Chopped parsley

Directions:
In saucepan, combine the cornstarch, or flour, with some of the broth. Combine all remaining ingredients and bring to a boil, stirring constantly, until mixture is thickened. Add chopped parsley just before serving.

**In making any type of gravy, a quick way to thicken if it seems too thin: just stir in a few tbsp. of instant mashed potatoes and cook until thickened.

Writing recipes, that's my 'druther.
Yet, one topic leads to another—
I'm beginning to sound
As this keyboard I pound
More and more like someone's Grandmother!
(And I AM!)

Hospitality

Do we know what it means? The dictionary simply states that it is the act of being generous and friendly to guests.

At first glance this would seem to imply that the guests would receive the advantage, the host and hostess being the givers.

But the longer hospitality is exercised, the more one realizes that there are rich returns; a treasure house of rewards. In cultivating the many avenues of hospitality, we come to realize that they result in some of the happiest times of our lives.

It seems evident that in order to be genuinely hospitable, one needs to "walk in another's shoes;" to be truly concerned about making another comfortable and at ease. This then, would not restrict the practice to our homes, but anywhere we would chance to meet a friend, or a stranger.

If we so choose, we may treat any passing stranger as our "guest." It's simple to give away a warm smile, and that can be done anywhere. Even on a bad day, it won't crack your face. The harried checkout clerk needs one; the surly teen lounging on the corner, or the bag lady with the shades drawn over her soul. There are little windows of opportunity everywhere, and we will see them if we are cultivating a generous and a friendly heart.

For quite some time, Richard and I had dreamed, planned and saved for a motor trip across the "good old U.S.A." Several years ago we accomplished this, and I am now reminded of some events that took place on that trip. One evening we found ourselves in a small town in the lovely state of Vermont. We took note of a charming little restaurant called "Jana's Kitchen." As we waited to be seated, we exchanged small talk with a local family. We then proceeded to enjoy a wonderful meal, and to relax and take in the "atmosphere." When nearly finished, the lady with whom we had chatted appeared at our table. She presented us with a local map, well marked with special points of interest Since she nursed at a local clinic, she gave us her phone number and offered assistance should we need medical aid while in the area. You can well imagine that we left that restaurant warmed within and without, and holding a lasting memory to cherish.

Supper Smoke

We encountered a number of delightful strangers such as she. There was the matronly waitress in North Dakota who, while serving Richard one of the hugest breakfast entrees I have ever seen, also took the time to regale us with awesome snowstorm and blizzard encounters.

We recall warmly the black bus driver who, just outside Washington D.C., took the time to thoroughly explain the intricacies of the metro system, thus assuring us safe and trouble-free passage to the inner city and back out.

I recall the handsome young executive, his tie whipping in the exhilarating drafts of downtown Boston, who paused on the street to tell us how to find his favorite vacation spot on Cape Cod.

And there was Monica, a British tourist who seated herself beside us as we lunched at Quincy Market, and who entertained us with such boisterous and flat-footed opinions that neighboring diners bent their ears to listen. We laugh at her memory still!

We will never forget Miss Kitty, a devout member of the Daughters of the Confederacy, who swept us off on a priceless tour of her quiet Southern town. She was like an animated history book, each page as fascinating as the last.

Each time I think of her, my heart is warmed in the memory of Fan, who shared her front porch, her recipes, and finally even a soft and chocolaty hug that I prize to this day.

We could never leave out the Zimmermans, who shared a Sunday dinner with us in Up-State New York. They included, in their table prayer, a request for "traveling mercies", a term we had never heard. We felt we were blessed with those "mercies" throughout the rest of our journey.

We began to realize as we traveled that the warm social contacts we were encountering were priceless, compared to the spectacular scenery we enjoyed. We need to remember that we may have opportunities to extend just such gifts in our own hometowns.

Of course, hospitality includes the sharing of our homes and table. If we are motivated by a heart that cares, we may find that our meal and our table decor will vary in consideration of our varied guests.

If we have "walked in their shoes" we sometimes may find ourselves setting out our chipped ironstone on a vinyl cloth, and serving bread and soup. In another instance we may feel justified in using our best china, cloth napkins and a floral centerpiece. We will feel happy in either setting because we sincerely wish our guests to feel relaxed and at home with us. This would also include being honest and as open as possible with our guests. Stretching our food budget well beyond our means, or becoming harried over excessive preparations is going to defeat its own purpose. Neither our guests nor we will be able to relax.

There once was a bride of resources
Who planned a fine meal of six courses.
She went into orbit
Between meatballs and sorbit,
And now she's consumed with remorses.

We need to remember that whatever we can reasonably manage, in regards to menu and setting will be ENOUGH, if offered in sincerity and without apology. If our budget, at this time, allows only simple fare then remember this old adage:

The people who mind, don't matter
And the people who matter, don't mind.

Years ago we moved to California in search of better job opportunity. We were hardly settled when a neighboring young couple invited us over to share their evening meal. I have recalled that evening many times through the years. The meal consisted of biscuits and gravy. We've enjoyed more elaborate meals with this same couple many times, when fortune began to smile upon them, but this one stands out as one of the very best. It was offered in genuine friendliness. And too, it was simply all they had.

Bread and Beyond

"Throw a loaf of bread and a pound of tea in an old sack and jump over the back fence."

-John Muir

Back of the loaf is the snowy flour
Back of the flour, the mill
And back of the mill is the wheat and the shower,
The sun, and the Father's will.
                              -Louis P. De Gouy

Bread making may be called a skill, an experience, or an art, but I am confident that it is a privilege. If you use the right ingredients, bread is an important part of our nutrition. It is not surprising that it is often called the "staff of life."

I have read that in the Eastern countries, those who sell bread go about the streets calling. "Allah Karim," meaning "God is merciful." Surely we need give Him thanks for our daily bread.

Bread is not only a vital part of our sustenance, but there is also a great satisfaction in turning out a "good loaf."

When you have measured, stirred, kneaded, shaped, and baked; and then pulled a big brown loaf from your oven and let the warm savory aroma drift through your abode; how easy it is to thank God for His bounty, and to offer it to your family with joy and quiet satisfaction!

A house can become a home in the time it takes for loving hands to create one loaf of bread!

Supper Smoke

Pioneer Bread

Ingredients:
1/2 cup warm water
3 tbsp. dry yeast
1/3 cup butter or margarine
1 3/4 cups buttermilk
2 tsp. salt
1/2 cup+2 tbsp. honey
1 cup old-fashioned oatmeal
2 eggs
1/2 cup corn meal
2 cups whole-wheat flour
1 cup Grape Nuts (not flakes)
2 to 4 cups white bread flour
1/2 cup chopped walnuts

Directions:
Dissolve yeast in warm water. Set aside to rise. In saucepan, melt butter. Add buttermilk, salt, honey, and oatmeal. Cook 5 to 10 minutes, or until thickened. Set aside to cool. In large mixing bowl, beat eggs. Add oatmeal mixture and yeast and blend well. Add the corn meal and the whole-wheat flour, beating with mixer. Add Grape Nuts and begin to work in white flour and nuts, adding enough flour to make a soft dough. Continue to knead until smooth and elastic. Lightly oil dough and let rise. Punch down and shape into 2 loaves. Place in greased bread pans and let rise again. Bake at 350 degrees for 40 to 45 minutes.

I love healthy, chewy breads, and so I worked out this recipe, and the one following, myself. They are both hearty. This one'll nearly grow hair on a snake's chest; the other will rare you right back on your haunches. Take your pick. (They're WONDERFUL for toast.)

Settler's Bread

Ingredients:
1/2 cup warm water
2 tbsp. yeast
2 1/2 cups whole-wheat flour
1/2 cup quick oats
1/2 cup wheat germ
2 tsp. salt
2 bananas
1/4 cup butter or margarine
1 cup milk
1 cup small curd cottage cheese
1/4 cup honey
2 tbsp. molasses
2 eggs
3 to 4 cups white flour

Directions:
Dissolve yeast in warm water. In large bowl, combine the whole-wheat flour, oats, wheat germ, and salt. Set aside. In saucepan, heat together the butter, milk, cottage cheese, honey and molasses. Add to mashed banana and beat well. Add eggs and yeast mixture, blending well. Beat in the flour mixture and continue to stir in white flour until you have a fairly stiff dough. Turn out on floured board and knead 'til your forehead gets dewy. Cover and let rise. You can punch this down and knead as many times as you want, the more the better, but once WILL suffice. When you're out of zip, or time, or both, roll out and shape into loaves, place in greased loaf pans, and let rise again. Bake at 350 degrees for 30 to 40 minutes.

Supper Smoke

Potato Bread

Ingredients:
1/2 cup warm water
2 tbsp. dry yeast
1 tbsp. sugar
1/4 cup margarine
1 cup milk
1 tsp. salt
1 cup mashed potatoes
1 egg
Approximately 4 or 5 cups flour

Directions:
In small bowl, dissolve yeast in warm water, sprinkling sugar over the top. Set aside to rise. In saucepan, melt margarine. Add milk, salt, and mashed potatoes and heat to lukewarm. In large mixing bowl, beat egg. Add potato mixture and yeast and blend well. Stir in flour, a little at a time, to make a soft dough. Turn out on floured board and knead until smooth and elastic. Cover and let rise. Punch down and shape into loaves. Place in greased pans to rise. Bake at 350 degrees for 20 to 30 minutes.

To the novice bread maker: What does "smooth and elastic" mean? Well, at first the dough feels just like a blob. But after kneading for awhile it begins to feel just a bit like...chewing gum...YES! Kind of like that and when it is risen and ready to bake it feels like chewing gum with SASS!

Oatmeal Bread

Ingredients:
1/2 cup warm water
2 tbsp. dry yeast
1/4 cup margarine, melted
1/3 cup brown sugar, packed
1 tsp. salt
2/3 cup quick oats
3/4 cup boiling water
1 egg, beaten
White flour

Directions:
In small bowl, dissolve yeast in warm water and set aside to rise. In large mixing bowl, combine margarine, brown sugar, salt and oatmeal. Pour boiling water over all and stir well. With mixer, beat in egg. Add yeast mixture and blend well. Add enough flour to make soft dough. Turn out on floured board and knead until smooth and elastic. Cover and let rise. Punch down and shape into loaf, Place in greased baking pan and let rise again. Bake at 350 degrees for 20 to 30 minutes.

Supper Smoke

Buttermilk Wheat Bread

Ingredients:
3/4 cup warm water
2 tbsp. yeast
1/4 cup margarine
2 tbsp. molasses
1 1/4 cups buttermilk
2 tsp. baking powder
2 tsp. salt
1/2 cup wheat germ
2 cups whole-wheat flour
2 1/2 cups white flour

Directions:
In small bowl, dissolve yeast in warm water, setting aside to rise. In saucepan, melt margarine. Add molasses and buttermilk and heat to lukewarm. Pour into large mixing bowl and add yeast mixture, baking powder, salt and wheat germ. Blend well. Beat in the whole-wheat flour and work in enough white flour to make soft dough. Turn out on floured board and knead until smooth and elastic. Let rise. Punch down and shape into loaves and let rise in greased baking pans. Bake at 350 degrees for 20 to 30 minutes.

Harvest Bread

Ingredients:
1/2 cup warm water
2 tbsp. dry yeast
1/4 cup shortening
1 medium onion, grated
1 cup cottage cheese
1 cup buttermilk
1/4 cup sugar
4 tsp. dill weed
2 tsp. salt
2 eggs, beaten
About 5 cups flour

Directions:
In small bowl, dissolve yeast in warm water, and set aside to rise. In saucepan, melt shortening. Add onion and sauté until soft, but not browned. Add cottage cheese and buttermilk and heat to lukewarm. Pour into large mixing bowl. Add yeast mixture, sugar, dill weed, and salt, blending well. With mixer, beat in eggs and continue to beat in enough of the flour to make very soft batter. Beat well. Stir remaining flour in by hand, kneading it until it becomes smooth and elastic. Cover and let rise. Punch down, shape into loaves and place in greased pans. Let rise again. Bake at 350 degrees for about 30 minutes.

Italian Parmesan Bread

Ingredients:
2 cups warm water
2 tbsp. dry yeast
1/2 cup butter or margarine, softened
2 eggs
1/4 cup sugar
2 tsp. salt
3 tsp. dry onion flakes
1 tsp. Italian seasoning
1 tsp. garlic salt
6 cups flour
3/4 cup Parmesan cheese
4 cups flour
1/4 cup melted butter or margarine
Parmesan cheese

Directions:
In small bowl, dissolve yeast in warm water, setting aside to rise. In large mixing bowl, combine softened butter, eggs, sugar, and the four seasonings. Add yeast mixture and 2 cups of the flour. With mixer, beat at low speed until all is blended, then on high for 2 minutes. Stir in remaining flour and cheese. Knead until smooth and elastic. Let rise and punch down, then shape into 2 loaves and rise again. Brush each loaf with melted butter and sprinkle with Parmesan cheese. Bake at 350 degrees for 30 minutes or until golden brown.

Mackie's Bundt Bread

Ingredients:
2 loaves frozen bread dough, partially thawed
1 1/2 cubes (3/4 cup) butter
Parmesan cheese, garlic salt, and parsley, to taste

Directions:
Grease bundt pan. Slice each loaf into 8 slices. Melt butter and add seasonings to taste. Roll each of the 16 pieces in butter mixture and layer in pan. Let rise to the top of the pan. Bake at 350 degrees for about 35 minutes. Turn out on platter and serve warm.

This was served at a recent Seaman Cousins reunion. It went over big!

Supper Smoke

Fiona's French Bread

Ingredients:
½ cup warm water
2 tbsp. yeast
1 tbsp. sugar
1/3 cup oil
3 tbsp. sugar
1 tbsp. salt
2 cups hot water
6 cups white flour

Directions:
Dissolve yeast in warm water, sprinkling sugar over top. Set aside to rise. In large mixing bowl, combine oil, sugar and salt. Add hot water and stir well. Add yeast and , with mixer, beat in 3 cups of the flour. Stir in enough remaining flour to make soft dough. Let rise and stir down every 10 minutes for 5 times. Divide into 2 parts and roll each into a 9 by 12 rectangle. Roll up into long loaves. If you're lucky enough to have a SHARP knife then wait 'til the loaves have risen and carefully make slashes diagonally across loaves. I, seldom having a sharp knife, make the slashes BEFORE the loaves have risen, or not at all. Bake at 350 degrees for 20 minutes.

I don't know any Fiona's. I just thought it sounded good.

French Bread Fillings

These fillings are meant to be spread on the bread dough after you have rolled it out to a rectangle. After spreading, then roll up the long way, as for regular French bread and proceed with same instructions. Each recipe is enough for two loaves.

Parmesan Herb Filling
1/2 cup Parmesan cheese
2 tbsp. dried parsley flakes
1 tsp. garlic powder
2 tsp. seasoning salt

Cream Cheese Filling
1 8 oz. pkg. cream cheese, softened
1 tbsp. dried parsley flakes
1 tsp. onion salt
1 tsp. garlic powder
1 tsp. Italian seasoning

** Butter Mix: Mix together one pound of butter, one pound of soft margarine, and a little milk. Blend well and store in margarine containers. It's soft enough to spread, economical and delicious.

Good Old Potato Buns

Ingredients:
1/2 cup warm water
2 tbsp. yeast
1 tbsp. sugar
1/4 cup butter or margarine
1/4 cup sugar
1 tsp. salt
1 cup buttermilk
2 eggs
¾ cup mashed potatoes
About 5 cups flour

Directions:
Dissolve yeast in warm water, sprinkling sugar over all. Set aside to rise. In saucepan, melt butter. Add sugar, salt, and buttermilk and heat to lukewarm. In large mixing bowl, beat eggs. Add mashed potatoes and blend well. Add buttermilk mixture and yeast. Mix well. Work in enough flour to make soft dough, knead, cover and let rise. Punch down and shape into rolls and place on greased baking sheets to rise. Bake at 350 degrees for 10-15 minutes

These are plain, down to earth rolls and they're just simply good. I've made hundreds of 'em. They also go over very well for sandwich buns. Shape the rolls bigger and whap them down flat with a floured, flat-surfaced bowl, let them rise and bake.

Pluckets

Ingredients:
1 recipe Good Old Potatoes Buns
1/2 cup butter or margarine
1 cup sugar
2 1/2 tsp. cinnamon

Directions:
When bun dough has risen, grease several pans or a bundt cake pan well. Melt butter. In a small mixing bowl, combine sugar and cinnamon. Form dough into walnut size pieces and dip each in butter, then sugar mixture. Layer in the greased pans and let rise. Bake at 350 degrees for 15 to 20 minutes, depending how big the pan. Cover lightly with foil if they begin to brown too fast. Turn out on platter, pour coffee, and pig out.

The aroma of these, just out of the oven, is enough to melt hearts of stone. Make a batch and invite all your enemies.

Supper Smoke

BEST Whole Wheat Buns

Ingredients:
1 cup warm water
2 tbsp. yeast
1 cup salad oil
2/3 cup sugar
2 1/2 tsp. salt
1 cup boiling water
2 eggs
1 to 1 1/2 cups whole-wheat flour
4 to 5 cups white flour

Directions:
In small bowl, sprinkle yeast over warm water and set aside to rise. In large mixing bowl, combine oil, sugar and salt. Pour boiling water over all and let cool to lukewarm. Beat in the 2 eggs and the whole-wheat flour. Work in enough white flour to make soft dough. Cover and let rise. Punch down and shape into buns, place on greased baking sheets and let rise again. Bake at 350 degrees for 10 to 15 minutes, or until golden brown.

I do love this recipe. It's from my dear friend Nettie, and I think of her each time I make them. You may think of whomever you wish, while you make them, perhaps even a Russian Czar, but you won't be disappointed in the buns.

Favorite Oatmeal Rolls

Ingredients:
3 tbsp. butter or margarine
2 cups boiling water
1 cup oatmeal
2/3 cup brown sugar
1 1/2 tsp. salt
1/3 cup warm water
2 tbsp. yeast
1 tbsp. sugar
2 eggs
5 to 6 cups flour

Directions:
In saucepan, melt butter. Add water and bring to a boil. Add oatmeal and cook 'til thickened. Remove from heat and add brown sugar and salt. Set aside to cool 'til lukewarm. Meanwhile, dissolve yeast in water, sprinkling sugar over all. In large mixing bowl, beat eggs. Add cooled oatmeal mixture and dissolved yeast and mix well. Continue beating in flour, and stir in enough flour to make a soft dough. As you begin to knead this dough, it will be sticky, so it helps to oil your hands. Cover and let rise. Dip fingers in oil, and shape dough into buns. Place on greased sheets and let rise again. Bake at 350 degrees for 10 to 15 minutes.

These aren't much fun to make as the dough WILL be sticky, but they are so good that they're worth the trouble.

Cheesy Spud Buns

Ingredients:
1/3 cup warm water
2 tbsp. yeast
1 tbsp. sugar
1/4 cup butter or margarine
1/4 pound Velveeta cheese, cut in small chunks
1 tsp. salt
3 tsp. dry onion flakes
1 tbsp. Italian seasoning
1 tsp. garlic powder
1 tsp. dry mustard
2 eggs, beaten
3/4 cup mashed potatoes
4 to 5 cups flour
1/4 cup butter or margarine
Parmesan cheese

Directions:
In small bowl, dissolve yeast in warm water, sprinkling sugar over top. Set aside to rise. In saucepan, melt butter and Velveeta cheese. Add the next five seasonings.

In large bowl, beat eggs. Add mashed potatoes, then yeast and cheese mixtures, blending well. Beat and stir in 4 to 5 cups flour, making a soft dough. Knead and let rise. Shape into buns and place on greased pans to rise. Brush with melted butter and sprinkle with Parmesan cheese. Bake at 350 degrees for 10 to 15 minutes.

Ranch Rolls

Ingredients:
1/2 cup water
2 tbsp. yeast
1/4 cup margarine or butter
1/4 cup sugar
1 tsp. salt
1 pkg. dry Ranch dressing mix
2 cups cottage cheese
2 eggs, beaten
4 to 5 cups flour
1/4 cup butter or margarine
1/4 tsp. garlic salt

Directions:
In large bowl, dissolve yeast in warm water. Set aside to rise. In saucepan, melt butter. Add sugar, salt and dressing mix, the cottage cheese and beaten eggs. Add yeast mixture and blend well. Beat and knead in flour until it becomes a soft dough. Lightly oil dough, cover and let rise. Punch down and shape into buns, placing on greased baking sheet. Melt butter and add garlic salt. Brush on raised buns and then bake at 350 degrees for 10 to 15 minutes or until golden brown.

Supper Smoke

Marlyn's Rolls

Ingredients:
1/2 cup warm water
2 pkgs. yeast
1 1/2 cups scalded milk
1/2 cup sugar
2 1/2 tsp. salt
1/2 cup oil
2 eggs, beaten
6 to 7 1/2 cups flour

Directions:
Dissolve yeast in warm water. Scald milk and add sugar, salt and oil, stirring well. Add beaten eggs and yeast mixture. Beat as much of the flour in as you can, then stir in the rest with wooden spoon, and work in with fingers. Let rise. If you have time, punch down and let rise again. Shape into rolls and place on greased baking pans. Let rise. Bake at 350 degrees until golden brown; 15 to 20 minutes.

These are some of the best dinner rolls I've ever eaten. That is, if I eat them at Roy and Marlyn's house. When I use Marlyn's recipe, mine are good too, but not AS good! She tells me she always raises her roll dough in the oven. She turns the oven on to around 200 degrees while mixing up the dough. When oven is heated, she turns it OFF. Then places the roll dough, covered, in the oven and shuts the door to raise.

Italian Bread Sticks

Ingredients:
1/2 cup warm water
1 tbsp. yeast
1 tbsp. sugar
1/3 cup oil
3 tbsp. sugar
1 tbsp. salt
2 cups hot water
6 cups flour
1/2 cup butter or margarine
1 tbsp. dried parsley flakes
1 tsp. onion salt
1 tsp. garlic powder
1 tsp. Italian seasoning

Directions:
In small bowl, dissolve yeast in warm water, sprinkling sugar over top. Set aside to rise. Combine oil, sugar, and salt in large mixing bowl. Add hot water. Beat in flour, several cups at a time, and continue working in flour until it forms a soft dough. Knead and let rise. If you have the time, punch down and let rise several times. Divide dough into 40 small balls. On slightly oiled counter top, roll each ball under fingers to make a long rope, 5 or 6 inches long. Place on greased pans and let rise. Bake at 350 degrees just until set, but NOT browned, about 7 minutes. At this point you may set them aside until just before serving, or freeze them. When ready to serve, preheat oven to 400 degrees. Melt butter and add seasonings. Place in long, narrow pan and dip each bread stick in mixture. Place on greased pans and bake 'til golden brown.

Serve hot. A good way to sup your soup.

Supper Smoke

Italiano Cheese Twists

Ingredients:
1/2 cup warm water
2 tbsp. dry yeast
1 tbsp. sugar
1/3 cup oil
3 tbsp. sugar
1 tbsp. salt
1 1/2 cups hot water
5 to 6 cups white flour
1 cup sour cream
1 tsp. onion salt
1 tsp. garlic powder
2 tsp. Italian seasoning
1/2 cup parmesan cheese
1/3 cup melted margarine or butter and Parmesan cheese

Directions:
In small bowl, dissolve yeast in warm water. Sprinkle sugar over yeast and set aside to rise. In large mixing bowl, combine oil, sugar and salt. Add hot water and stir well. Beat in flour, several cups at a time, and continue working in until making a soft dough. Oil dough, cover, and let rise. Meanwhile combine the sour cream, seasonings and Parmesan cheese.

When dough has risen, roll out on floured board to a 12 by 18 rectangle. Spread seasoned filling over dough. Working from the long side of rectangle, fold over 2 times, making a long 18-inch roll. With floured knife, cut into 25 slices, twisting each slice to make a strip. Place on greased baking pans, brush with melted butter and more Parmesan cheese. Let rise and bake at 350 degrees for 15 minutes or until golden brown.

Mama Mia!

Bonanza Bread Bowls

Ingredients:
1/2 cup water
2 tbsp. dry yeast
4 tbsp. butter or margarine
1/4 to 1/2 cup chopped onion
1/4 cup sugar
1 tbsp. salt
1 1/2 cups milk OR 1 can cheddar cheese soup
1 1/2 cups corn meal
2 eggs
White flour

Directions:
In small bowl, dissolve yeast in warm water. Set aside to rise. In saucepan, melt butter. Sauté onion until clear. Add sugar and salt, then milk or cheese soup, and blend well. Stir in corn meal and heat to thicken. Remove from heat and cool to lukewarm. In large mixing bowl, beat eggs. Add cornmeal mixture and yeast. Mix well and then continue to add white flour to make a soft dough,. Knead, cover, and let rise. Punch down dough and divide into 10 or 12 balls. Roll out each ball on floured surface in a circle. Fit each circle over a greased, upturned, ovenproof soup bowl, or aluminum foil meat pie pan. Space each upturned bread bowl on greased cookie sheets and bake at 350 degrees for 15 minutes or until golden brown. Remove bread bowls immediately and upturn to cool

Taco soup tastes quite special in these bowls and your guests will think you went to a whole lot of trouble, which you did.

Supper Smoke

Whole Wheat Bread Bowls

Ingredients:
2 cups warm water
2 tbsp. yeast
2 eggs
2 tsp. salt
1/2 cup honey
1/2 cup oil
3 cups whole wheat flour
3 cups white flour

Directions:
In small bowl, dissolve yeast in warm water. In large mixing bowl, beat the eggs. Add the salt, honey and oil and blend. Add the dissolved yeast mixture. Beat in as much of the flour as you can with a mixer, then continue by hand. Knead in enough flour to make a stiff dough. Grease dough, cover and let rise. Punch down and let rise again. Punch down and shape into large buns (4 to 5 inches in diameter). Place on greased baking sheets, several inches apart. Press down slightly with fingers to flatten buns somewhat. Let rise and bake at 350 degrees for 15 minutes, or until golden brown. Cool. To serve, score with sharp knife approximately 1 inch form outer edge in a circle. Either remove enough bread to make a bowl, or allow your guests to do so. Serve hot chowder or soup.

Lot's of fun!

Bread and Beyond

Saturday Sweet Rolls

Ingredients:
2 tbsp. butter or margarine
2 tbsp. flour
1/4 tsp. salt
Juice and pulp from one large orange (to equal 1/2 cup)
1/3 cup sugar
1 (8 oz.) can crushed pineapple, with juice

....

2 tbsp. dry yeast
1/3 cup warm water
1 cup warm water
1 cup milk
1 tsp. salt
1/4 cup sugar
1/4 cup oil
1 egg
3 1/2 to 4 cups flour
Sugar and cinnamon
Maraschino cherries, optional

....

1 tbsp. butter or margarine
¼ cup cream cheese
Confectioner's sugar
1 tsp. vanilla
Milk

Directions:
For filling: Melt butter in saucepan. Add flour and heat to a bubble. Remove from heat and add next four ingredients. Return to heat and cook and stir until thickened. Cool.

For rolls: Dissolve yeast in water. In saucepan, warm milk, then add salt, sugar and oil. In large mixing bowl, beat egg. Add the yeast and milk mixtures and blend well. Add one or two cups of the flour and beat well. Stir in enough remaining flour to make soft dough. Cover and let rise. Roll out dough on floured surface to form a rectangle. Sprinkle with water and then with brown sugar and cinnamon. Roll up and seal edges. With thread, cut into 12 to 14 slices. Place each on greased baking pan, patting each out flatter with fingers. Let rise a little. Then, with fingers, press down a little circle in center of each roll. Spoon cooled fruit filling

Supper Smoke

in each hollow and let rise until rolls are light. Bake at 350 for 10 to 15 minutes. Let cool in pans.

For frosting: Soften butter and cream cheese. Add sugar, vanilla and milk, stirring until fairly stiff. Carefully spread frosting around outer edge of roll, leaving filling to show. Garnish with maraschino cherries if you wish.

Cinnamon Rolls

Ingredients:
2 tbsp. yeast
1/2 cup warm water
1 cup milk
1 cup water
1/2 cup sugar
2 tsp. salt
1/2 cup oil
2 eggs
6 to 6 1/2 cups flour
Brown sugar and cinnamon

Directions:
In small bowl, dissolve yeast in water. In saucepan heat milk and water together. Add sugar, salt, and oil. In large mixing bowl, beat the eggs. Add the milk and yeast mixtures. With mixer, begin to beat in flour, one cup at a time until too thick to beat. Continue to stir in enough flour to make a SOFT dough…in fact…soft enough to seem more like thick batter. Cover and let rise. Pour out on floured surface and gently roll out in rectangle, about 1/2 inch think. Dampen dough with warm water; then sprinkle generously with brown sugar and cinnamon. Roll up the long way, like a jellyroll. *Cut in slices and lay on greased baking pans. Let rise and bake at 350 degrees for 15 to 20 minutes. While still warm, frost with your favorite icing.

*Instead of using a knife, which sort of mashes the dough down, I use a strong thread. Work a long piece under the dough, then bring up each end and pull threads together, and voila! A clean cut!

Hot Cross Buns #1

Ingredients:
1/2 cup warm water
2 tbsp. dry yeast
1 cup milk
1/3 cup shortening
1/3 cup sugar
1 1/2 tsp. salt
2 eggs
2/3 cup chopped dates
1 tbsp. cinnamon
1/2 tsp. nutmeg
4 1/2 to 5 cups white flour
Powdered sugar and milk

Directions:
In small bowl, dissolve yeast in warm water and set aside to rise. In saucepan, scald milk and add shortening, sugar and salt. In large mixing bowl, beat eggs. Add dates, cinnamon, and nutmeg. Add liquid ingredients and yeast and blend well. Beat in 1 or 2 cups of the flour, then stir in the rest to make a soft dough. Knead until soft and elastic. Cover and let rise. Shape into buns and place on greased baking pans. Brush with milk and let rise. Bake at 375 degrees for 15 to 20 minutes. Frost with simple powdered sugar/milk frosting.

Supper Smoke

Hot Cross Buns #2

Ingredients:
1 1/2 cups chopped dates, or 8 oz. pkg.
Boiling water
1/2 cup warm water
2 tbsp. yeast
1/4 cup butter or margarine
1/3 cup sugar
1 tsp. salt
1 cup buttermilk
2 eggs
3/4 cup mashed potatoes
1 tbsp. cinnamon
1/2 tsp. nutmeg
5 to 6 cups flour
1 1/2 cups powdered sugar
1/4 tsp. salt
2 tsp. vanilla
1/4 tsp. cinnamon
1/8 cup milk or cream

Directions:
In large mixing bowl, pour just enough boiling water over dates to barely cover. Set aside. In small bowl dissolve yeast in warm water. In saucepan, melt butter. Add sugar, salt and buttermilk and heat to lukewarm, stirring to dissolve sugar. In date bowl, beat eggs. Add the mashed potatoes, seasonings, buttermilk mixture, and yeast. With mixer, beat in 2 or 3 cups flour, then stir in enough more to make soft dough. Knead until smooth and elastic. Cover and let rise. Shape into buns and let rise again on greased baking sheets. Bake at 350 degrees for 10 to 15 minutes. While still hot, frost with the glaze of powdered sugar, salt, vanilla, cinnamon and milk. When cool, make a stiff frosting of powdered sugar, salt and milk, and make crosses on each bun.

Bread and Beyond

Country Corn Bread

Ingredients:
1 cup yellow corn meal
1 1/4 cups flour
3 tbsp. sugar
1 1/2 tsp. salt
1 1/2 tsp. baking powder
1/2 tsp. baking soda
2 large eggs
1 1/4 cups buttermilk
1/4 cup salad oil

Directions:
In large mixing bowl, combine all dry ingredients. In a separate bowl, beat eggs and add buttermilk and oil, blending well. Combine with dry mixture and turn into greased 9-inch square pan. Bake at 375 degrees for 20 to 30 minutes.

I suppose nearly every cook has a favorite corn bread recipe. I'll submit three of my favorites, but I'll confess that I've never met a slab of corn bread I didn't like.

Crunchy Sweet Cornbread

Ingredients:
1 cup sifted flour
3 tsp. baking powder
1/2 tsp. salt
1/2 cup sugar
1/2 cup yellow cornmeal
1 cup milk
1 egg, well beaten
1 tbsp. melted shortening

Directions:
Sift flour; then sift together with baking powder, salt and sugar. Stir in cornmeal. In separate bowl, beat egg and add milk and shortening. Blend with flour mixture. Turn into greased 8 inch pan and bake at 375 degrees for about 20 minutes.

Mexican Corn Bread

Ingredients:
1 cup corn meal
2 tbsp. flour
2 tbsp. sugar
1 tsp. salt
½ tsp. baking soda
2 eggs
1 cup buttermilk
1 can cream-style corn
1/4 cup bacon grease, softened
1 medium onion, chopped
1 small can (or less) jalapeno peppers, drained
1 cup grated longhorn cheese.

Directions:
In large mixing bowl, combine all dry ingredients. In a separate bowl, beat eggs and add the remaining ingredients EXCEPT the cheese.

Combine with flour mixture, blending just until moistened. Pour half the mixture into a greased pan; sprinkle with the cheese, and cover with remaining batter. Bake at 375 degrees for about 20 minutes or until golden brown.

This recipe is from our daughter Tamara, who hails from the heart of Tex/Mex country. While visiting over Christmas, we once had the privilege of enjoying hot tamales for Christmas breakfast. They certainly warmed the day!

Michelle's Biscuits

Ingredients:
1/2 cup butter or margarine
3 cups flour
2 tbsp. baking powder
2 tbsp. sugar
1 tsp. salt
Buttermilk
1 egg

Directions:
In small saucepan, melt the butter and set aside. In large mixing bowl, combine the dry ingredients. Pour enough of the butter to just cover the bottom of a 9 by 13 inch baking pan. To the remainder, add 1 egg and 1/2 cup buttermilk, blending well. Pour this mixture over the dry ingredients and combine, adding enough more buttermilk to make a soft dough, about brownie consistency. Pour this batter out on floured board and knead until smooth and springy. Pat out with fingers to about 1/2 inch thick.. Cut in shapes you desire. Place each biscuit in buttered pan and flip over to coat. Continue until all are coated, trying to leave a little space between. Bake at 400 degrees for 10 to 15 minutes.

Michelle is a dear friend, and I delight in her sense of humor and fun-loving spirit. She is courageously raising her five children alone and she presides over a lively household. Michelle loves to cook, and does so with a liberal and innovative hand. Her table fairly rocks with good food and good fun, and we love to shove our feet under it and enjoy! Just before serving us another tasty meal, she threw these biscuits together and served them hot. Without question, they are the best I've ever eaten. She does not use recipes, per se (the best cooks don't), but patiently tried to tell me just what she had done. I'll have to admit, mine weren't quite as good. Good Luck!

Supper Smoke

Farmhouse Biscuits

Ingredients:
2 cups flour
4 tsp. baking powder
1/2 tsp. salt
1/2 cup shortening
2/3 cup milk (approximately)

Directions:
In mixing bowl, combine the first three ingredients. Work the shortening into flour mixture with your hands until crumbly—NOT too fine. Add milk, stir, and place on floured board. Knead about 18 times. Pat down lightly to 1/2 inch thickness. Cut and bake on greased pans at 400 degrees until golden brown.

Call your farmer.

Quickie Cheese Biscuits

Ingredients:
1 1/2 tsp. baking powder
1/4 tsp. salt
Flour to make 1 cup
1/2 cup milk
2 tbsp. mayonnaise
1/2 cup shredded cheddar cheese

Directions:
Measure the baking powder and salt into a 1 cup measure. Add enough flour to make one level cup. In small mixing bowl, combine milk, mayonnaise and cheese. Add flour mixture and stir with fork. Knead, roll out and cut in shapes. Bake at 425 degrees until brown.

Light Baking Powder Biscuits

Ingredients:
2 cups sifted flour
4 tsp. baking powder
1/2 tsp. cream of tarter
1/2 tsp. salt
1 tbsp. sugar
1/2 cup shortening
2/3 cup milk
1 egg, unbeaten

Directions:
Sift dry ingredients together and place in large mixing bowl. Add shortening and blend. Make a well in the flour mixture and pour in the milk and add the egg. Stir to make a stiff dough. Knead about 5 times. Roll on floured surface to about 1/2 inch thick. Cut and bake on greased baking sheets at 400 degrees for 10 to 15 minutes

Your biscuits will be better if the shortening you use is cold.

Butter Dips

Ingredients:
2 1/4 cups flour
2 tbsp. sugar
1 tsp. salt
3 tsp. baking powder
1 cup milk
1/3 cup butter or margarine

Directions:
In mixing bowl, combine first four ingredients. Stir in milk and knead dough 10 times on floured surface. Roll dough out to 1/2 inch thickness and cut in narrow rectangles. Melt butter. Dip each rectangle in melted butter and lay, spaced apart on baking pan. Bake at 400 to 450 degrees for 5 to 10 minutes, or until golden brown.

Mary's Brown Soda Bread

Sure and 'twas a fair September morn that found us on the third floor of Dennis and Mary O'Connor's Bed and Breakfast in Dingle, Ireland! What a panorama lay below our high gabled window! Many colorful fishing boats were moored in the quiet harbor, and the smooth water reflected the green, green hills beyond. To the west, the clouds were tinged in a peachy glow, and the sea gulls dipped and soared over all. To top that off, Mary's delicious breakfast awaited us below! She shared her delicious soda bread recipe with me and here it is. The top o' the mornin' to you, too!

Ingredients:
1 1/2 cups whole wheat flour
1 1/2 cups white flour
1/2 cup bran
1/4 cup wheat germ
1 tsp. sugar
1 tsp. salt
1 tsp. baking soda
2 tbsp. margarine
2 cups lukewarm buttermilk

Directions:
In large mixing bowl, combine all dry ingredients, mixing well. Work the margarine into flour mixture until well blended. Make a well in the center of flour mixture and pour in the buttermilk. Mix well, until it resembles thick porridge. Grease well a round casserole dish or bread pan. Bake at 400 degrees for 45 minutes. Mary says—Turn out immediately and cool wrapped in a clean towel.

St. Joseph's B&B
Rooms en-suite
Tel: 087 6356437

Cheese Crunchies

Ingredients:
2 cups flour
1/2 tsp. salt
1/4 tsp. cayenne or chili powder, or to taste
1 cup butter or margarine, softened
A few drops Tabasco sauce, to taste
8 to 10 oz. sharp chedder cheese, grated
2 cups rice krispies
Paprika

Directions:
In mixing bowl, combine dry ingredients. Blend in butter, then Tabasco sauce and cheese, Stir in rice krispies and, with fingers, form into small balls. Place on ungreased baking pans. Flatten somewhat with fork tines and sprinkle with paprika. Bake at 350 degrees for about 10 minutes.

Supper Smoke

Coffee Cake Muffins

Ingredients:
2 tbsp. butter or margarine, softened
1/3 cup brown sugar, packed
3 tbsp. flour
1/2 tsp. cinnamon
1/2 cup chopped walnuts
1 3/4 cup flour
1 tbsp. baking powder
1 tsp. cinnamon
1/4 tsp salt
1 small pkg. instant vanilla pudding mix
1/3 cup butter or margarine, softened
1/4 cup sugar
1 egg, beaten
1 tsp. vanilla
1 1/4 cup milk

Directions:
In small mixing bowl, combine the first four ingredients, blending well. Add walnuts and set aside for topping. In a separate bowl, combine flour, baking powder, cinnamon, salt and pudding mix. In large mixing bowl, combine butter, sugar, egg, vanilla, and milk. Stir in the flour mixture and blend well. Spoon into greased muffin cups and sprinkle topping over all. Bake at 350 degrees for 15 to 20 minutes.

We think these muffins are special. Though a little more fuss to make, we savor them as a Sunday morning treat.

Banana Cream Muffins

Ingredients:
1 cup mashed banana, (about 2 medium)
1 tsp. water
1 tsp. baking soda
1/2 cup vegetable oil
1 cup sugar
1 egg, beaten
1/4 cup sour cream
2 tsp. vanilla
1 3/4 cups flour
1/8 cup wheat germ

Directions:
In small bowl, mash banana and set aside. In larger bowl, dissolve baking soda in water. Add oil, sugar, egg, sour cream, banana and vanilla. Blend well. Stir in the flour and wheat germ. Spoon into greased muffin cups and bake at 350 degrees for 15 to 20 minutes.

Supper Smoke

Oaty-Apple Muffins

Ingredients:
1 egg
1/4 cup salad oil
1/4 cup honey
3/4 cup milk
1/2 cup grated apple
1 cup flour
1 tbsp. baking powder
3/4 tsp. cinnamon
1/2 tsp. salt
1/4 cup packed brown sugar
1/3 cup unprocessed bran
1 cup uncooked oatmeal
Chopped nuts and/or raisins may be added

Directions:
In large mixing bowl, combine egg, oil, honey and milk. Add grated apple. In a separate bowl, combine all the dry ingredients, blending well. Make a well and pour the liquid mixture in and stir, just until moistened. Add nuts or raisins if preferred, and bake at 350 degrees for 15 to 20 minutes.

Buttermilk Bran Muffins

Ingredients:
4 cups All-Bran cereal
2 cups 100% Bran
4 tsp. salt
2 cups boiling water
1 quart buttermilk
3 cups sugar
1 cup shortening
4 eggs
5 cups flour
5 tsp. baking soda

Directions:
In large mixing bowl, combine the Brans and salt. Pour the boiling water over and mix well. Add the buttermilk, blend well and cool to lukewarm. In separate bowl, cream the sugar and the shortening. Beat in eggs, one at a time. Stir in Bran mixture. Add the flour and baking soda.

This is a huge recipe, as you can see, but it keeps well in a covered container in the refrigerator. This way you can pop a few muffins in the oven any time. When the children were still home, I used to grease a cookie sheet and drop batter on just like cookie dough and bake. They flatten out a bit and you scoop them off and butter while hot, and they are GOOD.

The Great Pumpkin Muffin

Ingredients:
1/4 cup sugar
2 tbsp. flour
1/2 tsp. cinnamon
4 tbsp. butter or margarine
2 1/2 cups flour
2 cups sugar
1 tbsp. pumpkin pie spice
1 tsp. soda
1/2 tsp. salt
2 eggs
1 cup pumpkin
1/2 cup vegetable oil
2 cups peeled, chopped apple

Directions:
In small bowl, combine sugar, flour and cinnamon. Cut in the butter and set aside for topping. In large bowl, combine the next five ingredients. In separate bowl, beat eggs, then add pumpkin, oil, and apple. Stir into dry mixture, only until moistened. Spoon into greased muffin tins and sprinkle topping over each. Bake at 350 degrees for 15 to 20 minutes.

Chocolate Chip Banana Muffins

Ingredients:
1 1/2 cups flour
3/4 cup sugar
1 tsp. baking powder
1 tsp. baking soda
1/2 tsp. salt
1/2 cup melted butter or margarine
1 egg, beaten
1 1/2 cups mashed banana (about 3 medium)
1/2 cup chopped nuts
1 cup chocolate chips

Directions:
In large mixing bowl, combine dry ingredients. Make well in center. In smaller bowl, combine the butter, egg and banana. Stir in the nuts and chocolate chips. Pour into flour well and stir only until moistened. Spoon into greased muffin cups and bake at 350 degrees for 15 to 20 minutes.

I hope you and yours are skinny 'cause there are calories creeping all through these. That's why they're so good.

Blueberry Muffins

Ingredients:
1/4 cup butter or margarine, softened
1/2 cup sugar
1/3 cup flour
1/2 tsp. cinnamon
1/3 cup sugar
1/4 cup butter or margarine, softened
1 egg
2 1/3 cups SIFTED flour
4 tsp. baking powder
1/2 tsp. salt
1 cup milk
1 tsp. vanilla
1 1/2 cups blueberries

Directions:
In small mixing bowl, combine the first four ingredients and set aside for topping. In larger bowl, combine sugar and butter, beating until fluffy. Beat in egg. In separate bowl, combine the sifted flour, the baking powder, and salt. Add to creamed mixture alternately with milk, beginning and ending with flour. Stir in vanilla and blueberries. Spoon into greased muffin tins and sprinkle topping over each. Bake at 375 degrees for 15 to 20 minutes.

Hearty Bran Muffins

Ingredients:
1 1/4 cup unprocessed bran
1 cup wheat germ
1 cup brown sugar
2 1/2 cups whole-wheat flour
2 1/2 tsp. baking soda
1/2 tsp. salt
2 eggs
1/2 cup honey
1/4 cup molasses
1/2 cup oil OR applesauce
2 cups buttermilk
1 cup boiling water
1 tsp. maple flavoring

Directions:
Combine first six ingredients in large mixing bowl. Make a well in center. In another bowl, beat eggs, then add remainder of ingredients and pour in flour well. Stir just 'til moistened. Bake at 350 degrees for 10 to 15 minutes.

I have searched at length for a really good bran muffin recipe. I thought once that I had found it, served in a café. But the cook said it was a mix! At last I have found these two and I love them both. Which one do you like best?

Best Bran Muffins

Ingredients:
1 cup flour
1/2 cup oatmeal, dry
1 cup whole-wheat flour
1/2 cup All Bran cereal
1/2 tsp. salt
1 tsp. baking powder
1 tsp. baking soda
1 egg, beaten
1/4 cup vegetable oil
1/2 cup molasses
3/4 cup buttermilk
1 (8 oz.) can crushed pineapple, undrained
1/2 cup chopped nuts, dates, or raisins (OPTIONAL)

Directions:
In large mixing bowl, combine all dry ingredients. In another bowl, beat eggs. Add all the rest of ingredients. Make a well in center of flour mixture. Pour in liquid mixture and stir gently, only until moistened. Bake at 375 degrees for 10 to 15 minutes.

Lemon Poppy Seed Muffins

Ingredients:
1 pkg. lemon cake mix
1 pkg. (3.4 oz.) instant lemon pudding mix
1 cup water
1/2 cup vegetable oil
4 eggs
1/4 cup poppy seeds

Directions:
In large mixing bowl, combine cake mix and pudding mix. Add the rest of ingredients and blend well. Grease or paper muffin cups and fill 1/2 to 3/4 full. Bake at 350 degrees for 10 to 15 minutes.

Magnificent Muffins

Ingredients:
2 1/2 cups white flour
2 tsp. soda
2 tsp. cinnamon
1/2 tsp. salt
1 cup brown sugar, packed
2 cups shredded carrots
1 cup shredded apple
3/4 cup raisins
1/3 cup walnuts or pecans, chopped (optional)
1/4 cup coconut
1 (8oz.) can crushed pineapple, drained
1/3 cup oil
1/3 cup applesauce or apple butter
2 tsp. vanilla
2 large eggs
2 egg whites

Directions:
In large mixing bowl, combine the first five ingredients and stir well. Add the next six ingredients and stir to coat. In small mixing bowl beat together the next five ingredients. Make a well in center of flour mixture, pour in egg mixture and stir only 'til flour is moistened. Spoon into greased or lined muffin cups and bake at 350 degrees for 15 to 20 minutes.

Muffin batter does NOT need much stirring. IF you do, there'll be tough ones occurring.

Supper Smoke

Momovers

Ingredients:
2/3 cups flour
1/4 tsp. salt
1/3 cup milk
1/3 cup water
2 eggs
1/2 cup shredded sharp cheddar cheese
Melted butter or margarine

Directions:
In mixing bowl combine flour and salt. Add milk and water and blend well. Beat in eggs, one at a time. Fold in shredded cheese. Spread melted butter in bottom and up the sides of muffin cups, being sure to cover well. Spoon in batter and bake at 400 degrees for about 20 minutes.

These behave like regular popovers, so don't be dismayed when they sort of cave in. They're champions for cheesy and chompy.

Apple Streusel Coffee Cake

Ingredients:
2 1/4 cups flour
3/4 cup sugar
3/4 cup butter or margarine
1/2 tsp. baking powder
1/2 tsp. baking soda
1 egg, beaten
3/4 cup buttermilk
1 (20oz.) can apple pie filling
1/3 cup raisins

Directions:
In large mixing bowl, combine flour and sugar. Cut in butter until mixture is crumbly. Set aside 1/2 cup of this mixture for topping. Add baking powder and soda to flour mixture. In small bowl, combine egg and buttermilk. Add to dry ingredients, stirring just until moistened. Spread 2/3 of batter in greased and floured 9-inch square pan. Spread filling and raisins over batter. Spoon rest of batter over filling; then crumb mixture over all. Bake at 350 degrees for 20 to 30 minutes.

Honey Bun Cake

Ingredients:
1 yellow cake mix, with pudding
4 eggs
2/3 cup vegetable oil
1/3 cup water
1 cup sour cream (8oz.)

....

1 cup brown sugar
1/4 cup flour
1 tbsp. cinnamon
1/4 cup butter or margarine, softened
1/2 cup chopped nuts

....

1 cup powdered sugar
2 tbsp. milk
1/2 tsp. vanilla

Directions:
Combine first five ingredients in large mixing bowl, beating until smooth with mixer. Set aside. In small bowl, combine the next five ingredients and set aside. Pour half the batter in a greased and floured 9 by 13 inch pan. Sprinkle half the filling mixture over batter. Spoon rest of batter over, then repeat with filling on top. Swirl batter with a knife. Bake at 350 degrees for 30 to 35 minutes, or until toothpick inserted in center comes out clean. Combine last 3 ingredients and drizzle over cake while still warm.

Just Plain Good Coffee Cake

Ingredients:
1/2 cup brown sugar
2 tbsp. flour
2 tsp. cinnamon
2 tbsp. melted butter or margarine
1/2 cup chopped nuts

....

1 1/2 cups flour
3 tsp. baking powder
1/2 tsp. soda
1/4 tsp. salt
3/4 cup sugar
1/4 cup shortening
1 egg
1/2 cup buttermilk or sour cream
1 tsp. vanilla

Directions:
In small bowl, combine first five ingredients and set aside for filling. Sift flour once, and then measure. Sift together with next four ingredients. Place in large mixing bowl. Cut in shortening until mixture is like fine cornmeal. In small bowl, combine egg, buttermilk, and vanilla. Fold into flour mixture and stir, just until blended. Spoon half of batter into greased and floured loaf pan. Sprinkle streusel filling over batter. Spoon rest of batter over top and bake at 350 degrees for 25 to 30 minutes.

Fruit-filled Coffee Cake

Ingredients:
1/2 cup brown sugar
2 tbsp. flour
2 tsp. cinnamon
2 tbsp. butter, softened
1/2 cup chopped nuts

....

1 1/2 cups sugar
3/4 cup butter or margarine
3 eggs
1 tsp. almond flavoring
3 cups flour
1 1/2 tsp. baking powder
1 1/2 tsp. soda
3/4 tsp. salt
1 1/2 cups sour cream (you may substitute a blend of 1 cup mayonnaise and 1/2 cup buttermilk)
1 can fruit pie filling, or whole cranberry sauce

Directions:
In small bowl, combine the first five ingredients and set aside for topping. In larger bowl, cream sugar and butter 'til light. Add eggs, one at a time, beating well after each addition. Blend in flavoring. Sift dry ingredients together. Add to creamed mixture alternately with sour cream, blending well. Spoon half the mixture into greased and floured loaf pan. Spread fruit filling carefully over batter, then other half of batter. Sprinkle topping over all, and bake at 350 degrees for 25 to 35 minutes, or until pick comes out clean.

Breakfast Cake

Ingredients:
1 egg
1/4 cup cooking oil
3/4 cup water
1/2 to 1 tsp. nutmeg OR cinnamon
1 pkg. yellow cake mix, regular size
....
3 tbsp. butter or margarine, softened
1/3 cup sugar
1 tbsp. cinnamon

Directions:
In mixing bowl, beat egg. Add oil, water, nutmeg and cake mix, blending well. Pour into greased and floured 9 x 13 inch baking pan. Combine last three ingredients and sprinkle over top. Bake at 350 degrees for 15 to 20 minutes.

Edith's Banana Bread

Ingredients:
3 very ripe bananas
3/4 cup sugar
1/8 tsp. salt
1 egg, beaten
1/4 cup butter or margarine
1 tsp. soda
1 tbsp. water
2 cups sifted flour

Directions:
In large mixing bowl, mash bananas. Blend in sugar, salt and beaten egg. Melt butter and stir into banana mixture. Dissolve soda in water and add, with sifted flour. Mix well and pour into greased and floured bread pan. Bake at 350 degrees for 40 to 50 minutes.

This is one of the very few recipes I have from my Mother-in-law Edith. Her cooking was simple and good, but it was her snappy Irish wit that spiced each meal she served!

Boston Brown Bread

Ingredients:
2 eggs
1/2 cup sugar
1/2 cup molasses
1 tsp. soda
1/2 cup milk or buttermilk
1 tsp. salt
1 cup corn meal
1 cup whole wheat flour
1 cup white flour

Directions:
In mixing bowl, beat eggs, then add sugar and molasses and blend well. Dissolve soda in milk and add. Then add the last four ingredients and blend well. Grease and flour 2 small coffee cans and divide batter between them. Bake at 350 degrees until toothpick comes out clean.

Homemade Noodles

Ingredients:
2 beaten eggs
1 tsp. salt
1/4 cup top milk, or cream
2 cups sifted flour

Directions:
Combine eggs, salt and milk in mixing bowl. Add enough flour to make a stiff dough. On floured surface, roll out dough very thin, flouring both sides more if needed. Let stand for 20 minutes. Then roll up and cut in 1/8 inch slices. Toss all on floured surface and then let dry several hours.

This is my mother's recipe. She added these to many of her soups, or sometimes cooked them alone, and we ate them with butter and salt and pepper. Every time I make a batch of these, I think of Mom, and of the wonderfully good, simple meals she made for us, three times a day. When I was a child, it seemed her hands were often floury. Now it seems to me that her hands were dusted with love.

Supper Smoke

Heavenly Waffles

Ingredients:
1 egg
1/2 cup oil
2 cups Bisquick
1 1/3 cups club soda

Directions:
In mixing bowl, beat egg and add the remaining ingredients, and bake.

These are light and crispy, and so EASY.

**History lesson! I've read that the first waffles were made in the 13th century, in England. It seems a clumsy crusader, wearing his armor, sat down by mistake on some fresh oatcakes. The steel links made deep imprints and he and his wife were both found buttering them and grinning and chewing and calling them "warfries", which means flat honeycomb cakes! (I did NOT make this up!)

Corn Meal Mountain Pancakes

Ingredients:
1 egg
1 1/4 cups buttermilk (or more)
1/4 cup shortening, melted
1 tbsp. molasses
1 cup flour
1 tsp. salt
2 tsp. baking powder
1/2 tsp. baking soda
1/2 cup yellow corn meal

Directions:
In mixing bowl, beat egg and add the next 3 ingredients. In separate bowl, combine all dry ingredients. Add to milk mixture, and stir just until moistened.

Overnight Pancakes

Ingredients:
1 tbsp. dry yeast
1/4 cup warm water
4 cups flour
2 tbsp. baking powder
2 tsp. baking soda
2 tsp. sugar
1 tsp. salt
6 eggs
1 quart buttermilk
1/4 cup vegetable oil

Directions:
In a small bowl, dissolve yeast in water. Set aside to rise. In a large mixing bowl, combine all dry ingredients. In separate bowl, beat eggs, and add buttermilk and oil. Combine with dry ingredients and add yeast. Store in refrigerator, covered.

These are very good, and besides that, the whole idea cuts down on early morning stress, of which we all need less.

Supper Smoke

Rose Petal Jelly

Ingredients:
Petals from 5 or 6 RED fragrant roses*
1 1/2 cups apple juice
1/4 cup lemon juice
1/4 cup water
1 pkg. MCP pectin
7 1/3 cups sugar
1 drop red food coloring

Directions:
Cover rose petals with water and bring to a boil, stirring for about 5 minutes. Strain through a cloth and reserve rose petal juice and discard pulp. In large kettle, measure 2 1/2 cups rose petal juice. Add apple juice, lemon juice and water, blending well. Sprinkle MCP pectin over mixture and blend well. Place kettle over heat and bring to a boil. Add the sugar, stirring well, and return to a boil. Boil 4 minutes. Remove from heat and add food coloring, being careful to not add too much. Ladle into hot, sterilized jars and seal.

Have fun experimenting with various rose petal colors and different juices, but be sure to use CLEAR fruit juice.

*Try to gather rose petals in early morning when roses and fragrance are at their best.

Dandelion Jelly

Do you yearn to savor all the golden Springtime?
Catch the lazy beauty of a summer day?
Sally forth and gather globes of sunshine:
Cook and hoard them for a wintry day!

Ingredients:
1 quart fresh dandelion blooms, pressed down somewhat
3 tbsp. lemon juice
1 box powdered pectin
5 1/2 cups sugar

Directions:
Rinse dandelion blooms in cold water to remove soil. Boil washed blooms for 3 minutes in 2 quarts water. DO NOT USE ALUMINUM KETTLE. Strain mixture through a cloth, pressing to remove all juice. Measure sugar and set aside. Measure 3 cups juice into large kettle. Add lemon juice and pectin. Bring mixture to a full rolling boil, then add sugar. Return to boil, stirring constantly, and boil for 3 minutes. Pour into hot sterilized jars and seal. Makes about 6 half-pints.

Grapefruit Jelly

Ingredients:
1 (12oz.) can frozen grapefruit juice
2 cans water
1 pkg. powdered pectin
5 cups sugar
1 or 2 tbsp. red Jell-O, dry

Directions:
Dilute the frozen juice with the two cans of water. Place four cups of this juice in large kettle. Slowly add pectin, stirring to dissolve. Measure sugar and set aside. Bring juice to a full rolling boil, stirring constantly. Add measured sugar and bring to a boil again. Continue to boil and stir for two minutes. Remove from heat and add dry Jell-O, stirring to blend. Pour into hot sterilized jars and seal.

Supper Smoke

The Gift of Listening

One of the finest ways to show generosity and true friendship is through the gift of good listening. There is hardly a way to estimate the value of such a gift. If our heart is in the right place and we care enough to want to "walk in another's shoes," then this gift is within the reach of any of us.

If we begin to sense that our friend wants and needs to talk, we should try to arrange a place where he can do so, without interruptions. Usually a neutral place is best, like a quite café or an outdoor area. Depending on the person, sometimes a good brisk walk together works well.

We need to remember that we need to listen to them from where THEY are. They may not have the same thoughts or ideas as we do, nor the background of experience we have had, but we need to withhold judgments and listen with an open mind. We need to remember that each person, created by God, is unique. We all see life through a somewhat different lens, changed and colored by what life has handed us, and by our own personal characteristics.

Sometimes our friend may be saying a lot more than his words tell us. If we really care, we will be listening for the unsaid words and the cry of the heart.

We need to resist the urge to "jump in" and finish his thought for him. That feels like a wet blanket when one is trying to express himself, and he may not want to say what you thought he did. When he finally gets it said, you may be surprised. You might even learn something!

You don't need to look him in the eye constantly, but you do need to let him know that he has your undivided attention. If you're not sure what he means, ask him to repeat his thought. It helps you to understand better, and lets him know that you're trying to stay on the "same page."

We need to resist the urge to fill every silence with your thoughts and answers. He may be trying to sort something out in his mind. Give him time. If he seems confused, try to repeat back to him what he has been saying as you understood it.

Try not to analyze what he has been saying. If he felt he needed a counselor, chances are he would have gone to one. He may want your advice or opinion, but don't be hasty with it. He may just want you to HEAR him. There's a good chance he knows the answer already; he just hasn't realized it yet. A quiet sounding board is many times all it takes for the answer to surface. If we find ourselves formulating answers before he is even finished, then we aren't really listening.

His thoughts were slow
His words were few
And never seemed to glisten
But he was a joy to all his friends
You should have heard him listen!
*   -Source unknown*

Vegetables

I think the good Lord meant for us
To eat our veggies raw.
They're all so fresh and crunchy then,
With nary a cooking flaw.
If He had only made them grow
With creamy, seasoned crust,
'Twould thus enhance the flavors,
Since chewing them, we must.
Yet, if you're not a veggie soul,
No need to roll your eyes,
Do skip this section, dear one,
And turn to Cakes and Pies.

Zippy Potatoes

Ingredients:
2 tbsp. cooking oil
1/4 tsp. browning sauce
1 tsp. paprika
1 tsp. garlic salt
8 peeled and quartered potatoes
Parsley

Directions:
In flat microwave pan, stir the oil, browning sauce, paprika and garlic salt. Blot quartered potatoes with paper towels. Place in pan and stir to coat with mixture. Cook, covered on HIGH for about 3 minutes, turn and cook about 3 minutes more. Sprinkle with parsley and serve.

** If you have trouble with your stored potatoes sprouting, place an apple in with them.

Tex Mex Potatoes

Ingredients:
1/2 cup flour
1/2 cup corn meal
1 1/2 tsp. salt
1 1/2 tsp. chili powder
6 to 8 peeled potatoes
1 to 1 1/2 cubes melted butter or margarine

Directions:
In mixing bowl combine first four ingredients. Cut potatoes in half, lengthwise and blot dry with paper towels. Dip in melted butter and then in flour mixture. Place in single layer on greased baking pan. Bake at 350 degrees for 40 to 45 minutes.

**For really creamy, rich tasting mashed potatoes without added calories, just add some non-dairy coffee creamer.

Scalloped Potatoes

Ingredients:
1 can cream of mushroom soup
1/2 cup milk
1/8 tsp. pepper
4 cups thinly sliced potatoes
1 small onion, chopped or sliced thin
1 cup shredded cheddar cheese
1 tbsp. butter or margarine
Dash of paprika

Directions:
In large mixing bowl combine the soup and milk, stirring until smooth. Add all the rest of the ingredients, except butter and paprika. Pour into buttered 1 1/2 quart casserole. Dot with butter and sprinkle with paprika. Cover and bake at 375 degrees for 1 hour. Uncover and bake 15 minutes more.

This recipe is old as the hills, or our marriage at least. It's one of the dishes I served guests (poor souls) when I was first learning to cook.

Tater Kryspies

Ingredients:
2 cups mashed potatoes
1 cup chopped ham, or crumbled cooked bacon
1 cup (4 oz.) shredded cheddar cheese
1/4 cup mayonnaise
1 egg, beaten
1/4 cup chopped onion
1 tsp. prepared mustard
1/2 tsp. salt
1/4 tsp. pepper
2 cups crushed cornflake crumbs
1/4 cup melted butter or margarine

Directions:
Combine all ingredients except margarine and crumbs. Set aside. Melt margarine and combine with crumbs. Place in a flat pan. Form 6 to 8 patties and coat with buttered crumbs. Place on greased cookie sheet and bake at 350 degrees for 20 to 30 minutes.

Good way to use up leftover mashed potatoes and they're yummy too. You can also shape these patties the night before and refrigerate. Then, in the morning, pop them in the oven while you're setting the table, scrambling eggs and fixing juice and VOILA…an impressive breakfast.

Vegetables

Onion Bag Potatoes

Ingredients:
1/4 cup flour
1 large oven bag
1/2 to 1 pkg. dry onion soup mix
8 to 16 medium peeled potatoes
1/4 to 1/2 cup sliced butter or margarine

Directions:
Place flour and dry onion soup mix in oven baking bag. Tumble to mix. Add potatoes and tumble to coat. Slice butter or margarine over potatoes in bag. Close and place in flat roasting pan. Make slits in bag as directed. Bake at 250 degrees for 2 1/2 hours or 350 degrees for about 1 hour.

This is a favorite company recipe. I put them and the meat I plan to serve both in the oven before leaving for church. Add a veggie and/or salad and the meal is complete, and so simple.

Supper Smoke

Potato Cheese Casserole

Ingredients:
1/2 cup butter or margarine
1/2 cup onion, chopped
1/2 cup flour
2 tsp. salt
1 tsp. dry mustard
4 cups milk
1 1/2 cups shredded cheese (6 oz.)
1 tbsp. dry parsley
16 to 24 small potatoes, peeled, cooked and shredded coarsely
1/4 cup butter or margarine, melted
2 cups crushed corn flake crumbs

Directions:
In saucepan, melt margarine and sauté onion until clear. Add flour, salt, and dry mustard, stirring well. Slowly add milk and bring to a boil, stirring constantly. Add cheese and parsley. In 9 by 12 inch buttered baking pan, arrange shredded potatoes. Pour sauce over all. Combine margarine and crumbs and sprinkle over potatoes and sauce. Bake at 350 degrees for 1 hour or until brown and bubbly.

I have served this to many, many guests and they never throw it back.

Vegetables

New Pan Potatoes

Ingredients:
Raw, quartered new potatoes
1 cube butter or margarine
Salt and pepper to taste

Directions:
In a deep 9 by 13 inch baking pan, layer quartered potatoes. Season with salt and pepper. Slice cube of butter or margarine over all. Cover and bake 1 to 1 1/2 hours. Stir and serve.

So simple and so good. What more can I say? If you prefer plain, old, fried potatoes from scratch, try sprinkling a little flour on the raw chunks. Makes them crispier!

**Did you find a good buy on yams or sweet potatoes? Either boil or bake them, then cool, wrap in foil, and freeze them.

Harvard Beets

Ingredients:
1 tbsp. vinegar
1 tbsp. sugar
1/2 tsp. salt
1/8 tsp. pepper
1 tbsp. cornstarch
1 pint, or can beets

Directions:
Combine first five ingredients. Add beets, including liquid. Bring to a boil, stirring constantly and cook until thickened.

I remember first trying this at my sister-in-law Wilma's, who was a marvelous cook. This dish reminds me of the pickled beets my mother used to serve her guests years ago.

Supper Smoke

Jazzy Carrots

Ingredients:
10 to 12 medium carrots (about 2 pounds)
1 small green pepper, chopped
1 medium onion, chopped
1 can tomato soup, chopped (NO, NO! Just kidding!)
1/2 cup oil
1 cup sugar
3/4 cup vinegar
1 tsp. dry mustard
1 tsp. Worcestershire sauce
1/2 tsp. salt
1/4 tsp. pepper

Directions:
Peel and slice carrots in rounds and cook in salted water until barely tender. Combine remaining ingredients and pour over drained carrots. Marinate at least 6 hours, or overnight. Heat and serve.

This makes a nice big batch. If you want to add color to the dish, you may add 1 can drained green beans just before heating.

Vegetables

Green Bean Supreme

Ingredients:
2 cans green beans, French style or regular
2 tbsp. butter
3 tbsp. minced onion
1 tbsp. flour
1/2 tsp. salt
1/4 tsp. dry mustard
1/2 tsp. paprika
1/2 tsp. Worcestershire sauce
1 cup milk or cream
1 cup grated cheese
2 tbsp. fine breadcrumbs or finely crushed corn flake crumbs

Directions:
Drain green beans and set aside. In saucepan melt butter and sauté onion until clear. Blend in flour and all seasonings. Heat until bubbly, stirring constantly. Gradually add milk or cream. Stir and heat to boiling. Add beans to sauce. Pour into greased, one-quart casserole. Sprinkle with cheese, then crumbs. Place in hot oven just until cheese is melted and crumbs are browned.

Barbeque Green Beans

Ingredients:
4 slices bacon, shopped
1/4 cup onion, chopped
1/2 cup catsup
1/4 cup brown sugar
1 tbsp. Worcestershire sauce
2 (16 oz.) cans green beans, drained

Directions:
Cook bacon and onion in medium saucepan until bacon is crisp. Drain. Add catsup, brown sugar and Worcestershire sauce; bring to a boil. Stir to dissolve sugar. Stir in green beans. Return to boil, reduce heat, and simmer, uncovered for 10 minutes, stirring occasionally. Serves 6 to 8.

Supper Smoke

Veggie Dip or Vegetables Incognito

Ingredients:
2/3 cup mayonnaise
1/3 cup sour cream
1/2 tsp. flavor enhancer
1 tbsp. minced onion
1 tbsp. dried parsley
1 tsp. dill weed
1/2 tsp. rooster sauce (I get tired of spelling it!)
2 tsp. hot pepper sauce
1 tsp. seasoning salt

Directions:
Combine all ingredients and chill. In the meantime, fix a tray of radishes, carrot rounds, tomato slices, cauliflower, cucumber, and all that kind of stuff. If you arrange the tray prettily and plop the dip in the middle of it all, the adults will crunch on it, to be polite if nothing else, and children MIGHT at least consume one radish.

**Some folks like to cook cauliflower a bit for this tray. If you do, add 1/2 tsp. sugar, which keeps cauliflower white.

Baked Beans

Ingredients:
3 to 4 cups dry navy beans
1 whole onion, chopped
1 tsp. dry mustard
2 to 3 tsp. salt
1/2 tsp. pepper
1 cup brown sugar, firmly packed
1 to 2 cups tomato juice, sauce, or soup
A blurb of molasses
A chunk of ham or bacon
A few drops liquid smoke

Directions:
Wash beans and soak overnight. Bring to a boil and cook slowly until tender. Drain. Add all remaining ingredients and place in covered roaster or bean pot. Bake at 300 degrees at least 4 hours or very slow oven, 180 to 200 degrees, overnight.

As a young bride, I tried and tried to bake beans and dumped out every batch; until my own dear sister thought to tell me that the beans MUST FIRST be cooked until tender before they are baked. Take heed, young bride!

**Wash a potato and toss it in any pot of beans you are cooking. Throw the potato out when beans are done. Less gas!

Supper Smoke

Shortcut Baked Beans

Ingredients:
2 cans (1lb.14oz.) pork and beans
1 can tomato sauce
1/2 onion, chopped
1 tsp. salt
1/2 tsp. pepper
1 tsp. dry mustard
Brown sugar to taste
Bits of cooked ham or bacon, if you have it

Directions:
Combine all ingredients (draining some of the pork and bean liquid if you wish.) Bake in covered dish at 300 degrees for 2 hours.

It might not fool your mother-in-law, but it'll stand you in good stead if you get in a bind.

Cheddar Cheese Sauce

Ingredients:
1/2 cup butter or margarine
1/2 cup flour
1 tsp. salt
1/2 tsp. pepper
4 cups milk
2 cups (8oz.) shredded cheddar cheese
1 tbsp. prepared mustard

Directions:
In saucepan, melt butter. Add flour salt and pepper and stir 'til smooth. Gradually add milk and bring to a boil, stirring constantly. Continue cooking until thickened. Add cheese and mustard and stir until cheese is melted.

This is a versatile little sauce that goes good over baked potatoes, eggs or veggies.

North Dakota Tomato Jam

(Don't knock it 'til you've tried it!)

Ingredients:
3 cups peeled, chopped tomatoes and their juice
1/3 cup lemon juice
1 pkg. Sure-Jell
1/2 tsp. margarine
4 1/3 cups sugar

Directions:
In large kettle, combine all ingredients EXCEPT sugar. Bring mixture to a boil, while stirring constantly. Add sugar. Continue stirring and cook until mixture comes to a full rolling boil. Cook 1 minute. Ladle into hot jars and seal.

Lookie here, child…you haven't tasted anythin' 'til you bite into fresh, home baked bread from Mama's wood stove, slathered with butter and tomato jam!

Supper Smoke

Grandma Amelia Amoth's Beet Pickles

Ingredients:
Beets
2 cups water
2 cups vinegar
2 1/2 cups sugar
1 tbsp. pickling spice

Directions:
Wash beets, but DON'T cut off the roots or tops. (All the nice red juice will ooze out if you do.) In large kettle, place beets and cover with water. Bring to a boil, and cook until tender when poked with fork. Drain water, and then dump all in sink and cover with cold water to cool. The skins will easily slip off. Also cut off the roots and the tops. If beets are small, leave whole, or if larger, slice evenly, or quarter. In large cooking pot. Combine water, vinegar, sugar and spices. Bring to a boil and add enough beets so that liquid covers them. Bring to a boil again and boil 5 minutes. Ladle into hot, sterilized jars, leaving at least 1/2 inch space at top. Screw on hot lids and rings and let stand to seal.

My grandmother, Amelia Halvorsen, married my grandfather, Martin Amoth, in the Lutheran church close to Franklin, Minnesota. Two children were born to them there. Then Grandmother bid her family goodbye, and with her young husband and children, began a pioneer journey. I wonder if she suspected that she would never again see her girlhood home.

They settled near Langdon, North Dakota, and in a sod house on the open prairie, they began pioneer living. Five more children were born here, the third oldest being my father, Albert. At a young age, grandfather Martin began suffering the effects of what is now known as multiple sclerosis. My father and his older brother took over the work of the farm as young boys, and they learned the meaning of hard work and of hardship. Grandfather Martin passed away at the age of forty-five, and Grandmother never married again. Though life was hard, my father often recalled happy times together as a family.

Mom's Tomato Sauce

Ingredients:
10 pounds ripe tomatoes
2 green peppers
4 large onions
2 cloves garlic
2 tbsp. salt
2 tbsp. celery salt
1 tbsp. chili powder
1 tsp. basil
1 tsp. pepper
2 tsp. paprika
1/4 cup oil
1/4 cup sugar

Directions:
Wash, stem, and cut up the tomatoes, mashing to make juice. Cook, stirring constantly, until soft, (May have to add a little water.) Run tomato mixture through a food mill, reserving juice and discarding pulp. Grind, or chop peppers, onions, and garlic and add to tomato juice. Add all of remaining ingredients. Bring to a boil, stirring constantly and then simmer for 1 hour, stirring occasionally. While mixture is hot, pour into pint jars, seal, and process in water bath for 20 minutes. Makes 8 or 9 pints.

This was my Mom's recipe and I'd hardly know how to cook without it.

Supper Smoke

Zucchini Relish

Ingredients:
10 cups ground zucchini squash, rind and all
4 cups ground onions (put a clothes pin on nose!)
2 large sweet peppers, ground
2 large green peppers, ground
2 1/4 cups vinegar
6 cups sugar
1 tbsp. nutmeg
1 tbsp. dry mustard
1 tbsp. turmeric
1 tbsp. cornstarch
2 tsp. celery seed
1/2 tsp. pepper

Directions:
Combine the first four ingredients and let stand overnight. Drain, rinse in cold water, and place in large kettle. Add all remaining ingredients. Bring to a boil, stirring constantly and then cook slowly for 30 minutes. While mixture is hot, pour into hot jars and seal. Makes about 7 pints.

This is really good stuff. Hubby hardly thinks he can live without it, so I try to make several batches at once.

Vegetables

My Psychiatrist

Yes, the other day I had another visit with him. We have had many sessions together, but this particular one became so impressive, that I thought I would like to share it with you.

Perhaps a few words of commendation for my doctor would be in place. Without question, he is the greatest psychiatrist the world has ever known. His office is never closed. He is there, waiting to give council and support, even in the long, silent hours of the night. One needs no appointment, and he has no waiting room. Each patient steps in immediately with all that troubles him. He is genuinely interested in them all. He has all the time in the world – and more- to listen. And listen he does, in such a kind, caring way.

Of particular interest to me is that he knows my history so thoroughly. He has files on all my ancestors. He knows what kind of baby I was; every detail of my childhood and adolescence. Each major and minor incident of my life is recorded; why it happened, and how I reacted.

So you see, it is with complete confidence that I go to him, knowing that he understands me, even far better than I understand myself.

His services are free. His only requisite is a faithful following of his prescription. Sometimes his therapy seems hard to grasp, sometimes not. But it never fails to answer my need. Perhaps, by now, you have guessed his name.

It is Jesus.

This consultation would be of interest to mothers, and young mothers in particular. I came to Him feeling extremely tired and depressed. I told him so.

"Why?" He wanted to know. "Just relax and tell me all about it."

"Well, it seems like the task before me looks so BIG. What a terrible time to raise a family! There are so many pitfalls, and the world around us grows so dark. I feel afraid, sometimes, for my family, and for myself. I don't feel I have the wisdom to guide them in safe paths, and I feel weak and confused. I worry a lot, and I'm always so BUSY. There seems never enough time, and I feel I'll never catch up. Then I get cross and impatient, and I feel so bad about that. I vow to do better, but so often I fail again. And it seems to me there are so many problems in life that have no answers, that I can see. They just go on and on. Sometimes life looks like a huge mountain that I have to climb. It looks so dark, and so steep. I suppose that's why I'm so tired all the time. I don't really feel like I'm walking up the path anymore. It seems more like I'm crawling. OH! How WILL I ever make it?"

Supper Smoke

I find myself sobbing...into a warm and caring silence. I know He has heard, and that He understands. I seem to feel a hand on my shoulder, and He quietly waits 'til I'm through.

And now it's my turn to listen.

"Yes, my child, I have looked at this mountain with you. Truly it does look huge and forbidding. No wonder you have been so tired and troubled. You should have come sooner," He gently chided. "But, I'm so glad you came in time. Some of my patients wait so long that they lose hope, and are filled with despair. Some of them never come to me again."

And so he gave me my prescription. "Look it over," He said, "and see if you have any questions."

I'm puzzled. What did I see? It appears to be a picture – a beautiful one – and so restful. There is a little green hill with a path meandering to the top. It's a sunny day, and there's a little breeze, so the grass looks like rippling waves. It all looks so peaceful, and quiet.

"But, what of the mountain?" I cried. "Where is it? I have to climb it, don't I?"

"Now child, I don't want you to look at that mountain again. I've taken it away. You were trying to live your whole life every day. I want you to live just one day at a time. Look...this little green hill is one day. Does this seem too hard to climb?"

"Why, of COURSE not!" I cried.

"That's all that I ask of you. You must never try to climb more than one hill at a time." He pointed out to me that, indeed, there were a few rocks and rough places. And there were some clouds too, but He showed me a pleasant little meadow that I hadn't seen before. It was beautiful there – so cool and shady – and here He wanted me to rest.

"You passed many a little meadow on your way up that dark mountain," He said, "But you didn't see them. You were too tired, and your head was bent so low."

Then, too, He showed me others climbing, their burdens larger than mine. I felt urged to help them along, as we climbed.

"You passed these too, before, but you huddled your pitiful strength around you, afraid that if you spent it on others, there would not be enough for you. Now, as you give your strength to others, you'll find that your own is increased."

"Now, my child, go out into this day, and come again to report of your travel."

And so I came in the evening to tell Him.

"Yes, it was MUCH easier! With just one little hill to climb, I felt much more relaxed, and rested. My family noticed, and they were happier too! I even left some of my work and took a little walk with the children. We found wild flowers, and we watched a Blue Jay. On the way home we held hands, and we laughed and sang together. I felt so rested that I was SURPRISED how quickly the work was finished. Then I realized that I had passed through the little meadow you had prepared for us to enjoy."

"But, still, at the crest of the hill, in the evening, I knew that I had stumbled sometimes through the day. But, as your prescription says – one day at a time – I felt an urge to make amends where necessary, so I'd be prepared to start a fresh green hill tomorrow. In my heart there is new hope!"

And He seemed to smile, and together we look ahead. "Now you must know that some of these hills will not be so bright and sunny. Some will be dark and difficult all the way to the top. But NEVER like that mountain. I'll never ask more than one hill for each day. You will learn to watch for the meadows. They are so easily missed, but are so very important for renewing your strength."

"Some day, my child, you'll leave it all behind…the hills and the mountain. And all at once…and FOREVER, your heart will swell with rapture, and you will be joined in such a harmony that you will need a new body to contain the joy!"

"And this wondrous singing, swelling joy, shall know no bounds, and shall never, ever end."

> One day at a time, I will follow.
> One day at a time, by His side.
> 'Twill bring me great joy in the morning,
> When He says, "Come to me, and abide."
> **R.A.S.**

Supper Smoke

Child of a King

There's a King in a far away country of love,
Who reigns from a throne of pure gold.
'Tis a country whose battles were furiously fought,
And whose victory has often been told.

Now this King, in that country so far, far away,
('Tis strange as I tell it, I know)
He yearns to adopt all the children He finds,
And thus His great kingdom doth grow.

Long ago, this King, and beloved own Son,
Reigned together, as though they were one.
Yet they framed a great plan to adopt all of man,
But 'twas death to His own blessed Son.

Now, you'd think, would you not, that a King such as He?
With vast warriors in ranks, trained above,
Would reign with a force as would quell every foe?
Yes, He DOES! For his ensign is love.

"Twas this love won my heart, and adopted was I.
I'd possessed a huge debt that He paid.
I'm the child of a King! And great riches are mine,
All because of this plan that they made.

I dwell in an embassy, far from that land.
There are enemies here, everywhere.
But ambassadors too, and we share as we toil.
As for armor, we're girded with prayer.

I rejoice each new day, though perils abound,
And my duties demand that I trust;
That I lean on His wisdom, and further His work,
I'm the child of a King, and I must!

So I lift up my head, secure in His realm.
To Him every honor I bring
There's no time to worry, and no need to doubt,
For I am the child of a King.

Vegetables

*Some day I will climb the most beautiful stairs,
And survey vast domains, on the wing,
Forever I'll praise Him. Forever we'll reign,
For I am a child of a King!*

R.A.S.

Just Desserts

An elderly fellow kept roaring
To his wife, that evenings were boring.
She called friends for treats,
Served coffee and sweets,
And they stayed half the night…
She kept POURING!

Norwegian Apple Pie

Ingredients:
1 egg
3/4 cup sugar
1 tsp. vanilla
1 tsp. baking powder
1/4 tsp. salt
1/2 cup flour
1/2 cup chopped nuts
1 cup fresh diced apples

Directions:
In large mixing bowl, combine all ingredients in order given. Mixture will be stiff. Turn into buttered 9-inch pie pan. Bake at 350 degrees for 30 minutes or until brown.

Serve warm with whipped cream topping, or ice cream.

If you're Norwegian, like my father was, then you'll know how to tell amusing stories and slap your leg joyously when you come to the punch line. Then you pause for another bite of cake and a long slurp of coffee, and then…another story!

**When whipping cream for any dessert-topping try adding a couple tablespoons instant vanilla puddings mix. Extra taste and the whipped cream is nice and stiff and won't weep.

Strawberry Angel Food

1 angel food cake
1 large pkg. strawberry Jell-O
2 1/2 cups boiling water
2 (10oz.) pkgs. sliced, frozen strawberries, thawed
2 tbsp. sugar
1/4 tsp. salt
1 pint whipping cream

Directions:
In large mixing bowl, dissolve Jell-O in boiling water, stirring to dissolve well. Stir in thawed berries, sugar and salt, stirring well again to dissolve. Let cool until mixture begins to thicken. In a separate bowl, whip cream and fold into Jell-O mixture. Cover bottom of large, flat dessert pan with half of the angel food cake, torn into fairly small pieces. Pour half the strawberry mixture over cake. Make another layer of cake, using other half. Then pour the remaining strawberry mixture over all. Refrigerate 4 to 5 hours before serving.

This is a light and delicious dessert. We love to serve it to guests and always hope there is a goodly amount left over!

Supper Smoke

Huckleberry Cake Dessert

Ingredients:
1 white cake mix
1 (8oz.) pkg. cream cheese, softened
1/2 cup sugar
1 tsp. vanilla
2 cups whipping cream

1 cup sugar
3 tbsp. cornstarch
1 cup water
3 cups huckleberries

Directions:
Mix the cake mix according to box directions and bake. When cool, crumble into a 9 by 13 inch pan. In mixing bowl, thoroughly combine cream cheese, sugar and vanilla. In another bowl whip cream until stiff peaks form. Add to creamed cheese mixture. Pour over cake crumbs. Prepare huckleberry topping by combining next four ingredients in saucepan. Cook over medium heat, stirring constantly, until mixture thickens and boils. Cool. Carefully spoon over cream mixture. Chill to serve.

Huckleberry Marshmallow Dessert

Ingredients:
4 or 5 tbsp. butter or margarine, melted
3 tbsp. sugar
20 graham cracker squares, crushed

1 cup sugar
5 tbsp. cornstarch
Dash of salt
3/4 cup water
2 to 3 cups huckleberries
1 tsp. lemon juice

1 cup milk
50 large marshmallows
1/2 pint whipping cream

Directions:
Combine butter, sugar and graham crumbs. Press into a greased 9 by 13 inch baking pan and bake at 350 degrees for 10 to 15 minutes. Remove from oven and cool.

In saucepan, combine sugar, cornstarch, and salt. Slowly add water and then huckleberries. Cook over medium heat until mixture boils and is thickened. Add lemon juice and set aside to cool.

In double boiler, put milk and marshmallows. Melt and cool. Whip cream and add to cooled marshmallow mixture. Spread over graham cracker crust. Let set until firm. Spread cooled huckleberry mixture over all.

You may use various fruit mixtures in this recipe, such as cherry pie filling, or even chocolate pudding.

Chocolate Peanut Supreme

Ingredients:
1/3 cup butter or margarine, melted
1/2 cup chunky style peanut butter
1/2 cup brown sugar
1 1/2 cups crushed graham crackers (24 squares)

1 1/2 cups sugar
1/2 (rounded) cup flour
1/2 cup dry cocoa
1 tsp. salt
2 1/2 cups water
3/4 cup coffee
3 tsp. vanilla
3 to 4 tbsp. peanut butter
12 oz. Cool Whip OR 1/2 pint whipping cream +1/4 cup sugar
1 cup chopped peanuts

Directions:
Combine first four ingredients and press into 9 by 13 inch pan.

Combine sugar, flour, cocoa, salt, water and coffee, blending well. Cook until mixture thickens and boils, stirring constantly. Add vanilla and peanut butter and cool, stirring occasionally. When cooled, spread over graham crust and top with Cool Whip, or whipping cream, whipped and sweetened. Garnish with peanuts and chill to serve.

Marlyns's Fluted Cake Dessert

Ingredients:
1 yellow, or white cake mix
4 oz. cream cheese, softened
2 tbsp. milk
3/4 cup sugar
6 to 8 oz. Cool Whip (no more)
Cherry, or huckleberry pie filling

Directions:
Grease and flour 2 fluted cake pans. Mix cake mix as directed on box. Pour into prepared pans and bake at 350 degrees, approximately 20 minutes, or until toothpick comes out clean. Remove from oven and cool about 10 minutes. Then turn out on serving platters. In mixing bowl, whip together the cream cheese and milk until smooth. Slowly add the sugar and bend well. Add the Cool Whip. Carefully spoon cream cheese mixture into fluted cake. Top with pie filling. Chill.

Try to loosen the edges of cake a bit before turning out on platter, and be sure and hold your face just right! These desserts look so pretty and taste wonderful. Thanks Marlyn!

Fruit Pizza

Ingredients:
1 cup flour
1/2 cup butter or margarine
1/2 cup powdered sugar
8 oz. cream cheese, softened
1/2 cup powdered sugar
1 cup fruit juice
1/4 cup sugar
2 tsp. cornstarch
Various fruits, such as pineapple chunks (drained), oranges, bananas, grapes, strawberries, kiwi…whatever you have on hand. If using bananas, be sure to dip slices in lemon juice before layering.
Maraschino cherries are nice for garnish

Directions:
In mixing bowl, combine flour, butter and powdered sugar, making a soft dough. Press into a greased 12 inch pizza pan and bake at 350 degrees for 15 minutes. Cool. In another bowl, combine cream cheese, and powdered sugar. Spread over cooled crust.

In small saucepan, combine juice, sugar and cornstarch and cook until mixture thickens and boils. Cool.

Arrange peeled and sectioned fruits in circles, starting at outer edges and using color contrast. Spread cooled fruit juice mixture over fruit arrangement.

This always goes over big. Color has a lot to do with appetite, don't you think? This dessert just wouldn't taste the same if fruit colors were brown, tan, ishy yellow, and gray.

Come to think of it, would Eve even have looked twice at that apple had it been brown?

Cranberry Apple Crisp

Ingredients:
2 1/4 cups quick oats
2 cups brown sugar
3/4 cup flour
3/4 cup butter or margarine, melted
1 can whole fruit cranberry sauce
2 cups apples, peeled and shredded

Directions:
In mixing bowl, combine the oatmeal, brown sugar, flour, and butter. Reserve 1 cup. Press remaining crumbs into well greased 9 by 13 inch pan. In another bowl, combine cranberries and shredded apples. Spread over crumbs. Top with remaining crumbs. Bake at 400 degrees for 15 to 20 minutes, or until mixture begins to bubble. Serve warm with ice cream, or whipped topping.

Supper Smoke

Bread Pudding

Ingredients:
4 cups bread cubes, crust removed
3 cups milk
3/4 cup firmly packed brown sugar
1/2 cup raisins
1/4 cup butter or margarine
1 tsp. vanilla
1/4 tsp. salt
1/4 tsp. nutmeg
3 eggs

Directions:
Place bread in a 2-quart, buttered baking dish. In a saucepan, scald milk. Stir in sugar, raisins, butter, vanilla, salt, and nutmeg. In another bowl, beat eggs. Gradually blend in milk mixture. Pour over bread. Set dish in a shallow pan with hot water about 1 inch deep. Bake at 350 degrees for 1 hour, or until knife inserted near center comes out clean.

This is humble fare. We ate it often as children, and, in my opinion, it is one of the best comfort foods this world will ever know! Some folks seem to feel even more comforted by serving this with cream, or ice cream, but I never do. Why tamper with perfection?

Chocolate Marshmallow Dessert

Ingredients:
4 tbsp. butter or margarine, melted
2 tbsp. sugar
24 chocolate graham cracker squares, crushed (or add 3 tbsp. cocoa to regular grahams)
1 cup milk
50 marshmallows
1 cup chocolate chips
1 cup whipping cream
1/4 to 1/2 cup chocolate chips
1/2 cup chopped nuts

Directions:
Combine butter, sugar and graham crackers. Spread in a buttered 9 by 13 inch pan and bake at 350 degrees for 10 to 15 minutes. Cool.

In double boiler, add milk, 1 cup chocolate chips and marshmallows. Place over heat and stir until melted. Cool. In small bowl, whip cream and add to cooled marshmallow mixture. Spread over cooled crust and sprinkle with chocolate chips and chopped nuts. Chill to serve.

Supper Smoke

Chocolate Date Dessert

Ingredients:
40 Hydrox cookies, crushed
1 cup water
1 cup chopped dates
40 marshmallows
1 cup chopped nuts
2 cups whipping cream
1/4 cup powdered sugar

Directions:
Place all but 1/3 of crumbs in well buttered 9 by 13 inch pan. In saucepan, measure the water and dates. Cook, stirring constantly for 1 minute. Remove from heat and add marshmallows. Cover and let stand until marshmallows melt. Blend together and spread over crumbs. Sprinkle with chopped nuts. Cool. Whip cream until soft peaks form. Gradually add sugar and whip until stiff. Spread over all and sprinkle with remaining crumbs. Refrigerate several hours or freeze. If frozen, take out a little while before serving.

Éclair Torte

Ingredients:
1 cup water
1/2 cup BUTTER
1/4 tsp. salt
1 cup flour
4 eggs
1 pkg. (8oz.) cream cheese, softened
2 pkgs. (small) instant vanilla pudding mix
3 cups cold milk
1 (12oz.) carton whipped topping
Chocolate syrup

Directions:
In a saucepan, combine water, butter and salt. Bring to a boil. Add flour all at once; stir and cook until mixture forms a smooth ball. Remove from heat and let stand five minutes. Add eggs, one at a time, beating well after each addition. Spread into greased 9 by 13 pan. Bake at 400 degrees for 30 to 35 minutes, or until puffy and golden brown. Cool. In mixing bowl combine cream cheese, pudding mixes, and milk. Beat until smooth. Spread over cooled crust and refrigerate for 20 minutes. Spread with whipped topping and chill. Drizzle with chocolate syrup just before serving.

Supper Smoke

Cherry Torte

Ingredients:
6 egg whites
1 tsp. cream of tartar
2 cups sugar
2 cups soda crackers, broken in pieces (44 squares)

3/4 cup chopped nuts
2 tsp. vanilla
1 large container Cool Whip
1 can cherry pie filling

Directions:
In mixing bowl beat egg whites until frothy. Add cream of tartar and beat until stiff. Gradually add sugar, beating as you add. Beat until whites stand in peaks. Fold in soda crackers, nuts, and vanilla. Bake in 9 by 13 inch greased pan at 350 degrees for 20 to 25 minutes. Cool five or six hours, or overnight. Top with Cool Whip and cherry pie filling, or the other way around. Chill at least 2 hours.

This is one of our favorite company desserts. You can vary this one a lot by using different fruit pie fillings, or chocolate pudding or lemon pie filling. We like 'em all.

Heavenly Raspberry Crunch

Ingredients:
1 cup flour
1/2 cup butter or margarine
1 tbsp. sugar
1/2 cup crushed almonds

1 (8oz.) pkg. cream cheese
1 cup powdered sugar
1 cup Cool Whip

1 1/2 cups water
5 tbsp. cornstarch
1 1/2 cups sugar
4 cups raspberries

1 cup whipping cream
1/4 cup powdered sugar

Directions:
For crust, blend first four ingredients and spread in greased 9 by 13 inch pan. Bake at 350 degrees for 20 minutes. Cool.
In mixing bowl, beat together cream cheese and powdered sugar until well blended. Fold in Cool Whip and spread on cooled crust. Chill.

In saucepan, combine water, cornstarch and sugar and cook, stirring constantly, until mixture is clear and thickened. Add berries. Cool, and then spread over cream cheese mixture. Whip cream until soft peaks form. Gradually add sugar and beat until stiff. Spread over berry filling. Chill to serve.

This recipe comes from Bruce and Tonya, two of my favorite people. They have a lovely little family and I feel fortunate to call Bruce my nephew. You too, will feel fortunate, when you sit down to a square of this dessert.

Thanks Bruce and Tonya!

Supper Smoke

Huckleberries 'N Cream Supreme

Ingredients:
1 box white cake mix
1 (8oz.) pkg. cream cheese
1 cup powdered sugar
1 (8oz.) container Cool Whip, thawed
1 small pkg. grape or blueberry Jell-O
1 3/4 cup sugar
5 tbsp. cornstarch
2 cups boiling water
4 cups huckleberries

Directions:
Grease and flour a 9 by 13 inch pan. Prepare cake mix as directed on pkg. Pour 2/3 of batter in pan. Bake at 350 degrees for 20-25 minutes. Cool completely. Meanwhile combine cream cheese and sugar and beat until fluffy. Fold in Cool Whip. Spread on top of cooled cake. Refrigerate. In a saucepan combine Jell-O, sugar and cornstarch. Add boiling water and cook 2 minutes. Cool completely and stir in fruit. Carefully spread on top.

Other fruits, such as raspberries, may be used, using a Jell-O flavor that compliments the fruit.

I enjoyed this tasty dessert at a wedding reception. It was a lovely experience, but I don't recall the bridal pair!

River Picnic Dessert

Ingredients:
1 cup chopped pecans
1 cup shredded coconut
1 pkg. German chocolate cake mix
1 (8oz.) pkg. cream cheese, softened
4 cups powdered sugar
1 tsp. vanilla
Whipped cream, optional

Directions:
Grease a 9 by 13 inch pan. Sprinkle nuts and coconut on bottom. Prepare cake mix as directed. Pour over nuts and coconut. Do not stir. In a separate bowl, combine cream cheese, sugar and vanilla. Beat until creamy. Carefully dab spoonfuls over batter. Bake at 350 degrees for 30-35 minutes. Serve with whipped cream if desired.

We recently enjoyed a lovely Sunday picnic beside the gently rippling Moyie River. The day was enhanced by the presence of very dear friends who all shared in providing the meal. Jeanette brought this lovely offering, which outshone all the other desserts. Whip this up soon, and then find yourself some friends, and a river.

Supper Smoke

The River Time

Oh! A wonderful stream is the River Time,
    As it runs through the realm of tears,
With a faultless rhythm, a musical rhyme,
And a broader sweep and a surge sublime,
    As it blends with the ocean of years.

How the winters are drifting like flakes of snow
    And the summers, like birds between,
And the years in the sheaf-- how they come and they go,
On the river's breast, with its ebb and its flow,
    As it glides in the shadow and sheen.

There's a magical isle up the River Time,
    Where the softest of airs are playing;
There's a cloudless sky and a tropical clime
And a song as sweet as a vesper chime,
    And the Junes with the roses are straying.

And the name of the isle is Long Ago,
    And we bury our treasures there;
There are brows of beauty, and bosoms of snow;
There are heaps of dust - oh, we loved them so!
    There are trinkets and tresses of hair.

There are fragments of songs that nobody sings,
    There are parts of an infant's prayer;
There's a lute unswept, and a harp without strings;
There are broken vows, and pieces of rings,
    And the garments our loved ones used to wear.

There are hands that are waved, when the fairy shore
    By the mirage is lifted in air;
And we sometimes hear, through the turbulent roar,
Sweet voices we heard in the days gone before,
    When the wind down the river was fair.

Oh, remembered for aye be that blessed isle,
    All the day of our life till night;
And when evening glows with its beautiful smile,

And our eyes are closing in slumbers awhile,
>May that Greenwood of souls be in sight!
>>Benjamin Franklin Taylor, 1819-1897

Early Morning Walk—October in North Idaho

The hills are shadowed in somber blue.
> *And thoughts wake, weary, to face the dawn.*

But, HARK! Though cloudy, the sun breaks through,
> *And golden fingers, search over and yon,*

Like streams of hope from a warming cup
> *My glad heart wakens, as doubting stills*

My soul is lifted; my eyes look up,
> *As Tamaracks shout from awakening hills!*

R.A.S.

"Let them eat cake!"

(Generally attributed to Marie Antoinette after her arrival in France in 1770)

Oh, cakes and friends we should
    choose with care,
Not always the fanciest cake
    that's there
Is the best to eat! And the plainest
    friend
Is sometimes the finest one,
    in the end!

        -Margaret E. Sangster 1894

Fudge Nut Cake

Ingredients:
1/4 cup shortening
1 1/2 cups sugar
2 egg yolks, beaten
1 3/4 cups flour
1/2 cup cocoa
3 tsp. baking powder
1/2 tsp. salt
1 1/2 cups milk
1 tsp. vanilla
1 cup chopped nuts
2 egg whites
1/2 cup sugar

Directions:
In large mixing bowl, cream together the shortening and sugar until light and fluffy. Blend in egg yolks. Set aside. Sift together the flour, cocoa, baking powder and salt. Add to creamed mixture alternately with milk. Blend in vanilla and nuts. In separate bowl, beat egg whites until fluffy. Slowly add sugar, beating well as you add, until mixture is stiff and glossy. Carefully fold into batter. Pour into greased loaf pan or two 8-inch layer pans and bake (loaf pan) at 350 degrees for about 25 to 30 minutes.

I always frost this cake with Angel Feather Icing (see frosting section.)

This recipe has been a family favorite for years. It comes from Richard's Aunt Dorothy, who lived in the little lumber town of St. Maries, Idaho. Richard spent most of his childhood there, and what a carefree childhood it was! Most of it was spent plunging in and out of the St. Joe River.

Aunt Dorothy was a chocoholic, besides being more fun than a barrel of monkeys, so we always looked forward to a visit at her house!

"Let them eat cake!"

Caramel Fudge Cake

Ingredients:
1 pkg. chocolate cake mix
Water, oil and eggs, as called for
1 can (14oz.) sweetened condensed milk*
1 jar (17oz.) caramel ice cream topping
1/2 to 1 pint whipping cream
Powdered sugar
Chopped nuts, toffee chips or mini chocolate chips

Directions:
Grease and flour a 9 by 13 inch baking pan. In large mixing bowl, prepare cake batter as directed on package. Bake as directed. Cool 15 minutes. With top of wooden spoon, poke cake every 1/2 inch. Drizzle condensed milk over cake and let stand until soaked into holes. Carefully spread caramel sauce over cake. Chill 2 hours. Whip cream, sweetening with powdered sugar to taste. Sprinkle nuts, toffee chips, on chocolate chips over whipped cream, or leave plain.

At this point, cake can be frozen and unthawed an hour or so before serving.

*Sweetened condensed milk (easier on the budget)
1 cup instant nonfat dry milk
2/3 cup sugar
Pinch of salt
3 tbsp. margarine or butter, melted
1/3 cup boiling water
Combine all in blender and process 'til smooth. Same as 14oz. can.

Supper Smoke

June's Chocolate Sour Cream Cake

Ingredients:
1 pkg. chocolate sour cream cake mix
2 (4oz.) pkgs. Bakers German Sweet Chocolate
3/4 cup butter or margarine, softened
1/2 cup chopped, toasted almonds
1 (8oz.) container Cool Whip
Shredded chocolate bar

Directions:
Bake cake as directed on package. Cool cake layers. Meanwhile, prepare filling: Melt 1 1/2 pkgs. of the chocolate over low heat. Cool and beat in butter. Add almonds and chill one hour. Carefully cut each layer of cooled cake in half. Spread chocolate filling and Cool Whip alternately between layers. Spread Cool whip thickly on top. Garnish with shreds of remaining chocolate bar. Chill.

June has shared with us all the stresses and the delights of a journey to a far-away tropical land, and we are the better friends for the journey. Thus she has passed the acid test of a true friend, and it seems mundane to speak of cake! Yet, it is such a good cake and such a good friendship!

"Let them eat cake!"

Chocolate Brownie Loaf

Ingredients:
3/4 cup butter or margarine
3/4 cup brown sugar, packed
3/4 cup white sugar
1 tsp. vanilla
2 eggs
1 3/4 cups flour
1/2 cup cocoa
1 tsp. baking powder
1/2 tsp. baking soda
1 (8oz.) container plain yogurt OR sour cream
1 cup chopped walnuts

1/4 cup butter or margarine
1/4 cup cocoa
3 tbsp. milk
1/2 tsp. vanilla
1 1/2 cups powdered sugar
Walnuts, chopped coarsely

Directions:
In large mixing bowl, combine butter, sugars, and vanilla, beating 'til creamy. Add eggs, one at a time, beating well after each addition. Sift together the dry ingredients and add in thirds, alternately with yogurt. Stir in walnuts. Pour into greased and floured 9 by 5 inch loaf pan. Bake at 350 degrees until tests done with a toothpick, about 50 to 60 minutes. Invert and cool.

Frosting:
Cream together the butter, cocoa, milk and vanilla. Add powdered sugar and blend well. Frost top of loaf and allow frosting to drizzle down sides of loaf. Sprinkle chopped walnuts on top.

Supper Smoke

Good Old Chocolate Cake

Ingredients:
1 cup shortening
2 cups sugar
2 eggs
1 cup buttermilk
2 1/2 cups flour
1/2 cup cocoa
2 tsp. baking soda
1/2 tsp. salt
1 tsp. vanilla
1 cup boiling water (I like to use boiling coffee)

Directions:
In large mixing bowl, cream together the shortening and sugar until light and fluffy. Add eggs one at a time, beating well after each addition. Add buttermilk. Set aside. Stir dry ingredients together and add, alternately with milk, to creamed mixture. Blend in vanilla. Add boiling water and mix well. Pour into greased and floured 9 by 13 inch baking pan and bake at 350 degrees for 15 to 20 minutes, or until toothpick comes out clean. Use frosting of your choice.

**In cake mixing instructions, I have recently read that you should, when combining wet and dry ingredients, always begin and end with the dry. The explanation made good sense, but I forgot what it was. So…..JUST DO AS I SAY!

"Let them eat cake!"

Moist Chocolate Cake

Ingredients:
2 cups flour
1 tsp. salt
1 3/4 cups sugar
1/2 cup margarine
2 eggs
1/2 cup cocoa
1 cup hot coffee
1 tsp. soda
1/2 cup boiling water
3/4 cup chopped nuts, optional

Directions:
Sift together the flour and salt and set aside. In large mixing bowl, cream together the sugar and margarine. Beat in the eggs, one at a time, beating well after each after each addition. In small bowl, combine cocoa and coffee. Add to creamed mixture. Add dry ingredients gradually, blending well. Dissolve the soda in boiling water and add, mixing well. Add nuts if desired. Bake at 350 degrees for 15-20 minutes, or when tested done with toothpick. This one is easy to over-bake.

**Unless specified otherwise, always use large eggs in any baking recipe.

Chocolate Date Dandy Cake

Ingredients:
1 1/4 cups boiling water
1 1/2 cups chopped dates (about 1/2 pound)
1 pkg. chocolate cake mix
1 (6oz.) pkg. chocolate chips
1/2 cup chopped walnuts

Directions:
In large mixing bowl, pour boiling water over chopped dates. Cool. Prepare cake mix according to package directions, using date mixture in place of water called for. Pour into greased 9 by 13 inch pan. Sprinkle chocolate chips and nuts over batter. Bake at 350 degrees for 35 to 40 minutes.

Supper Smoke

Absolutely Divine Devil's Food Cake

Ingredients:
1 (8oz.) can sliced beets, shredded and reserved with juice
2 cups unsifted flour
2 tsp. baking soda
1 tsp. salt
1/2 cup unsalted butter, softened
2 1/2 cups packed brown sugar
3 eggs
3 squares (1oz. each) unsweetened chocolate, melted
1/2 cup buttermilk
2 tsp. vanilla

Directions:
Grease bottom and sides of two 9-inch cake pans. Line bottoms with waxed paper, grease, and flour pans. Prepare beets and set aside.

In small bowl, combine flour, soda and salt. In large mixing bowl beat sugar and butter until fluffy. Add eggs, one at a time, beating well after each addition. Blend in melted chocolate. Beat in flour alternately with buttermilk, beginning and ending with flour. Beat until smooth. Stir in beets and vanilla. Pour into prepared baking pans and bake at 350 degrees for 30 to 40 minutes, or until toothpick comes out clean. Cool in pans for 10 minutes, then turn out on racks and peel off waxed paper. Cool completely before frosting.

Fudge Frosting:
Heat 2 cups heavy cream in saucepan just to boiling point. Stir in 2 pkgs. semi-sweet chocolate chips and 2 tsp. vanilla. Stir until mixture is smooth and chocolate is melted. Beat over ice until of spreading consistency.

This recipe is from Sis Phyllis. Refer to recipe title and heat up your oven!

Chocolate Apple Cake

Ingredients:
2 cups sugar
1 cup butter or margarine
3 eggs
2 1/2 cups flour
1/4 cup cocoa
1 tsp. soda
3/4 tsp. cinnamon
1/2 tsp. allspice
1/2 cup water
2 cups peeled, shredded apple
1 cup chopped nuts
1/2 cup chocolate chips

1 tbsp. butter or margarine
1 tsp. vanilla
1 1/2 cups powdered sugar
1 or 2 tbsp. water

Directions:
In large mixing bowl, cream together the sugar and butter until light and fluffy. Add eggs, one at a time, beating well after each addition. Sift together the dry ingredients and add alternately with water. Fold in the apple, nuts and chocolate chips. Pour into a greased and floured tube, or bundt pan. Bake at 325 degrees for 35 to 45 minutes or until toothpick comes out clean. Cool 15 minutes and then invert on serving plate.

To make glaze, combine butter, vanilla and powdered sugar, slowly adding water to spreading consistency. Drizzle over warm cake.

Supper Smoke

Strawberry Cake

Ingredients:
1 small box strawberry Jell-O
1 box white cake mix
1/2 cup oil
1/2 cup buttermilk OR strawberry yogurt
1 tsp. vanilla
4 eggs
1 cup sliced strawberries
1 cup chopped nuts
1 cup coconut

Directions:
Grease and flour 3 round cake pans. Cut wax paper to fit bottoms, insert and grease again. In mixing bowl, combine Jell-O, cake mix, oil, buttermilk, and vanilla, blending well. Add eggs, one at a time, beating well after each addition. Lightly coat strawberry slices with flour (so they don't sink to the bottom) and fold in, along with nuts and coconut. Bake at 350 degrees for 10 to 15 minutes.

Frost with frosting of your choice. If using frozen and thawed strawberries, add flavor to frosting by substituting some of the drained strawberry juice for some of the liquid.

"Let them eat cake!"

Sour Cream Cake

Ingredients:
2 1/2 sifted flour
1 1/2 tsp. baking powder
1 tsp. soda
1 tsp. salt
3 eggs
1 1/3 cups sugar
2 tsp. vanilla
1 1/3 cups sour cream

Frosting:
2 cups sugar
2/3 cup water
1 1/2 tbsp. corn syrup
4 tbsp. butter or margarine
Dash of salt
6 tbsp cocoa
2 tsp. vanilla

Directions:
Sift together the flour, baking powder, soda and salt. Set aside. In small bowl, beat eggs until thick and creamy. Gradually add the sugar, beating constantly. Transfer egg mixture to a large mixing bowl. Stir in flour mixture alternately with vanilla and sour cream. Bake in greased and floured loaf pan at 350 degrees for 15 to 20 minutes.

Frosting:
While cake is baking, combine all ingredients, except vanilla, and bring to a boil. Cook, stirring occasionally, until soft ball stage. Remove from heat; add vanilla and LET SIT WITHOUT STIRRING until lukewarm. Then beat until spreading consistency.

Raspberry Cake

Ingredients:
2 cups sifted flour
3 tsp. baking powder
1/2 tsp salt
1/2 cup butter or margarine
1 cup sugar
2 eggs
1 cup milk
1 tsp. vanilla
2 cups fresh raspberries, lightly dusted with flour

Glaze:
1 tbsp. butter or margarine, melted
3 tbsp. cream
1/2 tsp. vanilla
1 1/2 to 2 cups powdered sugar
Coconut, optional

Directions:
Sift together the first three ingredients and set aside. In large mixing bowl, cream the butter and sugar together 'til light and fluffy. Add eggs, one at a time, beating well after each addition. Add sifted dry ingredients alternately with milk and vanilla, starting and ending with dry ingredients. Pour 2/3 of batter into a greased and floured 9 by 13 inch pan. Sprinkle raspberries over batter and spread remaining batter over all. Bake at 350 degrees for 25 to 30 minutes. Frost with powdered sugar glaze.

Glaze: Combine first three ingredients. Add sugar, beating well, until of spreading consistency. Sprinkle coconut over glaze if desired.

"Let them eat cake!"

Pig-Lickin' Good Cake

Ingredients:
1 yellow cake mix, dry
1 (11oz.) can UNDRAINED mandarin oranges
1/4 cup water
3 eggs
1/3 cup vegetable oil

1 (20oz.) can crushed pineapple, well drained
1 (10 or 12 oz.) container Cool Whip
1 small pkg. instant vanilla pudding mix

Directions:
In large mixing bowl, combine dry cake mix, mandarin oranges, AND juice, water, eggs and oil. Beat with mixer on low until blended, then on medium for 2 or 3 minutes. Pour batter into greased and floured 9 by 13 inch baking pan. Bake at 350 degrees for 25 to 30 minutes, or until toothpick comes out clean. Cool completely.

To make frosting, combine the pineapple and Cool Whip and blend well. Slowly add the pudding mix, blending well. Spread on cake and refrigerate.

This one's a winner at our house. Moist and delicious!

Supper Smoke

Double Lemon Cake

Ingredients:
1 pkg. yellow cake mix
1 small pkg. instant lemon pudding mix
4 eggs
1/4 cup oil
1 cup water

1 (6oz.) can frozen lemonade
1 cup powdered sugar

Directions:
In mixing bowl, combine cake mix, pudding mix, eggs, oil, and water. Beat with mixer at medium speed for 4 minutes. Pour into greased and floured 9 by 13 inch pan. Bake at 350 degrees for 25 to 30 minutes. Remove from oven and cool five minutes. Meanwhile mix lemonade and powdered sugar. Thoroughly prick warm cake with large-prong fork and pour lemonade mixture over hot cake. Return to oven and bake three to four minutes more.

"Let them eat cake!"

Spring Dream Cake

Ingredients:
1 pkg. white cake mix
1 small pkg. instant pistachio pudding mix
1 1/3 cups water
4 eggs
1/4 cup vegetable oil
1 1/2 cups coconut
3/4 cup chopped nuts

Directions:
In large mixing bowl, combine the dry cake mix and pudding mix. Add water, eggs and oil. Beat at medium speed for 3 minutes. Stir in coconut and nuts. Pour into 3 greased and floured cake pans. Bake at 350 degrees for 15 to 20 minutes. Cool in pans for 10 minutes. Turn out and cool completely.

I like to frost this one with Angel Feather Icing (see Frosting section) and add 2 drops of green food coloring.

Lemon Streusel Cake

Ingredients:
1 pkg. lemon cake mix with pudding
1/2 cup butter or margarine
3/4 cup milk
2 eggs
1/4 cup sugar
1 (8oz.) pkg. cream cheese, softened
1 tbsp. lemon juice
1 tsp. grated lemon rind
1/2 cup chopped nuts

Directions:
In mixing bowl, cut butter into cake mix until crumbly. Remove 1 cup for topping. To remaining ingredients, add milk and eggs. Beat on high with mixer for 2 minutes. Pour into greased and floured 9 by 13 inch pan. Set aside. For filling, cream together the sugar, cream cheese, lemon juice, and rind. Blend well. Drop by tsp. onto batter and spread across batter to edge of pan. Add nuts to reserved crumbs and spread crumb mixture over all. Bake at 350 degrees until tests done with toothpick.

Pineapple Torte

Ingredients:
1/2 cup butter or margarine
3/4 cup sugar
3 eggs, separated
1 (20oz.) can crushed pineapple, drained (reserve juice)
1 tsp vanilla
2 ½ cups sifted flour
2 tsp. baking powder
1/2 tsp. baking soda
1/2 tsp. salt
3 egg whites
1/4 cup sugar

1 1/2 cups whipping cream
1/4 cup powdered sugar
1/2 tsp. almond extract
2 tbsp. slivered almonds

Directions:
In large mixing bowl, cream together the butter and sugar until light and fluffy. Beat in egg yolks, blending well. Meanwhile, drain pineapple, reserving 2/3 cup juice. In another bowl, combine the juice, 3/4 cup pineapple and vanilla. Sift together the dry ingredients. Add to creamed mixture alternately with pineapple mixture. In another bowl beat egg whites until soft peaks form. Add the sugar, 1 tbsp. at a time, beating until stiff. Fold into cake batter. Pour into two greased and floured cake pans. Bake at 350 degrees for 15 to 20 minute. Cool. Split layers and spread cream filling between layers and on top. Garnish with almonds.
Cream filling:
Whip cream until soft peaks form. Gradually add sugar while beating. Fold in extract and reserved drained pineapple.

Supper Smoke

Graham Streusel Cake

Ingredients:
3/4 cup butter or margarine, melted
3/4 cup brown sugar, packed
1 1/4 tsp. cinnamon
2 cups graham cracker crumbs (28 squares)
3/4 cups chopped nuts
1 cup water
1/3 cup vegetable oil
3 eggs
1 pkg. lemon cake mix
Powdered sugar
Milk
Vanilla

Directions:
In mixing bowl, combine first five ingredients and set aside for streusel. In another bowl, combine the water, oil, eggs, and cake mix and beat on low speed for 30 seconds. Beat on medium speed for 2 minutes. Grease and flour a 9 by 13 inch baking pan. Pour about 2 1/3 cups cake batter in pan. Sprinkle with 2 cups of the crumbs mixture. Pour remaining batter over crumbs and sprinkle rest of crumb mixture over all. Bake until cake springs back when touched…about 20 to 25 minutes at 350 degrees. Drizzle with powdered sugar glaze.

Pumpkin Cream Bundt Cake

Ingredients:
2 tbsp. butter or margarine, melted
1/2 cup packed brown sugar
1/4 tsp allspice
1 tsp. ground cinnamon
3 cups flour
1 tbsp. cinnamon
2 tsp. baking soda
1 tsp. salt
2 cups sugar
1 cup butter or margarine
4 eggs
1 cup canned pumpkin
1 cup (8oz.) sour cream
2 tsp. vanilla
Powdered sugar
Cinnamon
Milk

Directions:
Make streusel filling by combining first four ingredients and set aside. Sift together the flour, cinnamon, baking soda, and salt. In large mixing bowl, cream together the sugar and butter until light and fluffy. Add eggs, one at a time, beating well after each addition. Add pumpkin, sour cream and vanilla alternately with flour mixture. Grease and flour a bundt pan and spoon half the batter into pan. Sprinkle streusel filling over batter. Spoon other half over all. Bake at 350 degrees for 30 to 40 minutes, or until toothpick comes out clean. Cool 10 minutes and invert on serving plate. Make a glaze of powdered sugar, cinnamon and milk and drizzle over warm cake.

Supper Smoke

Cinnamon Bundt Cake

Ingredients:
1 yellow cake mix
1 pkg. instant vanilla pudding mix
1/2 cup vegetable oil
1 cup water
4 eggs
1 tsp. butter flavoring
1 tsp. vanilla
1/4 cup nuts
1/4 cup sugar
1 tsp. cinnamon
1/4 cup nuts

Directions:
In large mixing bowl, blend together the cake mix and pudding mix. Add oil and water and blend well. Add eggs, one at a time, beating well after each addition. Beat 6 minutes at high speed. Add the flavorings. Grease and flour a bundt pan. Sprinkle chopped nuts in pan. Set aside. To prepare filling, combine sugar, cinnamon and nuts. Pour half the cake batter into bundt pan. Sprinkle the filling over batter. Add the rest of batter. Bake at 350 degrees for 40 to 45 minutes. Let rest 15 minute before removing form pan.

"Let them eat cake!"

Lemon Glazed Nectar Cake

Ingredients:
1 pkg. lemon cake mix
1/2 cup sugar
1 cup apricot nectar
1/2 cup vegetable oil
4 eggs

1/4 cup lemon juice
1/8 tsp. salt
1 3/4 cups powdered sugar

Directions:
In large mixing bowl, combine the cake mix and sugar. Blend in apricot nectar and oil. Beat in eggs, one at a time. Beat at high speed for 6 minutes. Pour batter into greased and floured angel food cake pan. Bake at 350 degrees for 40 to 45 minutes. Cool on rack for 10 minutes. Invert on serving plate and frost with lemon glaze while cake is still hot.
Lemon Glaze:
Combine juice, salt and sugar and beat until smooth.

Carrot Layer Cake

Ingredients:
3/4 cup sugar
1 1/2 tbsp. flour
1/8 tsp. salt
3/4 cup canned milk
6 tbsp. butter or margarine
3/4 cup chopped nuts
1 tsp. vanilla

1 cup raisins with water
1 cup vegetable oil
1/4 cup raisin water
2 cups sugar
2 cups flour
2 tsp. cinnamon
2 tsp. baking powder
1 tsp. baking soda
1 tsp. salt
4 eggs
4 cups shredded carrots
1 cup chopped nuts

Directions:
To make filling, combine first five ingredients and bring to a boil. Reduce heat and simmer for 30 minutes, stirring occasionally. Remove from heat and add nuts and vanilla. Set aside.

To make cake, place raisins in small saucepan and barely cover with water. Bring to a boil and cook several minutes. Drain and reserve 1/4 cup water. In large mixing bowl, beat oil, raisin water, and sugar until light. In another bowl, combine flour, cinnamon, baking powder, soda, and salt. Add to creamed mixture alternately with eggs. Stir in raisins, carrots, and nuts. Pour into three greased and floured cake pans and bake at 350 degrees for 30 to 40 minutes, or until toothpick comes out clean. Cool in pans for 10 minutes; then invert and cool completely. Spread cooled filling between layers and frost with Angel Feather Icing.

"Let them eat cake!"

Lazy Carrot Cake

Ingredients:
1/4 cup cold water
4 eggs
1 1/4 cup salad dressing
2 tsp. cinnamon
1 pkg. yellow cake mix
2 cups shredded carrots
1 cup chopped raisins, divided
3/4 cup chopped walnuts

1 (8oz.) pkg. cream cheese, softened
1 tbsp. vanilla
3 to 3 1/2 cups powdered sugar
Chopped nuts

Directions:
In large mixing bowl, combine water, eggs, and salad dressing and blend. Add cinnamon and cake mix and beat until well blended. Stir in carrots, raisins and walnuts. Pour into greased and floured 9 by 13 inch baking pan. Bake at 350 degrees for 30 to 35 minutes.

To make frosting, cream together the cream cheese, vanilla and raisins. Slowly add powdered sugar 'til spreading consistency. Spread on cake and garnish with chopped nuts if desired.

**Before adding whole raisins to a cake batter, be sure to dust them with flour, to keep them from sinking to the bottom.

Supper Smoke

Jo's Applesauce Cake

Ingredients:
1 cup raisins
Water
2 1/2 cups flour
1/2 tsp. salt
1/2 tsp. cinnamon
1/2 tsp. cloves
1/2 tsp. allspice
1/2 cup shortening
2 cups sugar
2 eggs
1 1/2 cups applesauce
2 tsp. soda
1/2 cup reserved raisin water, boiling
1 cup chopped nuts

1/4 cup butter or margarine, softened
4 oz. cream cheese, softened
Powdered sugar
1 tsp. black walnut flavoring

Directions:
In small saucepan, barely cover raisins and bring to a boil. Set aside. Sift dry ingredients and set aside. In large mixing bowl, cream together the shortening and sugar until light and fluffy. Add eggs, one at a time, beating well. Beat in applesauce. Drain raisins and reserve water to make 1/2 cup or a little more. Bring to a boil and add soda. Add to creamed mixture. Add dry ingredients and then the raisins and nuts. Bake in greased and floured 9 by 13 inch pan at 350 degrees for 35 to 40 minute.

Frosting: Cream together the butter and cream cheese. Gradually add sugar, beating well, until of spreading consistency. Add flavoring and frost.

Jo was a cousin of Richard's and grew up as part of their family. Richard's parents took an exceedingly casual attitude about discipline, and what little was done, was accomplished out of sheer frustration by Jo and her sister Peg! Most of their effort was to no avail and it's no wonder they both left home at a young age. However, Richard and I both remember Jo with great fondness. Besides having cheerfully surmounted a great many difficulties, she developed a generous spirit and was also a very good cook.

Pumpkin Roll

Ingredients:
3 eggs
1 cup sugar
3/4 cup canned pumpkin
1 tsp. lemon juice
3/4 cup flour
1/4 tsp. cloves
1/4 tsp. ginger
1/4 tsp. salt
1 cup chopped nuts

1/4 cup softened butter or margarine
4 oz. cream cheese, softened
1 cup powdered sugar
1/2 tsp. vanilla
Pinch of salt

Directions:
Grease and flour 10 by 15 by 2 inch jelly roll pan. Line bottom of pan with wax paper and grease again.

In large mixing bowl, beat eggs until pale and thickened. Slowly add sugar, beating constantly. Add the next seven ingredients, blending well. Pour into jellyroll pan and bake at 350 degrees for about 15 minutes (it's easy to over bake.) Remove from oven and flop over onto a towel sprinkled with powdered sugar. Peel off wax paper and roll up, as for jellyroll. Cool. Meanwhile, prepare filling, combining the butter, cream cheese, sugar, vanilla, and salt. Beat until creamy. Unroll cooled cake roll and spread filling within half inch of edges. Roll up and refrigerate until ready to serve.

Blue Ribbon Banana Cake

Ingredients:
3/4 cup shortening
1 1/2 cups sugar
2 eggs
1 cup mashed banana (about 2)
1 tsp. vanilla
1/2 cup buttermilk
2 cups sifted flour
1/2 tsp. salt
1 tsp. soda
1 tsp. baking powder
1/2 cup chopped nuts
1 cup coconut, divided

2 tbsp. butter or margarine, melted
1/2 cup cream
1/2 cup sugar
2 tbsp. flour
1/2 cup chopped nuts
1/4 tsp. salt
1 tsp. vanilla

1 egg white
1/4 cup shortening
1/4 cup butter
1/2 tsp. coconut extract
1/2 tsp. vanilla
2 cups powdered sugar

Directions:
In large mixing bowl, cream together the shortening and sugar until light and fluffy. Add eggs; beat 2 minutes. Add banana; beat 2 more minutes. Sift together the dry ingredients and add to creamed mixture alternately with vanilla and buttermilk. Beat 2 minutes. Stir in nuts. Pour into 2 greased and floured cake pans. Sprinkle 1/2 cup coconut on each layer. Bake at 375 degrees for 25 to 30 minutes. Meanwhile, make filling. Combine butter, cream, sugar and flour in saucepan. Cook until thick. Add nuts, salt, and vanilla. Cool. Spread between cooled cake layers.

Frosting: Cream together all but sugar until fluffy. Add powdered sugar and beat 'til light and fluffy.

English Toffee Cake

Ingredients:
1 angel food cake, baked and frozen
2 cups whipping cream
1 tsp. vanilla
1/2 cup fudge OR butterscotch ice cream sauce
1/2 pkg. English toffee bits

Directions:
Carefully cut frozen cake in three layers, using toothpicks to mark accurate cuts. Beat whipping cream until soft peaks form. Add vanilla. Slowly add fudge or butterscotch sauce, blending well. Frost between layers, sprinkling toffee bits on each layer. Frost top and sides. Sprinkle remainder of toffee bits on top. Freeze until serving time.

**For a different look to a plain old angel food cake, swirl some dry Jell-O mix in the batter before baking.

Supper Smoke

Surprise Cupcakes

Ingredients:
1/2 cup shortening
1 1/2 cup sugar
2 eggs
1 tsp. vanilla
1/2 cup hot water
1/3 cup cocoa
1 3/4 cups flour
1 tsp. soda
1/2 tsp. baking powder
1/2 tsp. salt
1 cup buttermilk
1 (8oz.) pkg. cream cheese
1/3 cup sugar
1 egg
1/8 tsp. salt

Directions:
In large mixing bowl, cream together the shortening and sugar. Add eggs and vanilla and blend well. In small bowl, combine hot water and cocoa and blend in. Sift dry ingredients and add, alternately with buttermilk. Beat two minutes. In separate bowl, combine cream cheese, sugar, egg and salt for filling. Fill paper lined or greased cupcake holders 2/3 full. Drop one tsp. filling on top of each cupcake. Bake at 350 degrees for 40 minutes.

"Let them eat cake!"

Chocolate Pumpkin Cupcakes

Ingredients:
1 pkg. spice cake mix, dry
1 1/2 cups pumpkin
3 eggs
1/3 cup vegetable oil
1/3 cup water

1/4 cup butter or margarine
1/4 cup milk
1 cup white sugar
1 cup miniature marshmallows
1/2 to 3/4 cup chocolate chips
1 tsp. vanilla

Directions:
In large mixing bowl, combine the first five ingredients, and beat for 2 minutes. Fill greased or paper-lined cup cake holders 2/3 full and bake at 350 degrees for 10-15 minutes, testing with toothpick and being sure not to over bake. Cool.

Frosting: In saucepan, combine the butter, milk, and sugar. Bring to a boil and cook 1 1/2 minutes-no longer. Remove from heat and add marshmallow, chips, and vanilla. Mix until smooth and spread on cooled cupcakes at once.

Maple Carrot Cupcakes

Ingredients:
2 cups flour
1 cup sugar
1 tsp. baking powder
1 tsp. soda
1 tsp. cinnamon
1/2 tsp. salt
4 eggs
1 cup vegetable oil
1/2 cup maple syrup
3 cups grated carrots (about 6 medium)

1 (8oz.) pkg. cream cheese, softened
1/4 cup butter or margarine, softened
1/4 cup maple syrup
1 tsp. vanilla
Chopped nuts, optional

Directions:
In large bowl, combine the first six ingredients. In another bowl, beat together the eggs, oil, and syrup. Stir into dry ingredients, just until moistened. Fold in carrots. Fill greased, or paper-lined muffin cups 2/3 full. Bake at 350 degrees for 15 to 20 minutes, or until toothpick comes out clean.

Frosting: Combine all ingredients except nuts and beat until smooth. Frost cooled cupcakes and sprinkle with chopped nuts if desired.

"Let them eat cake!"

Lemon Pineapple Cupcakes

Ingredients:
1 box yellow cake mix
1 small box lemon Jell-O, dry
1/2 cup vegetable oil
4 eggs
1/2 cup cold water
1 tsp. vanilla
1 cup crushed pineapple, undrained

1/2 cup water
1/2 tsp. salt
2 tsp. vanilla
1/3 cup non-dairy creamer
3/4 cup shortening
5 cups powdered sugar (more or less)

Directions:
In large mixing bowl, combine cake mix and Jell-O. Add oil, eggs, water and vanilla and beat well. Blend in the pineapple. Pour batter into greased or paper-lined muffin cups, filling each 2/3 full. Bake at 350 degrees for 10 to 15 minutes. Remove from muffin cups to cool.

Frosting: In large bowl, combine all but powdered sugar, blend well and beat for 3 or 4 minutes. Add sugar, one cup at a time, and beat on high for 5 to 7 minutes.

Supper Smoke

Applesauce Cupcakes

Ingredients:
1 cup raisins
Water
2 1/2 cups sifted flour
1 tsp. soda
1 tsp. baking powder
1/2 tsp. salt
1/2 tsp. nutmeg
1/4 tsp. cloves
1 tsp. cinnamon
1/2 cup shortening
1 cup sugar
2 egg yolks
1 cup applesauce
1 tbsp. grated lemon peel
1 cup chopped nuts
Powdered sugar, salt, milk, and vanilla

Directions: In small saucepan, barely cover raisins with water and cook 'til soft. Set aside. Sift together dry ingredients and set aside. In large mixing bowl, cream shortening and sugar until fluffy. Add egg yolks and blend well. Add applesauce to creamed mixture, alternately with flour mixture. Fold in lemon peel, drained raisins, and nuts. Fill paper-lined, or greased muffin cups 2/3 full. Bake at 375 degrees for 25 to 30 minutes. Remove from tins, and while cupcakes are still hot, make a glaze by combining the last four ingredients and spread over cupcakes.

Short Cake

Ingredients:
2 eggs
1 cup sugar
1 cup flour
1 1/4 tsp. baking powder
1/4 tsp. cream of tartar
1 tsp. vanilla
1/2 cup hot water

Directions:
In mixing bowl, beat eggs and sugar until light colored. Sift dry ingredients. Add to creamed mixture alternately with vanilla and water. Blend thoroughly. Bake in greased 8 by 8 inch pan at 350 degrees for 20 to 30 minutes.

Don't let this simple little recipe fool you. It turns out very well and so good with sliced fruit spilling over each square! Perhaps a dab of whipped cream on top.

Cake Mix Extender

Ingredients:
1 cake mix and the ingredients called for
ADD:
1 cup flour
3/4 cup sugar
1/2 cup water
1/3 cup oil
1/2 tsp. salt
1 tsp. vanilla

Directions:
Proceed with regular cake mix instructions, adding additional ingredients, in order given.

Do you need a bigger cake for a crowd? This will make a 12 by 16 inch sheet cake, enough to serve 24.

Angel Feather Icing

Ingredients:
2 egg whites
3/4 cup sugar
1/3 cup corn syrup
2 tbsp. water
1/4 tsp. cream of tartar
1/4 tsp. salt
1 tsp. vanilla

Directions:
Blend all but vanilla in top of double boiler. Place over boiling water and begin immediately to beat. Continue until mixture stands in stiff peaks. Remove from heat, add vanilla, and continue to beat until well blended and of spreading consistency.

This is number one favorite at our house. I've used the recipe for years and never had a flop.

**To save mess when frosting a cake, lay strips of waxed paper around edges of cake plate. Carefully lay bottom layer on the plate and begin to frost. When finished, carefully pull out the paper strips and you have a clean plate around the edges.

"Let them eat cake!"

Thrifty Frosting

Ingredients:
4 tbsp. flour
1 cup milk
1/2 cup butter or margarine
1/2 cup shortening
1 cup sugar
2 tsp. vanilla

Directions:
In small saucepan, cook flour and milk until thick, stirring constantly. Cool. In mixing bowl, cream together the butter and shortening. Add sugar and vanilla, beating until light and fluffy and sugar is dissolved. Add cooled mixture and beat together until smooth and well blended.

This recipe is large enough for a layer cake, and you might want to half the recipe for a loaf cake.

This frosting has a whipped cream texture.

Decorator Frosting

Ingredients:
1/2 cup water
1/2 tsp. salt
2 tsp. vanilla
1/3 cup non-dairy creamer
3/4 cup shortening
5 cups powdered sugar

Directions:
Measure all ingredients but powdered sugar into a large mixing bowl. Bend well. Beat with mixer at least 3 minutes. Slowly add sugar, beating on high, for 5 to 7 minutes. If too thin, add more sugar; if too thick, a drip or two of water.

Fudge Cream Frosting

Ingredients:
1 cup whipping cream
12 oz. semi-sweet chocolate chips
2 tsp. vanilla

Directions:
In saucepan, heat cream just until boiling. Remove from heat and add chocolate chips and vanilla. Stir until chips are melted and mixture is smooth. Place over ice and beat until spreading consistency.

Chocolate Chip Fudge Frosting

Ingredients:
6 tbsp. butter or margarine
6 tbsp. milk
1 1/2 cups sugar
1 cup chocolate chips
1 tsp. vanilla

Directions:
Combine butter, milk and sugar in saucepan. Bring to a boil, stirring constantly, and boil 3 minutes. Add chocolate chips and vanilla and beat 'til spreading consistency. Sets up fast!

"Let them eat cake!"

Quick Fudge Frosting

Ingredients:
1 cup sugar
1/2 cup cocoa
4 tbsp. butter or margarine
1/2 cup milk
2 tbsp. light corn syrup
1/8 tsp. salt
1 to 1 1/3 cups powdered sugar
1 tsp. vanilla
4 oz. cream cheese

Directions:
In a small saucepan, combine sugar and cocoa. Add butter, milk, syrup and salt. Heat mixture to boiling, stirring constantly. Boil 3 minutes, stirring constantly. Cool slightly. Beat in powdered sugar, vanilla, and cream cheese. Continue beating 'til thick enough to spread.

Chocolate Fudge Mallow

Ingredients:
1/4 cup butter or margarine
1/4 cup milk
1 cup sugar
1 cup miniature marshmallows
1/2 to 3/4 cup chocolate chips
1 tsp. vanilla

Directions:
In saucepan, combine butter, milk, and sugar. Bring to a boil and cook 1 1/2 minutes, no longer, stirring constantly. Remove from heat and add marshmallow, chips and vanilla. Stir until marshmallows and chips are melted. Beat until thick enough to spread.

Supper Smoke

German Chocolate Frosting

Ingredients:
1/2 cup butter or margarine
1 cup sugar
3 egg yolks
1 cup evaporated milk
1 tsp. vanilla
1 1/3 cups coconut
1 cup chopped walnuts or pecans

Directions:
In saucepan, combine butter, sugar, egg yolks and evaporated milk. Cook over medium heat until thickened, stirring constantly, about 10 or 12 minutes. Add vanilla, coconut and nuts and beat until thick enough to spread.

Angel Food Frosting

Ingredients:
1 cup whipping cream
1 cup milk
1 pkg. instant pudding mix, flavor of choice

Directions:
In large mixing bowl, combine all ingredients and mix well. Beat with mixer until light and fluffy.

This frosting is nice for angel food cake. Cake needs to be refrigerated after frosting though. Good excuse to eat it all at once!

"Let them eat cake!"

Cocoa Fluff

(Angel Food Cake Topping)

Ingredients:
1 cup whipping cream
1/2 cup powdered sugar
1/4 cup cocoa
Dash of salt
1 tsp. vanilla

Directions:
In chilled mixing bowl, combine all ingredients except vanilla. Beat until stiff peaks form. Add vanilla and blend. Chill.

Cinnamon Sauce

Ingredients:
1/2 cup sugar
2 tbsp. cornstarch
1/4 tsp. salt
2 cups water
1/4 cup butter or margarine
2 tsp. vanilla
1 tsp. cinnamon, or to taste
Dash of nutmeg

Directions:
In saucepan, combine sugar, cornstarch, and salt. Gradually stir in water. Bring to a boil, stirring constantly and cook about 5 minutes. Remove from heat and add butter, vanilla and spices.

Supper Smoke

Lemon Sauce

Ingredients:
1/2 cup sugar
1 tbsp. cornstarch
Pinch of salt
1 cup water
2 tbsp. butter or margarine
1 tsp. grated lemon rind
3 tbsp. lemon juice

Directions:
In saucepan, combine sugar, cornstarch and salt. Gradually add water and bring to a boil. Boil 5 minutes, stirring constantly. Remove from heat and add butter, lemon rind and lemon juice.

Caramel Butter Sauce

Ingredients:
1 cup brown sugar
1 cup white sugar
1 cup cream
1 cup butter
1 cup vanilla*
*(okay, okay, I just wanted to see if you were paying attention… It's really 2 tsp. vanilla)

Directions:
In saucepan, combine all ingredients except vanilla. Bring to a boil and cook 1 1/2 minutes, stirring constantly. Remove from heat and add vanilla. Makes about 2 cups.

"Let them eat cake!"

Crystallized Flowers

Ingredients:
Edible flowers*
2 tsp. dried egg whites (look for this in health food stores, or cake decorating shops)
2 tsp. warm water
Clean artist's brush

Directions:
It's best to pick flowers you plan to use in early morning while they are freshest. Be sure they haven't been sprayed with chemicals.

In a small bowl, combine egg white and water. Stir gently with wire whisk until all egg white is absorbed. Then beat until mixture is foamy. With artist's brush, lightly brush each flower with mixture. After brushing each, lightly sprinkle with granulated sugar. Place on waxed paper and let dry overnight. These flowers may be stored up to one week in tightly covered container.

Fun to make and to use in cake decorating, or to garnish a special salad.

*Edible flowers: Rose, carnation, pansy, chrysanthemum, daylily, honeysuckle, violet, gardenia, marigold, nasturtium, daisy, viola, peony, cornflower, lavender, apple blossoms, tuberous begonia, geranium, and lilac.

Toxic flowers: Daffodil, hydrangea, tulip, morning glory, primrose, iris, sweet pea, lily of the valley, larkspur belladonna, monkshood, tobacco, and foxglove.

If in doubt about a flower not listed, <u>please do research.</u>

Supper Smoke

An old Log House

There's an old log house
In a valley far away,
Where a white-headed child
Romps through a golden day.

There's a quiet little Mother
Who toils the hours old.
Yet she pauses, and she listens
To each trouble that is told

There's a glad-faced Papa
Whose eyes are twinkly kind.
He reads to us 'til storybooks
Store treasures in our mind.

There's a worn stair way
Where they creep for quiet prayer;
A hallowed spot on yonder floor,
They left their burden there.

There's a place in my heart
Where I see them still today,
Though their voices are stilled
And the house decayed away.

Oh yes, she's real….and so is he!
Though summer days are gone.
Their prayers still waft 'round heavens' throne.
Their message still lives on.

In troubles sore, I feel a hand;
I lift my head and know
Who guides my hands to yonder Book
That tells me how to go.

Their memory calls me back to prayer;
Some quiet, hallowed place.
They smile, they know, they understand
When I break through to "grace."

"Let them eat cake!"

I see her in my pondering dreams,
I hear his laughter still.
Their prayers warm all the days I live.
I know they always will.

R.A.S.

Whist!

Doff thy sighs;

Cook's bakin' PIES!

After the cooing and billing,
The bride made a pie, glad and willing.
It was two inches thick,
And it made hubby sick,
Because that was the CRUST, not the filling!

Pie Baking

If, years ago, my hubby or I could have seen myself writing out hints for better pie baking, well…we'd both have been totally astonished!

Richard, with a wicked grin, is fond of telling all about the first apple pie I attempted! Let it suffice to say, all you young brides who might be reading this, that…

If at first you don't succeed
    Why cry?
        Try
            Try
                Again

My mother was never great at pie baking either, God rest her soul. (I think she cut back too much on the shortening.) So I had to learn the hard way. I'm no champion yet, but when you start at the very bottom, there's lot's of room to climb higher, and hubby never complains anymore!

Somewhere in this book I'll include a few recipes for piecrust. Each to his own, but I like the oil and ice water one the best. Be sure the oil and shortening, but ESPECIALLY the water, is COLD. Also, the less handling, the better. When I think how I used to maul a poor crust around…it's no WONDER it turned tough on me!

I like to roll out the crust between two squares of waxed paper. This way, you don't end up with too much flour worked into the dough, and it's not as messy.

Ladies from "the old school" say that lard is the very best to use for the shortening. Others say that, for easy dishing out later it's best to add 2 tsp. sugar with the salt, when mixing crust. I'm also told that, for a flakier crust, one should substitute half of the water with vinegar, or lemon juice. (Be sure that is cold, too.)

And it could be that it all has something to do with the way you hold your face……

Supper Smoke

Cocoa Pie

Ingredients:
1 baked pie shell
1 cup sugar
5 heaping tbsp. flour
5 level tbsp. cocoa
1/2 tsp. salt
2 1/2 cups water (sometimes I use coffee)
2 tsp. vanilla
2 tbsp. butter or margarine
1 cup chocolate chips, optional
1 cup whipping cream or meringue

Directions:
In saucepan, combine dry ingredients. Add water and blend well. Bring to a boil, stirring constantly, and cook until thickened. Remove from heat and add vanilla and butter. Stir and cool. Add chocolate chips if you prefer. Pour into baked piecrust, top with meringue and bake, or whip cream, sweeten with sugar to taste and spread over filling. If you want to get really spiffy, garnish with shaved chocolate.

This pie always goes over well with guests, but not with hubby, who hates chocolate pie. How weird can you get?!

Michelle's Chocolate Pie

Ingredients:
Graham crackers (1 stack) crushed
3 tbsp. butter or margarine, melted
2 pkgs. Dream Whip
1 cup milk
1 tsp. vanilla
1 large pkg. instant chocolate pudding mix
2 cups milk

Directions:
Combine crushed graham crackers and butter and form into a pie pan. Set aside. In mixing bowl, combine Dream Whip, milk, and vanilla and beat until peaks form. In another bowl combine pudding mix and milk. Combine with Dream Whip and blend well. Pour into crust and cool.

Lemon Meringue Pie

Ingredients:
1 baked pie shell
3 eggs, separated
1/2 cup lemon juice
1 tbsp. grated lemon rind
1 1/2 cups sugar
1/2 cup cornstarch
1/4 tsp. salt
1 3/4 cup water
3 tbsp. butter or margarine
1/4 tsp. cream of tartar
1/3 cup sugar

Directions:
Carefully separate the eggs and set aside. Squeeze lemon or lemons to make 1/2 cup lemon juice. Grate lemon rind, being careful to only grate the outer, yellow part. Set these aside. In saucepan, blend together the sugar, cornstarch, salt and water. Bring to a boil, stirring constantly, until mixture is thickened. Slightly beat egg yolks and stir about half hot mixture into yolks. Blend and return to cornstarch mixture, blending well. Return to heat and bring to a boil, stirring constantly. Remove from heat and add the butter, reserved lemon juice, and rind. Blend well. Cool.

Meanwhile, in glass mixing bowl (at least not plastic) beat the reserved egg whites until soft peaks form. Add cream of tartar and blend. Slowly sprinkle in sugar, beating all the while, until mixture stands in stiff peaks.

Pour cooled lemon filling into baked piecrust. Carefully spoon meringue over pie filling, being careful that meringue comes clear to edges. Swirl with spoon and bake in 350 degree oven until light brown…about 10 minutes.

Lemon pie is kind of a pain to make, and it's far from my favorite besides; yet I've made dozens for hubby because they make him so happy! I hope I get at least a lemon-colored star some sweet day.

Banana Cream Pie

Ingredients:
1 baked pie shell
2/3 cup sugar
3 rounded tbsp. cornstarch
1/2 tsp. salt
3 cups milk
3 eggs, separated
1 tbsp butter or margarine
1 1/2 tsp. vanilla
2 or 3 bananas
Whipping cream, optional

Directions:
In saucepan, combine sugar, cornstarch, and salt. Gradually stir in milk. Cook over medium heat stirring constantly, until mixture thickens and boils. Boil 1 minute. Remove from heat and add half hot mixture to egg yolks, which have been slightly beaten. Blend well, return to heat and boil 1 minute more. Remove from heat and add butter and vanilla, blending well. Cool. Slice two or three bananas into baked pie shell. Pour cooled filling over bananas. Top with meringue or sweetened whipped cream.

Peanut Butter Cream Pie

Ingredients:
1 baked pie shell
1/2 cup chunky peanut butter
3/4 cup powdered sugar
1 large pkg. vanilla pudding mix
Cool Whip, or sweetened whipped cream

Directions:
In mixing bowl, combine peanut butter and powdered sugar, reserving one tbsp. for topping. Spread on bottom of pie shell. Cook pudding and cool. Spread on crust. Top with Cool Whip or sweetened whipped cream. Sprinkle reserved peanut butter crumbs on top. Chill.

Raisin Cream Pie

One baked pie shell
3/4 cup raisins
1/3 cup flour
3/4 cup sugar
1/4 tsp. salt
1 1/2 cups milk
1/2 cup raisin juice
2 eggs, separated
1 tsp. vanilla
2 tbsp. butter or margarine

Directions:
In small saucepan, barely cover raisins with water and cook until soft, reserving juice. In larger saucepan, combine flour, sugar, and salt. Gradually add milk and 1/2 cup raisin juice. Blend well. Add cooked raisins and cook, stirring constantly until mixture thickens. Remove from heat and add half the hot mixture to egg yolks, blending well. Return all to saucepan and cook again until thickened. Remove form heat and add vanilla and butter. Pour into baked pie shell.

Your may make a meringue with the two egg whites, or top with sweetened whipped cream.

Sour Cream Raisin Pie

Ingredients:
1 baked pie shell
1 cup raisins
1/2 cup sugar
1 tbsp. flour
1/2 cup white corn syrup
2 egg yolks
1 cup sour cream
1 tsp. cinnamon
1/4 tsp. cloves

Combine all ingredients and cook over medium heat, stirring constantly, until mixture is thickened. Pour into pie shell. Top with meringue and bake at 350 degrees for 10-12 minutes or until lightly browned.

Pineapple Cream Pie

Ingredients:
1 baked pie shell
1 20 oz. can crushed pineapple, drained
2/3 cup sugar
3 rounded tbsp. cornstarch
1/2 tsp. salt
3 cups milk
3 eggs, separated
1 tbsp. butter or margarine
1 1/2 tsp. vanilla
Meringue or 1 cup whipping cream, whipped and sweetened
Directions:
In saucepan, combine sugar, cornstarch, and salt. Gradually stir in milk, blending well. Cook over medium heat, stirring constantly, until mixture thickens and boils. Boil 1 minute. Remove from heat and stir half hot mixture into slightly beaten egg yolks. Blend well, return to heat, and boil 1 minute more. Remove from heat and add butter, vanilla, and drained pineapple. Cool. Pour into baked crust and top with meringue, or sweetened, whipped cream.

This recipe, the banana cream, and the lemon, are hubby's favorites, and if I had a dollar for every one I've made, I could've sailed the seven seas by now.

Supper Smoke

Gloria's Pumpkin Pie

Ingredients:
1 unbaked 9 inch pie shell
2 eggs, beaten
1 cup brown sugar
1/2 tbsp. flour
1/4 tsp. salt
1/4 tsp. nutmeg
1/2 tsp. cinnamon
1/2 tsp. Mapleine flavoring
1 1/2 cups pumpkin
1 cup milk

Directions:
In mixing bowl, combine in order given. Pour carefully into unbaked 9 inch pie shell. Bake at 425 degrees for 10 minutes; then 350 degrees for 30 minutes.

Thank you Gloria. I used to use a plain old pumpkin pie recipe. Then I ate pumpkin pie at your lovely home and since then I have always used your recipe. I think of you fondly on every Thanksgiving Day!

**Some cooks put a layer of small marshmallows in the crust of a pumpkin pie, then pour in the filling and bake. Forms a nice crust on top. (Oh, all right. HAVE your whipped cream then!)

Whist!

Light Pumpkin Pie

Ingredients:
1 graham cracker crust
1 large package instant vanilla pudding mix
1 large can pumpkin
2 tsp. pumpkin pie spice
1/2 cup milk
12 to 16 oz. Lite Cool Whip

Directions:
In large mixing bowl, combine all but Cool Whip, blending well. Fold in Cool Whip until well blended and pour into graham cracker crust. Chill at least 3 hours before serving.

Beatlenut Pie

Ingredients:
1 unbaked 9 inch pie shell
1/4 cup butter or margarine
1 cup sugar
3 tbsp. flour
1 tsp. vanilla
1/4 cup maple syrup
3 eggs, well beaten
1 cup milk
1/2 cup chopped walnuts
1/4 cup oatmeal
1/4 cup coconut

Directions:
In large mixing bowl, blend with mixer, the butter, sugar and flour. Add vanilla and syrup. Add the eggs and milk and blend well. Stir in the nuts, oatmeal, and coconut. Carefully pour mixture into UNBAKED 9 inch piecrust. Bake at 375 degrees for about 45 minutes. You may have to loosely cover with foil the last while so it doesn't get too brown.

Beatlenut pie has been a family favorite for years. I have no idea why it is named thus. It is very tasty but not as rich as pecan pie.

Tiny Pecan Pies

Ingredients:
1 (3oz.) pkg. cream cheese, softened
1 stick butter, softened
1 1/4 tsp. salt
1 cup flour
3/4 cup brown sugar
1 egg
1 tbsp. butter, softened
1 tsp. vanilla
1 cup chopped pecans

Directions:
In mixing bowl, combine cream cheese, butter, salt, and flour, mixing well with hands. Divide dough into 24 balls. Press (very thinly) into miniature cupcake pans.

For filling, combine sugar, egg, butter, vanilla, and pecans. Spoon small amount of filling in each pastry lined cup. Bake at 350 degrees for 25 to 30 minutes. Makes 24.

This recipe is from Cousin Carol Ann. I remember her as a beautiful girl who found great satisfaction in her nursing career at a leper hospital in Carville, Louisiana. She later married a southern lad and raised a family before she was killed in a tragic car accident.

Custard Mincemeat Pie

Ingredients:
1 cup sugar
2 tbsp. flour
1/2 tsp. salt
3/4 cup butter or margarine, melted
3 eggs
1 cup mincemeat
3/4 cup chopped nuts

Directions:
In mixing bowl, combine sugar, flour and salt. Add melted butter, blending well. Beat in eggs, one at a time. Add mincemeat and nuts. Pour into pastry-lined 9 inch pie pan. Top with lattice. Bake at 325 degrees for 40 to 50 minutes.

This recipe is handed down from Aunt Teg. She, Uncle Charles, and their two daughters Carol Ann and Charlene had a home on beautiful lake Coeur d'Alene. They were wonderfully hospitable people and hosted many a Seaman picnic there. Carol Ann was famous in the clan for having swum clear across the lake, which must have been almost 2 miles!

Supper Smoke

Fan's Pecan Pie

Ingredients:
2 eggs
2 half egg shells of milk
1/2 cup butter or margarine
1 cup brown sugar, packed
1 tbsp. flour
1/2 cup white sugar
1 cup pecans
Unbaked pie shell

Directions:
In large mixing bowl, combine all ingredients, stirring in whole pecans last. Pour into unbaked pie shell and bake at 225 degrees for 30 minutes, then 350 degrees for 30 minutes more.

While paying a visit to our daughter Marla, who was teaching in Alabama, she shared with me her friend Fan, who lived in a cottage nearby. Fan's real name is Ruby, like mine, and I very much enjoyed her company. Her skin is a lovely chocolate brown while mine is a pale pinkish white, but she didn't seem to mind. The morning we were to leave, we saw Marla off to her school, and then I took a walk, trying to reconcile myself to another long absence. I found myself on Fan's porch, pouring my heart out.

"Ah knows, child…ah knows" she quietly told me, as she stared into a troubled past I could not see. When I rose to leave, she enfolded me in a huge brown hug. It felt so warm and good that I have felt its comfort may times since! She not only shared her kind heart, but also her pecan pie recipe. THANK YOU, FAN!

Chocolate Pecan Pie

Ingredients:
Unbaked pie shell
3 eggs, slightly beaten
1 cup light OR dark corn syrup
1/2 cup sugar
1/2 cup semi-sweet chocolate chips, melted
2 tbsp. butter or margarine, melted
1 tsp. vanilla
1 1/2 cups pecan halves

Directions:
In mixing bowl, combine eggs, corn syrup, sugar, chips, butter and vanilla. Blend well. Stir in pecans. Pour into unbaked piecrust and bake at 350 degrees for 50 to 60 minutes. May have to cover loosely with foil during last of baking time.

Magnolia Pie

Ingredients:
2 cups sugar
1/2 cup butter, softened
4 tbsp. flour
3 eggs, beaten
1 cup buttermilk
1 1/2 tsp. vanilla
Unbaked pie shell

Directions:
In large mixing bowl, cream together the sugar, butter, and flour. Beat eggs and add, blending well. Add buttermilk and vanilla. Pour into pie shell and bake at 325 degrees for 50 to 60 minutes, or until pie appears set when you jiggle it slightly.

VERY rich
VERY good
Recipe from my dear sis, Phyllis

Supper Smoke

Green Tomato Mincemeat

Ingredients:
3 pounds green tomatoes
3 pounds tart apples
1 cup chopped suet (ask in the meat department)
Juice of one orange
Juice and grated rind of one lemon
1 1/2 cups apple cider vinegar
2 pounds brown sugar
2 tbsp. salt
2 tbsp. cinnamon
1 tbsp. nutmeg
2 tsp. cloves
2 pounds raisins

Directions:
Wash, core, and run tomatoes through food grinder. Drain. Cover with cold water and bring to a boil. Boil 5 minutes. Remove from heat and drain. Pare, core, and chop apples and add to tomatoes. Add all the rest of ingredients and blend well. Stir over heat, cooking slowly until mixture thickens, from 45 minutes to 1 hour. Pack in quart jars and process in pressure canner for 25 minutes at 10 pounds pressure. Makes about 4 quarts.

As you can see this is quite a process, so you may as well make a double batch while you're at it. Richard dearly loves mincemeat pie and none of the rest of the family can stand the stuff, so 8 quarts last a good long while…like about 8 years!

Lois's Rhubarb Pie

Ingredients:
4 cups cut-up rhubarb
Hot water
1 1/3 cups sugar
3 1/2 tbsp Instant Clear Jell
1/2 cup water
Red food coloring
Milk and sugar
Pastry for 2-crust pie

Directions:
Place cut-up rhubarb in large mixing bowl and cover with hot tap water. Set aside. In another bowl, mix together the sugar and dry Clear Jell. Blend WELL. Now prepare pastry for 2-crust pie. Set aside. Drain the rhubarb and add 1/2 cup water. Add sugar mixture and blend well. Stir in red food coloring. Assemble pie and brush top crust with milk and sprinkle with sugar. Bake at 425 degrees until juice starts to bubble (maybe 20 minutes?) Then lower heat to 300 degrees and bake 5 to 10 minutes more.

Lois, a neighbor and friend, is a wonderful cook, as was her mother Bertha, before her. Years ago, Richard and I received news that his father had been killed in a car accident in southern California. Crushed with pain, and totally bewildered, we needed to quickly get to his mother. While trying to place three small, crying children and scrape together some traveling money, a large food box was thrust upon us, prepared by Bertha. Within, as we traveled, were found a number of delicious food items, and we ate, only from that box, all the way to California. I know in my heart that it was prepared with love and prayers.

Close to forty years have gone by, and still my heart is warmed whenever I think of that box.

Though your act may seem small, never hesitate to reach out, in your own way, to someone in trouble.

Rhubarb Custard Pie

Ingredients:
2 eggs
1 3/4 cups sugar
1/3 cup flour
1/4 tsp. nutmeg
3 cups cut-up rhubarb
Pastry for 2-crust pie

Directions:
In mixing bowl, combine all ingredients in order given. Pour into unbaked pie shell, top with crust and bake at 400 degrees for 40 to 45 minutes.

Pineapple Mandarin Pie

Ingredients:
1 (20oz.) can crushed pineapple
1 (11oz.) can mandarin oranges, with juice
1 cup sugar
5 tbsp. cornstarch
¼ tsp. salt
1 tbsp. lemon juice
2 or 3 tbsp. butter or margarine
Pastry for 2-crust pie

Ingredients:
Drain the pineapple. In saucepan, combine mandarin oranges and juice, sugar, cornstarch, salt, and drained pineapple. Cook, stirring constantly, until thickened. Add lemon juice. Pour into unbaked pie shell and dot with butter. Top with crust, crimp and bake at 400 degrees for 25 to 30 minutes.

French Apple Pie

Ingredients:
5 cups tart apples, pared and sliced
1/2 cup sugar
1 tsp. cinnamon
1/8 tsp. nutmeg
1/2 cup packed brown sugar
3/4 cup flour
1/3 cup butter or margarine
Unbaked pie shell

Directions:
Arrange sliced apples in pastry-lined pan. In small bowl, combine sugar, cinnamon and nutmeg and sprinkle over apples. Combine brown sugar and flour. Cut in butter. Sprinkle over apples. Bake at 400 degrees for 40 to 50 minutes, or until apples are tender. You may have to loosely cover pie with foil during last of baking time, if it is browning too much.

Apple pie filling works fine too; just sprinkle the last four ingredients on top and lower baking time.

**When baking any apple pie, try sprinkling one-tablespoon dry lemon Jell-O over the apples before putting on the top crust. Nice flavor, and it helps so pie won't run over.

Supper Smoke

Huckleberry Pie

Ingredients:
1 cup sugar
1/8 tsp. salt
5 tbsp. cornstarch
3/4 cup water
2 or 3 cups fresh, or frozen huckleberries
1 tsp. lemon juice
Pastry for 2-crust pie

Directions:
In saucepan, combine sugar, salt, and cornstarch. Slowly add the water, stirring 'til smooth. Add huckleberries and place over heat, stirring constantly until mixture comes to a boil and thickens. Remove from heat and add lemon juice. Pour into unbaked piecrust, top with another crust, and bake at 400 degrees for 20 to 30 minutes.

Huckleberries abound in North Idaho. It's just that their abounding seems always to be done on extremely perpendicular slopes and, in some cases, miles between patches. A true friend will tell you where his patch is found. A non-friend will look shifty eyed and leave you to the bears.

To gain huckleberry heights, it's good to have a tough, beat-up 4-wheel drive pick-up, nerves of steel, and quick reflexes for dodging huge logging trucks. You also need a great deal of stamina for crashing up and down mountains, once you're on the hoof. A non-tippable huckleberry pail would be nice (though non-existent) and a huge water jug is a must, as well as a 5 pound lunch. O yes, and pepper spray for the bears.

We eat Huckleberry pie with respect and Godly fear.

Cherry Pie Filling

Ingredients:
1 1/2 cups sugar
5 tbsp. cornstarch
1/8 tsp. salt
1/2 cup water
2 to 3 cups fresh, pitted pie cherries
Several drops red food coloring
1 tsp. almond flavoring

Directions:
In saucepan, combine sugar, cornstarch, and salt. Slowly add cold water, blending well. Add pie cherries. Cook together, stirring constantly, until mixture is thickened. Remove from heat and add food coloring and almond flavoring.

**Do you plan to serve Pie a la mode? You can avoid stress if you make the scoops ahead, lay them in a pan, cover tightly and store in the freezer. Then you can just pop them on a pie slice when serving. Easy as Pie!

Supper Smoke

Jell-O Fruit Pie

Ingredients:
Crust:
1 1/2 cups flour
> 2 tbsp. sugar
> 1/8 tsp. salt
> 1/2 cup oil
> 2 tbsp. milk

Pie Filling:
> 1 cup sugar
> 2 1/2 tbsp. cornstarch
> 1 cup water
> 1 tbsp. lemon juice
> 3 tbsp. dry Jell-O, flavor of choice
> 2 to 3 cups fresh fruit, such as peaches berries, etc.
> Whipping Cream, optional

Directions:
Crust: Combine flour, sugar and salt. Pour in oil and milk. Stir and press into pie pan with fingers. Reserve a little of the mixture and press into another baking pan. Bake both until light brown. Reserve extra for crumbling on top.

Filling: Boil together the sugar, cornstarch, water and lemon juice. Add the Jell-O, stirring well. Cool. Meanwhile add diced peaches or other fresh fruit in cooled crust. Pour Jell-O mixture over fruit and chill. Garnish with crumbled piecrust and whipped cream, if desired.

Raspberry Dream Pie

Ingredients:
1 regular baked pie shell, or graham crust
1 (10oz.) pkg. frozen raspberries, thawed
1 small pkg. raspberry Jell-O
2 tbsp. sugar
1 cup heavy whipping cream

Directions:
Drain raspberries, reserving juice. Set aside. In large mixing bowl, combine the Jell-O and 1 cup boiling water, stirring well. To reserved raspberry juice, add water to make 3/4 cup. Stir into Jell-O mixture along with 2 tbsp. sugar and the raspberries. Refrigerate until mixture just begins to thicken. Whip cream until peaks form and fold into Jell-O mixture. Refrigerate again until it begins to jell. Spoon into piecrust.

Fresh Berry Pie

Ingredients:
1 baked pie shell
4 cups fresh berries, such as strawberries
1 cup sugar
3 tbsp. cornstarch (4 tbsp. for raspberries)
1 cup whipping cream, optional

Directions:
Crush 1 cup of the berries. Add sugar and cornstarch. Cook, stirring constantly until mixture is thickened and turns clear. Cool. Place remaining berries in baked pie shell. Pour cooled mixture over all. Garnish with sweetened whipped cream, if desired.

Supper Smoke

Fruit Measures

Apricots............…...	1 pound = 1 cup sliced
Plums................…...	1 pound = 3 cups, sliced or cut up
Strawberries..........…	1 pint = 3 1/4 cup whole
	= 2 1/4 cup sliced
Blueberries..............	1 pint = 2 1/2 cups
Peaches	
Or Nectarines......…	1 pound = 2 1/4 cups, peeled and sliced
Raspberries	
Or Blackberries...…	1 pint = 2 cups
Green grapes.........…	1 pound = 3 cups
Cherries...............….	1 pound = 3 cups; 2 cups pitted

Oil Piecrust

1 Crust:
- 1 cup + 1 tbsp. flour
- 1/2 tsp. salt
- 1/3 cup oil
- 3 tbsp. ice water

2 Crusts:
- 1 3/4 cups flour
- 1 tsp. salt
- 1/2 cup oil
- 4 tbsp. ice water

4 Crusts:
- 3 1/2 cups flour
- 2 tsp. salt
- 1 cup oil
- 6 tbsp. ice water

Directions:
In mixing bowl, blend flour and salt. Add oil and mix with fork to blend. Sprinkle ice water, 1 tbsp. at a time, mixing lightly with fork after each addition. Continue until flour mixture is taken up and forms a ball. Place one crust portion between squares of waxed paper. Lightly dampen tabletop to prevent slipping, and roll out to a circle. Peel top paper off and place paper side up, in pie pan, remove remaining paper. Pour in filling and, if there is a top crust, repeat process. Crimp edges, cut slits, and bake.

Supper Smoke

Vinegar/Egg Pie Crust

Ingredients:
3 cups flour
1 1/4 cup shortening
1 tsp. salt
1 egg, beaten
5 1/2 tbsp. ice water
1 tbsp. vinegar

Directions:
In mixing bowl, combine flour, shortening and salt with pastry blender. In another bowl, combine egg, water and vinegar. Sprinkle over flour mixture, a little at a time, until mixture forms ball and flour is absorbed. Makes 4 one-crust pie shells.

Meringue

Ingredients:
1 tbsp. cornstarch
2 tbsp. cold water
1/2 cup boiling water
3 egg whites
6 tbsp. sugar
Pinch of salt
1/2 tsp. vanilla

Directions:
Blend cornstarch and cold water in saucepan. Add boiling water. Stir over medium heat until mixture is clear and thickened. Cool (put it over ice if you're in a hurry.) Beat egg whites until foamy. Gradually add sugar and beat until stiff peaks form. At low speed, add salt and vanilla. At high speed, blend in cooled cornstarch mixture and blend thoroughly. Spread on pie filling and bake at 350 degrees for about 10 minutes.

In my sister Phyllis' words, "This is the best meringue recipe I have. Doesn't shrink. Doesn't weep bitter tears as it cools."
                                                           Thanks Phyllis.

**When cutting a pie with meringue, use a buttered knife. It cuts cleaner.

Foolproof Meringue

Ingredients:
3 egg whites
Dash of salt
1 cup (1/2 of 7oz. jar) marshmallow crème

Directions:
In mixing bowl, beat egg whites and salt until soft peaks form. Gradually add marshmallow crème, beating until stiff peaks form. Spread on pie filling, seal to edge of crust, and bake at 350 degrees for 12 to 15 minutes.

Meringue hint:
Beat egg whites until fluffy, but not stiff, THEN gradually add sugar and beat until peaks form.

Supper Smoke

The Weaver's Work

Dear friend, have you ever pondered
On past days…side by side?
I have…and it seems like weaving
A tapestry…long and wide.

There are, oh so many colors!
Some of them bright and gay.
Others are loosely woven, and dark.
I wish I could take them away.

There are some, I see, that are clear and true.
God's love has made them so.
It gives me pleasure to see them now,
And courage as on I go.

Look! Here are some warm and sturdy strands.
They've woven a beautiful view.
I know just how they were blended in.
These are the days that I spent with you!

I recall the gentle laughter;
And yes, there were tears shed too.
And so many prayers for each other!
These are all of a golden hue.

Me with my ironing, piled up high,
And you with your knitting there;
There were countless cups of coffee,
And that many thoughts to share.

Somehow our troubles, when shared this way,
Became a little smaller.
And the joys we shared, the courage gained,
Helped us stand a little taller

As my mind goes over these precious threads,
There's a quiet joy inside,
And a happy throb down in my heart,
Where dearest memories 'bide.

Whist!

And what of the future days, dear friend,
As the colors and weaving change?
There's none of the future that we can see,
Nor a pattern we can arrange.

Yet the Weaver's patient hands reach forth
O'er a future that's all obscure;
With a calm assurance, one day at a time,
And promises, solid and sure.

"You need not question the colors, child,
Though I know you cannot see,
Just how they'll blend in a pattern true.
They will, if you'll trust in me."

So let's be brave as we look ahead,
For the pattern yet to come.
Let's pray for each other often,
As the colors unfold, each one.

And when the pattern is finished,
And the Weaver's work is done,
We'll look back, and know the reason,
For the colors…every one.

R.A.S.

The Old Cookie Jar

Middle of the night and, we in our pajamas,
Guided by the light of a friendly star
Creeping down the stairway into the kitchen,
Filling our pockets from the old cookie jar.

You always chose those square little fig bars.
I liked caraways; they were so big!
Oh, the most delicious, raisin-filled brown ones
Away in the bottom and how we did dig!

Do you remember crouching in the doorway
Holding our breath, listening for a sound?
Someone is moving upstairs in the bedroom.
Oh, the disgrace if we should be found!

Silence again and, back in the kitchen,
Bare little feet know just where they are.
Round little faces, laughing in the darkness,
Dipping our hands in the old cookie jar.

>   -Betty Jo Hofstetter-
>   (My sister)

Old Fashioned Cookies

Ingredients:
1 cup shortening
2 cups sugar
2 eggs
1 cup sour cream
1 tsp. vanilla
1/2 tsp. salt
1/2 tsp. soda
4 tsp. baking powder
4 1/2 cups flour
3/4 cup chopped nuts

Directions:
In large mixing bowl, cream shortening and sugar. Beat in eggs, sour cream, and vanilla. Add dry ingredients, mixing well. Stir in nuts. Now, brace yourselves, kiddos. This is the old fashioned part. Roll out on a floured board, fairly thick. Cut with a large glass or round cookie cutter. Place on greased cookie sheets and bake at 350 degrees for 15 to 18 minutes.

Now wasn't that a nice, warm experience? (There's some flour on your nose.)

Mom's Molasses Cookies

Ingredients:
1 1/2 cups flour
3/4 tsp. soda
1/2 tsp. salt
1/2 cup solid shortening
1/4 cup molasses
3/4 cup sugar
1 egg

Directions:
Sift together the first three ingredients and set aside. In mixing bowl, blend together the last four ingredients. Stir in the flour mixture. Drop by spoonfuls on greased cookie sheets. Bake at 375 degrees for 10 minutes.

This recipe is an old family favorite. I remember eating them as a child, and I think Mom rolled them out on a floured surface and cut them, big and round. Sometimes she frosted them with a thin, white icing. That was over fifty years ago, and I can almost taste them still!

**If you hope to make cutout cookies try this. Roll out the dough between waxed paper and put in the freezer for a little while. The dough will cut easily, handle better, and you don't work so much flour into the dough.

Supper Smoke

Amish Sugar Cookies

Ingredients:
1 cup sugar
1 cup powdered sugar
1 cup margarine or butter
1 cup cooking oil
2 eggs
1 tsp. vanilla
1 tsp. baking soda
1 tsp. cream of tartar
4 1/2 cups flour

Directions:
In large mixing bowl, cream together the sugars, margarine and oil. Beat in eggs and vanilla, blending well. Add the remainder of ingredients. Shape dough into balls and place on ungreased cookie sheets. Flatten with sugared glass. Bake at 350 degrees for 10 to 12 minutes.

Aunt Florence's Tender Crisp Sugar Cookies

Ingredients:
1/2 cup butter
1/2 cup shortening
1/2 cup sugar
1/2 powdered sugar
1 egg
1 1/2 tsp. vanilla
1 1/4 cups sifted flour
1/2 tsp. soda
1/2 tsp. cream of tartar
1/2 tsp. salt

Directions:
Cream butter, shortening, and sugars 'til light and fluffy. Add egg and vanilla. Beat well. Sift dry ingredients. Add to creamed mixture. Mix thoroughly. Shape into 1 inch balls and place on lightly greased cookie sheets. Dip bottom of glass in granulated sugar. Press balls flat, redipping glass for each cookie. Bake at 375 degrees for 10 minutes, or until very lightly browned around edges. These are good plain, but even better with powdered sugar icing.

My Aunt Florence was a lovely lady, and a "maiden aunt" until, at the age of 69, her knight rode in on a shining steed (actually it was a Volkswagen.) He was then 81, but still full of the love of life. They joined hands in marriage and lived joyfully together for eight years, when he passed away. I rejoice in this sweet and tender story, just like her cookies!

Lemon Snaps

Ingredients:
2 cups Cool Whip, thawed
1 egg
1 pkg. lemon cake mix, dry
Powdered sugar

Directions:
In mixing bowl, combine Cool Whip, egg, and cake mix, blending well. Drop by teaspoons into powdered sugar. Roll to coat. Bake on greased cookie sheets at 350 degrees for 10 to 15 minutes.

Cinnamon Swirl Cookies

Ingredients:
1 cup white sugar
1 cup brown sugar
1 cup shortening
3 eggs
1 tsp. vanilla
1 tsp. soda
4 cups flour
3/4 cup chopped nuts
Cinnamon

Directions:
In large mixing bowl, cream sugars and shortening. Add eggs, one at a time, then continue adding all the rest of ingredients except nuts and cinnamon. On a floured board, roll out dough to a 12 by 20 inch rectangle. Sprinkle with cinnamon and nuts, pressing nuts into dough. Roll up carefully, as for jellyroll. Wrap in wax paper and chill. Slice and bake on greased cookie sheets at 350 degrees for 10 minutes.

Snow on the Mountain Cookies

Ingredients:
1/2 cup shortening, softened
1 cup sugar
1 egg
3/4 cup buttermilk, or sour milk
1 tsp. vanilla
1/2 tsp. soda
1/2 tsp. salt
1/2 cup cocoa
1 3/4 cups flour
1 cup chopped nuts, optional
Marshmallows

2 tbsp. butter or margarine
3 tbsp. cocoa
1/8 tsp. salt
1 tsp. vanilla
2 to 3 tbsp. hot coffee
2 to 3 cups powdered sugar

Directions:
In mixing bowl, combine shortening, sugar and egg and mix thoroughly. Add the next seven ingredients in order given, blending well. Chill dough. Drop by rounded spoonfuls on greased cookie sheets and bake at 375 degrees for 8 to 10 minutes. When barely done, take sheets from oven and carefully place 1/2 marshmallow on each cookie. Return to oven and bake, just until marshmallow puffs up. Cool and remove from pans.

Make a frosting by combining the butter, cocoa, salt, vanilla and coffee. Blend well and add enough powdered sugar to make spreading consistency. Carefully drizzle over cooled cookies, letting some of the marshmallow peek through. An old-time favorite at our house.

Supper Smoke

Fudge Nuggets

Ingredients:
1 cup sugar
3/4 cup shortening
1 egg
1 tsp. vanilla
6 tbsp. cocoa, dissolved in hot coffee
1/2 tsp. salt
1 1/2 cups flour
2/3 cup milk
1 1/2 cups quick oats
1/2 cup chopped nuts
Chocolate chips (a delicious addition, but optional)
Powdered sugar

Directions:
In mixing bowl, cream together the sugar and shortening. Add egg, vanilla and cocoa/coffee mixture and blend well. Stir in remainder of ingredients and drop by teaspoons on greased cookie sheets and bake at 350 degrees for 7 to 10 minutes. When cool, dip each cookie in powdered sugar.

Chocolate Crackles

Ingredients;
3/4 cup salad oil
3/4 cup cocoa
2 cups sugar
4 eggs
2 tsp. vanilla
2 tsp. baking powder
1/2 tsp. salt
2 cups flour
1/2 cup chopped nuts
Powdered sugar

Directions:
In large bowl, combine salad oil and cocoa, blending well. Beat in 2 cups sugar. Add eggs, one at a time, beating well after each addition. Stir in vanilla. Add dry ingredients and mix well. Stir in chopped nuts. Chill several hours or overnight. Form small balls and roll in powdered sugar. Bake on well greased baking sheets at 350 degrees for 10 to 12 minutes. DO NOT OVERBAKE. Cookies will have a puffy appearance when first out of the oven, but will "settle" to a brownie like texture.

Supper Smoke

Chocolate Peanut Clusters

Ingredients:
1/2 cup butter or margarine, softened
1 cup sugar
1 egg
2 oz. unsweetened chocolate, melted
1/3 cup buttermilk
1 tsp. vanilla
1 3/4 cups flour
1/2 tsp. soda
2 cups salted peanuts

2 squares unsweetened chocolate
2 tbsp. butter or margarine
3 tbsp. water
2 cups (about) powdered sugar

Directions:
In mixing bowl, cream together the butter, sugar, egg, and chocolate. Add buttermilk, vanilla, flour and soda and blend well. Stir in peanuts. Drop by spoonfuls on ungreased cookie sheets. Bake at 350 degrees for about 5 minutes, or until almost no imprint remains when touched. While still warm, make a frosting of the last four ingredients and spread.

Really Good Chocolate Chip Cookies

Ingredients:
3/4 cup butter-flavored shortening
1 1/4 cups packed brown sugar
2 tbsp. milk
1 tbsp. vanilla
1 egg
1 tsp. salt
3/4 tsp. soda
1 3/4 cups flour
1 cup chocolate chips
1 cup chopped nuts

Directions:
In mixing bowl, cream shortening and sugars. Add milk, vanilla and egg, blending well. Add dry ingredients. Stir in chocolate chips and nuts. Drop by spoonfuls on greased cookie sheets. Bake at 350 degrees for 8 to 10 minutes.

Chocolate Chip Meringues

Ingredients:
3 egg whites
1/8 tsp. salt
3/4 cup sugar
1 tsp. vanilla
1 (6oz.) pkg. chocolate chips

Directions:
In small bowl, beat egg whites and salt until stiff, but not dry. Add sugar, a little at a time, beating well after each addition. Mixture should be stiff and glossy. Stir in vanilla and fold in chips. Drop by teaspoons on oiled cookie sheets. Bake at 300 degrees for about 17 minutes, or until golden and firm to light touch.

Supper Smoke

Meringue Cookies

Ingredients:
2 egg whites
1 cup sugar
1 tsp. vanilla
1 cup coconut
2 cups rice crispies, or corn flakes, slightly crushed
1/2 cup chopped nuts

Directions:
In mixing bowl, beat egg whites 'til they hold strong peaks. Gradually add sugar, beating constantly. Stir in the remainder of ingredients. Drop by teaspoon on waxed, or well-oiled cookie sheets. Bake at 375 degrees for 5 minutes. Cool completely before carefully removing from pans.

Snickerdoodles

Ingredients:
1 cup shortening, softened
1 1/2 cups sugar
2 eggs
1/4 tsp. salt
1 tsp. soda
2 tsp. cream of tartar
2 3/4 cups flour

2 tbsp. sugar
2 tsp. cinnamon

Directions:
In mixing bowl, cream together the shortening, sugar and eggs. Add the next four ingredients in order given, blending well. Roll in balls the size of walnuts and then roll each in sugar/cinnamon mixture. Bake on ungreased cookie sheets at 400 degrees for 8 to 10 minutes (they will puff up and flatten out later.)

Can you go through childhood without warm snickerdoodles? This recipe always brings warm memories of Chuck, Richard's younger brother. He was a carefree and fun-loving young man who relished the joy in each new day. He loved these cookies, and since he died suddenly at 21 years of age, I'm glad for every cookie I baked for him.

Whole-Wheat Snickerdoodles

Ingredients:
1 1/2 cups sugar
1 cup butter or margarine, softened
1 egg + 1 egg white
1 tsp. baking soda
1/4 tsp. salt
1 1/2 cups whole-wheat flour
1 1/4 cups white flour

2 tbsp. Sugar
2 tsp. cinnamon

Directions:
In mixing bowl, cream sugar and butter. Beat in egg and egg white. Add the dry ingredients and blend well. Shape dough into small balls and roll in sugar/cinnamon mixture. Bake on ungreased cookie sheets at 375 degrees for 8 to 10 minutes.

Melting Moments

Ingredients:
1 cup butter (no substitutes)
1/3 cup sifted powdered sugar
1 1/4 cups flour
1/2 cup cornstarch

1/4 cup butter, softened
1 1/2 cups powdered sugar
2 tbsp. lemon juice

Directions:
In mixing bowl, combine butter and sugar, blending well. Add flour and cornstarch, mixing well. Shape cookies into small, walnut size balls and bake on ungreased cookie sheet at 350 degrees for 10 to 12 minutes. When cool, make a frosting of the butter, sugar and lemon juice and frost.

Peanut Crunch Cookies

Ingredients:
1 cup sugar
1 cup brown sugar
1 cup shortening
2 eggs, beaten
1 tsp. vanilla
1 tsp. baking powder
1 tsp. soda
2 cups flour
1 cup crushed corn flakes
1 cup oatmeal
1 cup salted peanuts

Directions:
In large mixing bowl, cream sugars and shortening together. Add eggs and vanilla, blending well. Continue adding dry ingredients, in order given. Stir in cornflakes, oatmeal, and peanuts. Shape dough in balls and roll in sugar. Press down with sugared glass bottom. Bake at 350 degrees for 8 to 10 minutes.

Supper Smoke

Peanut Butter Maple Cookies

Ingredients:
1 cup butter or margarine, softened
1/2 cup peanut butter
1 cup white sugar
1 cup packed brown sugar
2 eggs
1 tbsp. maple pancake syrup
2 tsp. vanilla
1 1/2 tsp. baking powder
1 tsp. soda
1 tsp. salt
2 cups flour
1 cup quick oats
1 pkg. peanut butter chips

Directions:
In large mixing bowl, cream together the butter, peanut butter, and sugars. Add eggs, syrup, and vanilla and blend well. Add dry ingredients in order given. Roll dough in balls and then in sugar. Press down with sugared glass. Bake at 350 degrees for 8 to 10 minutes.

Raisin-Filled Cookies

Ingredients:
3 cups raisins
3/4 cup sugar
3 tbsp. flour
3/4 cup water
2 tsp. lemon juice
1 cup chopped nuts, optional

1 cup shortening, NOT margarine or butter
1 cup white sugar
1 cup brown sugar
1 tsp. soda, dissolved in 1/2 cup warm water
1 tsp. salt
2 eggs
1 tsp. vanilla
4 cups flour

Directions:
With food grinder, grind up the raisins. In saucepan combine ground raisins, sugar, flour, water, and lemon juice. Cook over medium heat, stirring constantly, until mixture comes to a boil and thickens. Remove from heat, add chopped nuts, and set aside.

In large mixing bowl, cream together the shortening and sugars. Add soda dissolved in water, and salt. Mix well. Add eggs, one at a time, blending well. Beat in vanilla and then the flour. It helps to chill the dough at this point. Roll chilled dough into balls and place on greased cookie sheets. Flatten with bottom of floured glass. Place one heaping spoon of raisin filling on each cookie. Form a small ball of chilled dough in fingers and drop in flour. Shape a flat cookie top with fingers and place over top of filling, sealing edges with fingers or a fork. Bake at 350 degrees for about 10 minutes.

These were "special" cookies when I was a child at home. Now I am a granny, and they STILL are special. They're worth the extra effort.

Supper Smoke

Golden Carrot Cookies

Ingredients:
3/4 cup shortening
3/4 cup sugar
1 egg
1 1/4 cup grated carrots
1 tsp. vanilla
1/2 tsp. cinnamon
2 tsp. baking powder
1/2 tsp. salt
2 cups flour

1 1/2 cups powdered sugar
1/8 tsp. salt
1/2 tsp. cinnamon
2 or 3 tbsp. milk or cream

Directions:
In mixing bowl, cream shortening and sugar. Beat in egg. Stir in grated carrots and vanilla. Add the next four ingredients. Drop by teaspoons on greased cookie sheets. Bake at 375 degrees for 10-15 minutes. While still warm, make a glaze of the powdered sugar, salt, cinnamon and milk. Spread over cookies.

Gumdrop Cookies

Ingredients:
1 cup shortening
1 cup white sugar
1 cup brown sugar
2 eggs
1 tsp. vanilla
1 tsp. baking powder
1/2 tsp. soda
1/2 tsp. salt
2 cups flour
2 cups quick oats
1 cup shredded coconut
1 cup chopped gumdrops OR white baking chips

1 cup powdered sugar
1 or 2 tbsp. milk

Directions:
In mixing bowl, cream shortening and sugars. Beat in eggs and vanilla. Add next four dry ingredients, blending well. Stir in oats, coconut and gumdrops. Drop by spoonfuls onto greased cookie sheets. Bake at 350 degrees for 8 to 10 minutes. While cookies are still warm, make a glaze of powdered sugar and milk and drizzle over all.

Whoopie Pies

Ingredients:
6 tbsp. shortening
1 cup sugar
1 egg
1/2 cup cocoa
1/4 tsp. salt
1 tsp. vanilla
1/2 cup buttermilk
1 tsp. baking soda dissolved in 1/2 cup hot water
2 cups flour

3/4 cup shortening
2 1/2 to 3 cups powdered sugar
1 egg white
1 tsp. vanilla

Directions:
In mixing bowl, cream shortening and sugar. Beat in egg. Add cocoa, salt, vanilla, and buttermilk. Dissolve soda in hot water and blend in. Stir in flour. Drop by rounded spoonfuls on greased cookie sheets. Bake at 350 degrees for 8 to 10 minutes. Remove from sheets and cool. Meanwhile, beat shortening and one cup of the powdered sugar. Beat in egg white and vanilla. Then add rest of sugar. Frost flat side of one cookie, and top with another.

Gingerbread Whoopie Pies

Ingredients:
6 tbsp. butter or margarine, melted
1/4 cup sugar
3/4 cup molasses
1 tsp. ginger
1 tsp. cinnamon
1/2 tsp. baking soda
1/2 tsp. salt
1 egg
2 cups flour

6 tbsp. butter or margarine, softened
1 jar (7oz.) marshmallow crème
1/2 cup powdered sugar
1 tsp. vanilla

Directions:
In large mixing bowl combine first nine ingredients in order given, blending well. Chill. Meanwhile, combine butter, marshmallow crème, sugar and vanilla, for filling, and chill also. Form cookie dough in balls and pace on greased cookie sheets. Flatten with floured glass bottom and bake at 350 degrees for 7 to 10 minutes. Remove from pans and cool. Spread filling on a cooled cookie and top with another.

Lacey Oatmeal Cookies

Ingredients:
1/2 cup sugar
1/8 tsp. salt
1/2 cup margarine
1/2 tsp. vanilla
1 1/2 cups quick oats
1/2 cup finely chopped nuts, optional

2 tbsp. margarine or butter
1/4 cup chocolate chips

Directions:
In mixing bowl, combine sugar, salt and margarine. Stir in vanilla, oats and nuts. Form into small balls and place 2 inches apart on LIGHT COLORED, well greased cookie sheets. Press down each cookie with a sugared glass. Bake at 375 degrees for 8 to 10 minutes. WATCH CLOSELY. Cookies will "bubble" as they bake. When they stop bubbling and are BARELY browned around edges, they are done. Cool before carefully removing from pans. Melt margarine and chocolate chips, making a glaze. Drizzle over cooled cookies.

These are dainty little sweeties that taste wonderful. Just right for a tea party. Make sure to crook your little finger as you nibble on them.

Therapy Cookies

Ingredients:
1 cup brown sugar
1 cup butter or margarine
1 cup flour
1 tsp. soda
2 cups quick oatmeal

Directions:
WASH YOUR HANDS! In large mixing bowl, place all ingredients. Plunge in with your hands and work the ingredients with your fingers (don't lick!) until blended well. Shape 1-inch balls and place on ungreased cookie sheets. Sugar a flat-bottomed glass and whap each of them flat. Eat 'em all. EXCUSE ME. You've gotta bake 'em first. 350 degrees, 8 to 10 minutes. NOW eat 'em.

Double Chocolate Oatmeal Cookies

Ingredients:
1 1/2 cups sugar
1 cup butter or margarine, softened
1 egg
1/4 cup water
1 tsp. vanilla
1/3 cup cocoa
1/2 tsp. soda
1/2 tsp. salt
1 1/4 cups flour
3 cups oatmeal
1 (6oz.) pkg. chocolate chips

Directions:
In large bowl, cream together the sugar and butter. Add egg, water and vanilla and blend well. Add cocoa, soda, salt and flour, blending again. Stir in oatmeal and chips. Drop on greased cookie sheets and bake at 350 degrees for 7 to 10 minutes.

Oatmeal Cinnamon Cookies

Ingredients:
1 cup shortening
1 cup white sugar
1/2 cup brown sugar
1 egg, beaten
1 tsp. vanilla
1 tsp. soda
1 tsp. cinnamon
1 1/2 cups flour
1 1/2 cups quick oats
3/4 cup chopped nuts (optional)

Directions:
In mixing bowl, cream shortening and sugars. Add egg and vanilla and blend well. Stir in soda, cinnamon and flour, blending well. Add oats and nuts. Chill for one hour. Roll dough in walnut size pieces and place on greased cookie sheets. Flatten with greased, sugared glass. Bake at 350 degrees for 10 minutes.

Oatmeal Peanut Cookies

Ingredients:
1 cup shortening
1 cup sugar
1 cup packed brown sugar
2 eggs
1 tsp. vanilla
1 tsp. baking powder
1 tsp. baking soda
1 1/2 cups flour
3 cups oatmeal (old fashioned)
1 cup salted peanuts

Directions:
In large mixing bowl, cream shortening and sugars. Beat in eggs, one at a time. Add vanilla and blend well. Add baking powder, soda, and flour. Stir in oatmeal and nuts. Form into balls and place on greased cookie sheets. Press each one down somewhat, with a buttered, sugared glass bottom. Bake at 350 degrees for 7 to 10 minutes.

Oatmeal Fruit Cookies

Ingredients:
1 cup butter or margarine, softened
1 cup white sugar
3/4 cup brown sugar, packed
2 eggs
2 tsps. vanilla
1 tsp. baking powder
1 tsp. soda
1/2 tsp. salt
1/2 tsp. cinnamon
2 cups flour
1 1/4 cups quick oats
1 1/4 cups old-fashioned oats
2 cups dried fruit
1 cup raisins
1 cup chopped nuts
1/2 cup flaked coconut, optional

Directions:
In large mixing bowl, cream together the butter, sugars, and eggs. Add vanilla and blend well. Stir in the next five dry ingredients and combine. Stir in oats, dried fruit, raisins, chopped nuts, and coconut. Drop by heaping tbsp. on greased cookie sheets. Bake at 350 degrees for NO MORE than 10 minutes, or until lightly browned.

Supper Smoke

Spicy Molasses Drops

Ingredients:
1/2 cup shortening
3/4 cup sugar
1 egg
3/4 tsp. salt
1/2 tsp. soda
1 1/2 tsp. allspice
1 1/2 tsp. ginger
2 1/4 cups flour
1/2 cup molasses
1/4 cup boiling water
1 cup rolled oats
1/2 cup chopped nuts, optional

1/4 cup butter or margarine
1 1/2 cups powdered sugar
1 1/2 tsp. vanilla
2 tbsp. evaporated milk, or cream

Directions:
In mixing bowl, cream shortening and sugar. Beat in egg. Combine next five ingredients, blending well. Add molasses and boiling water. Stir in rolled oats and nuts. Drop by spoonfuls on greased cookie sheets. Bake for 7 to 10 minutes at 375 degrees.

In saucepan, brown butter, stirring constantly. Beat in rest of ingredients and spread over cooled cookies.

Molasses Oatmeal Treats

(Lo-Fat)

Ingredients:
1 cup whole wheat flour
1 cup quick oats
1/4 cup sugar
1 tsp. baking soda
1/4 cup + 2 tbsp. molasses
1/4 cup pancake syrup
2 1/2 tbsp. water
1 tsp. vanilla
1/4 cup wheat germ
1 cup Bran Flakes
2/3 cup raisins or chopped, dried fruit

Directions:
In mixing bowl, combine first four ingredients. Add molasses, syrup, water and vanilla. Blend well. Stir in wheat germ, Bran Flakes, and chopped fruit. Shape into balls and roll in sugar. Bake on greased cookie sheets at 275 degrees for about 10 minutes.

No-Bake Butterscotches

Ingredients:
1/2 cup margarine or butter
2 cups brown sugar, packed
1/2 cup canned milk
1 small pkg. instant butterscotch pudding mix
1/2 tsp. Mapeleine flavoring OR vanilla
3 cups quick oats
1/2 cup chopped nuts

Directions:
In large saucepan, melt margarine. Add sugar and canned milk and blend. Bring to a boil and cook, stirring constantly, for 3 minutes. Remove from heat and add the pudding mix and flavoring, stirring to blend. Add oats and nuts and stir quickly to blend well. While still very warm, drop by spoonfuls on waxed paper to cool.

Supper Smoke

North Dakota Date Bars

Ingredients:
1 pound dates, cut up
1 cup scalding water
1 tsp. soda
Butter or margarine, the size of an egg*
1 cup sugar
1 egg
1 tsp. baking powder
1 1/4 cups flour
1 cup walnuts
Powdered Sugar

Directions:
In mixing bowl, pour water over dates; add 1 tsp. soda and let cool. Add other ingredients in order given. Bake in greased 8 by 10 inch pan at 350 degrees for 20 minutes. Cut in bars and roll in powdered sugar.

* I think this would be about 1/4 cup. Come to think of it, though, this is a recipe from my own childhood, so it could be a dinosaur egg!

Cream Cheese Brownies

Ingredients:
1 box German chocolate cake mix
8 oz. cream cheese
1/2 cup sugar
1 egg
1 cup chocolate chips
1/2 cup chopped nuts

Directions:
Prepare cake mix as directed on package. Pour into a greased jellyroll pan. In small mixing bowl, combine cream cheese, sugar and eggs. Drop by spoonfuls onto cake batter, swirling to marble. Sprinkle chocolate chips and nuts over all. Bake at 350 degrees for 25 to 30 minutes.

Peanut-Butterscotch Bars

Ingredients:
1/2 cup butter or margarine
1/2 cup brown sugar, packed
1 1/3 cups flour
2/3 cup sugar
2/3 cup light corn syrup
1 cup butterscotch chips
1/2 cup peanut butter
2 cups corn flakes (NOT crushed)

Directions:
In mixing bowl, cream butter and sugar. Stir in flour. Press in lightly greased 9 by 13 inch pan. Bake at 350 degrees for 12 to 15 minutes. In saucepan, combine sugar and corn syrup; heat to boiling. Remove from heat and add chips and peanut butter. Stir until chips are melted and all is blended. Stir in corn flakes. Spread over baked layer. Cool and cut in bars.

Sharon's Brownies

Ingredients:
1/2 cup butter or margarine
1 cup sugar
2 eggs, slightly beaten
1 tsp. vanilla
2/3 cups flour
4 tbsp. cocoa
2/3 cup chopped nuts

Directions:
In mixing bowl, cream butter and sugar. Add eggs and vanilla. Stir in flour, cocoa and nuts. Spoon into greased 8 inch pan and bake at 325 degrees for NO LONGER than 25 minutes.

These were THE BROWNIES my family always enjoyed while still at home. I have used the recipe countless times, always with good success. Thanks Sharon!

Raisin Date Bars

Ingredients:
2 eggs, well beaten
1 tbsp. oil
1 tsp. vanilla
1 cup powdered sugar
1/4 cup flour
1/2 tsp. baking powder
1/2 tsp. salt
1/2 cup nuts
1/2 cup raisins
1/2 cup dates, chopped
Powdered sugar

Directions:
In mixing bowl, combine first four ingredients. In separate bowl, combine flour, baking powder, and salt. Add to first ingredients, blending well. Fold in the nuts, raisins and dates. Spread in greased 8-inch square pan. Bake at 325 degrees for 25 minutes or less. While still warm, cut in squares and roll in powdered sugar.

Chocolate Orange Brownies

Ingredients:
1/3 cup shortening
2/3 cup packed brown sugar
1 egg
1/2 cup milk
1/4 tsp. soda
1/2 tsp. salt
1 cup flour
1 1/4 cups quick oats
1 cup chocolate chips
1/2 cup sugar
3 tbsp. orange juice
1 tsp. grated orange rind

Directions:
In mixing bowl, cream together the shortening, sugar and egg. Add the next 6 ingredients, in order given. Spread batter in greased 9 inch baking pan. Bake at 375 degrees for about 30 minutes. JUST BEFORE BROWNIES ARE DONE, mix together the sugar, orange juice and rind. Bring to a boil, remove from heat and pour over brownies. Cool.

I've had this recipe ever since a new bride years ago. My husband's twin brother, single at the time, was very fond of these. He soon ventured forth to marry; a wonderful cook in the bargain, and has probably never thought of these since!

Supper Smoke

Chocolate Cream Cheese Bars

Ingredients:
1/2 cup butter or margarine
1 cup sugar
2 eggs
1 tsp. vanilla
1 oz. baking chocolate, melted
1 tsp. soda
1 cup flour
1/2 cup chopped nuts

1/4 cup butter or margarine, softened
1 (8oz.) pkg. cream cheese, reserving 2 oz.
1/2 cup sugar
1 egg
2 tbsp. flour
1/2 tsp. vanilla
1/4 cup chopped nuts

3 cups miniature marshmallows
1/4 cup butter, softened
2 oz. cream cheese, softened
1 oz. baking chocolate, softened
1 tsp. vanilla, softened (just kidding!)
2 tbsp. milk
3 cups powdered sugar

Directions:
Combine first 8 ingredients and spread on greased 9 by 13 inch pan. Combine the next 7 ingredients and spread over chocolate layer and bake at 350 degrees for 20 minutes. Remove from oven and sprinkle marshmallows over all. Return to oven for 2 minutes. Remove and swirl. Cool. Combine last 7 ingredients and swirl over all.

I feel like I've gained several pounds just typing this out.

Oatmeal Apple Bars

Ingredients:
2 cups flour
1 tsp. soda
1/4 tsp. salt
2 cups oatmeal
1 cup packed brown sugar
1 cup butter or margarine
4 apples, peeled and chopped
3 tbsp. butter or margarine
1 cup chopped nuts
1/2 cup sugar

Directions:
Sift flour, soda and salt. Place in large mixing bowl and add oatmeal, sugar and butter. Blend well with pastry blender. Pat HALF the mixture into a greased 10 by 15 inch pan. Cover mixture with apples. Dot with 3 tbsp. of butter. In small bowl, combine nuts and sugar and spoon HALF on apples. Pat on remaining crumb mixture and sprinkle on remaining sugar mixture. Bake at 300 degrees for one hour and 15 minutes.

Brittle Cookies

Ingredients:
40 saltine cracker squares (or one may use graham crackers)
1 cup butter (no substitutes)
1 cup brown sugar
1 (12oz.) pkg. chocolate chips
1 cup chopped nuts

Directions:
Layer foil on cookie sheet and spray well with vegetable spray. Layer crackers in single layer on foil. In saucepan, bring butter and sugar to a boil. Boil 3 minutes, stirring constantly. Pour over crackers. Bake 5 minutes more, or until crackers float. Remove from oven and sprinkle evenly with chocolate chips. When chips are softened, spread with a knife and immediately sprinkle with chopped nuts.

Sounds weird, but they're really yummy. The aspiring young cook in your household can do this one with aplomb.

Crunchy Marshmallow Bars

Ingredients:
1/2 cup butter or margarine
3/4 cup sugar
2 eggs
1 tsp. vanilla
3/4 cup flour
1/2 cup chopped nuts
1/4 tsp. soda
1/4 tsp. salt
2 tbsp. cocoa
2 cups miniature marshmallows
1 cup chocolate chips
1 cup peanut butter
1 1/2 cups rice crispy cereal

Directions:
In mixing bowl, cream the butter and sugar. Beat in eggs and vanilla. Stir in the flour, nuts, soda, salt, and cocoa. Spread on bottom of greased 9 by 13 inch pan. Bake at 350 degrees for 15 minutes or until done to touch. Sprinkle marshmallows evenly over top and bake 3 minutes more. Cool.

In saucepan, combine chips and peanut butter, stirring over low heat until melted and blended. Stir in cereal and spread over marshmallow layer. Chill and cut in bars.

Chocolate Oatmeal Bars

Ingredients:
3/4 cup butter or margarine, softened
1 cup brown sugar, packed
1 tsp. salt
1/2 tsp. soda
1 1/2 cups flour
1 1/2 cups oatmeal

3 tbsp. butter or margarine, melted
2 tsp. salad oil
3 tbsp. cocoa
1 tsp. vanilla
Powdered sugar
1 or 3 tbsp. milk

Directions:
In mixing bowl, cream butter and sugar until light and fluffy. Combine dry ingredients and add, blending well. Press half the batter into a greased 9 by 13 inch pan. Make chocolate filling by combining the butter, salad oil, cocoa, and vanilla. Stir in enough powdered sugar and milk to make a stiff filling. Spread over batter. Sprinkle remaining batter in small globs over all. Bake at 375 degrees for about 15 minutes.

*Fruit jams of various kinds also make a good filling. I like raspberry.

Famous Candy Bars

Ingredients:
1/2 cup white sugar
1/2 cup brown sugar
1 cup white syrup
1 cup peanut butter
6 cups corn flakes, crushed slightly
1 cup salted peanuts
1 (12oz.) pkg. chocolate chips OR
1(6oz.) pkg. chocolate chips AND
1 (6oz.) pkg. butterscotch chips

Directions:
In saucepan, combine sugars and syrup, bring to a boil and cook for 1 minute. Add peanut butter and blend well. In large mixing bowl, stir together the corn flakes and peanuts. Pour syrup mixture over all and blend. Place in greased 9 by 13 inch pan and firmly press with buttered fingers. Make a glaze of the chocolate chips, melted, and spread over all.

Supper Smoke

Chocolate Caramel Pecan Bars

Ingredients:
1 cup butter or margarine, cut in chunks
1 cup packed brown sugar
1 large egg yolk
2 tsp. vanilla
2 cups flour
2 cups chopped pecans or almonds

6 tbsp. butter or margarine
3/4 cup brown sugar, packed
3/4 cup light corn syrup
2 cups chocolate chips

Directions:
In mixing bowl, blend butter, brown sugar, egg yolk, and vanilla. Add flour and mix well. Press into bottom and sides of greased 10 by 15 inch pan. Sprinkle nuts over dough and press in with fingers. Bake at 350 degrees about 20 minutes, or until crust is golden brown.

Meanwhile make filling, by combining butter, sugar, and corn syrup. Bring to a boil and cook until soft ball stage, about 5 minutes. Spread while still hot, on baked crust. Sprinkle chips over all, and when they are soft, spread out and cool.

The Old Cookie Jar

Prairie School Teacher

There was a teacher long ago
Who taught a little prairie school;
She stood before the little ones
And said with them the spelling rule.
She bade them chant times tables when
Their slates were full, their writing done.
They wiggled through the tedious hours,
And how they stormed outside for fun!
Then sometimes when they trooped back in
She taught them some new song to sing.
And sometimes from a battered book
She read to them. Her voice would ring
To make the dead men's words alive,
'Til they were pictures fine and grand.
And sometimes she would catch them up
And journey to a far-off land!
But when she sent them home again
Across the prairies white with snow
(Or bright with flowers in the spring,)
She sometimes sighed to watch them go.
She wondered where their paths might land,
And if, perchance, some little part
Of all she taught might linger still
To guide a life or cheer a heart?
She wondered, but could little see
Beyond each day of good or bad…
She swept the floor and closed the door.
She was the teacher Grandpa had.

My grandpa wore a hearing aid
And cocked his head to hear your voice,
And yet he heard a-down the years
Old poems that made his tongue rejoice.
"Under the spreading chestnut tree,"
Quoth he, "The village smithy stands,
The smith! A mighty man is he!"
My grandpa spread expressive hands.
With sweet nostalgia he recalled,
"The house where I was born? Yes, child!

Supper Smoke

The little window where the sun
Came peeking in at morn!" he smiled.
And now we smile, remembering
Old poetry in Grandpa's voice.
Though he has silent grown and still,
The words sing on, and we rejoice.

My grandpa wore black spectacles,
And how he peered to see your face.
But, oh! The countries he had seen,
Yet strangely, never left his place.
He gazed upon the Emerald Isle,
Trekked white-robed Arabs' dusty trails;
He took a boat along the Nile,
Scaled mountains wearing clouds for veils.
He never met a stranger, but
He wished to know where they were from…
He traced the route that they would take
And knew the way that they had come.
My grandpa's eyes are closed in sleep,
His books are taken from the shelf,
And some of us have gone to see
The lands he never reached himself.

My grandpa's voice was cracked with age
We giggled so to hear his song!
And yet, so rollicking the tune
We could not help but sing along!
So in the low, green valley we
Would "while the happy hours away"
And sit beside the cottage door
Where (caroled he) lived Nellie Grey!
Then sang he of that happy land
Far, far away (lest we forget)
Where saints in glory praise and sing
Bright, bright as the day. (We hear him yet.)
Though Grandpa's voice is mute, it seems
That land is not so far away.
Because we hear among that throng
His voice, still singing praise for aye!

The Old Cookie Jar

*Some folks would say his life was small,
Bounded by miles he traveled here,
But I have yet to meet a man
Who held the joys he had more dear.
To have a poem in your heart,
A song to sing when days are drear,
A vision of some far-off place—
How full is life with hope and cheer.*

*Then let some teacher of this day
Who almost fears her work is vain,
Take hold! Take heart! And carry on
Her torch! Yea, hold it high again!
For who can know which word she reads
May hold for all life, some delight?
Or who can know which song she sings
May lead the children through the night?
What vision of a far-off place
May cheer some faltering spirit on?
Oh, who can know what shapes a life
And makes it fine, before it's gone?
Take hold! Take heart! Nor ask to know
The end of all you do. You see,
Some story's end may not be told
Until you reach eternity.*

    Tamara Seaman Koehn

Christmas

The day is done and the darkness
Falls from the wings of night,
As snowflakes wafted downward
From each wintry cloud in sight.

The golden lights from the brown house
Gleam through the snow and the mist,
And a feeling of gladness steals o'er me
That my soul cannot resist.

A feeling of gladness, and singing
That sets the heart aglow,
And resembles laughter only,
As the mists resemble the snow.

Come! Sing with us of the Christ child;
That simple and heart felt song;
It can soothe each restless longing,
And banish all thoughts of wrong.

It can heal a lonely heartache
When loved ones are far away,
And smooth each care and worry,
As we trust them to God each day.

At years end we pause to ponder
How quickly the days have flown;
Like golden leaves in the autumn skies
That fall winds have tossed and blown.

But each leaf's flight, the Father has known,
And the winds have a purpose sure.
With a song of love deep in our hearts,
We can feel each day is secure.

Supper Smoke

And the night shall be filled with music,
And the cares that infest the day,
Shall fold their books like carolers,
And silently steal away.

R.A.S.
Christmas 1987

(With apologies to Henry Wadsworth Longfellow)

Christmas

Norwegian Lefse

Ingredients:
4 cups mashed potatoes, including 4 tbsp. butter or margarine, 1 tsp. salt, and milk enough to mash
2 cups flour, about

Directions:
Mashed potatoes need to be room temperature (my sis, whose instructions these are, finds it best to use instant mashed potatoes, mixed according to instructions.) Add enough flour to make a non-sticky dough, about 2 cups. Add this gradually, using no more flour than necessary.

On a floured surface, shape dough into a long roll and cut into 24 equal pieces (each piece looks very small.) DO NOT COVER… Now preheat your griddle. Should be hot enough to make little brown "freckles" on bottom of lefse in 2 or 3 minutes. You'll have to experiment a bit. Now take a piece of the dough and shape, much as you would shape a dinner roll, making a round, smooth ball. Using plenty of flour, roll the ball out as thinly as possible, until about 10 inches in diameter. Be sure to keep enough flour under the dough so it won't stick. Use a LIGHT HAND on the rolling pin, don't bear down. Lift carefully, shake a bit to get rid of extra flour, and drop on griddle. Bake on one side 'til those brown spots appear, then turn and bake on the other side. When done, lay each out singly on dishtowel to cool. You may begin stacking them only AFTER they are cooled.
These may be frozen, laying waxed paper between every three or four. Take directly from freezer and arrange in single layer on cookie sheets. Bake in 300 degree oven JUST until warm.

They are the very best, hot off the griddle! Spread with butter, sprinkle with sugar and cinnamon, roll up, POUR COFFEE, and ENJOY!

Supper Smoke

Bunuelos

Ingredients:
1 cup water
2 tbsp. anise seed
4 cups flour
1 tbsp. baking powder
1/2 tsp. salt
2 eggs
Cooking oil
Cinnamon and sugar

Directions:
In small saucepan, combine water and anise seed and bring to a boil. Cook for a few minutes and then cool. In mixing bowl, combine flour, baking powder and salt. Add eggs and enough anise water to make a dough. Knead thoroughly. Pinch off little balls of dough and roll each out as thin as possible on floured surfaces. Fry in hot cooking oil. Remove from oil, drain, and sprinkle with cinnamon and sugar mixture.

Christmas in Mexico!

Clam Chowder

Ingredients:
5 medium potatoes, cut up
2 stalks celery, chopped
1 onion chopped
1 carrot, grated
4 medium potatoes, grated
2 or 3 cans minced or chopped clams, UNDRAINED
1/4 tsp. thyme
Salt and pepper to taste
Cooked and crumbled bacon
Cream, or top milk
2 to 4 tbsp. butter

Directions:
In stew kettle, place potatoes, celery, onion and carrot. Add water to cover and begin cooking. While first ingredients are beginning to cook, peel and grate other 4 potatoes. Add to cooking vegetables. Add clams and continue cooking until vegetables are done. Add seasonings, bacon and top milk. Bring to a simmer, but do not boil. Add butter and serve.

My dear friend Salinda shared this recipe with me long ago. We often enjoy it on Christmas Eve.

Supper Smoke

Layered Christmas Salad

Ingredients:
1 (6oz.) pkg. red Jell-O
1 small can crushed pineapple, well drained and reserving liquid
1 cup whipping cream
1 carton cream style cottage cheese
1 (6oz.) box lime Jell-O

Directions:
In mixing bowl prepare red Jell-O according to instructions. Pour into clear serving bowl and chill to set. Meanwhile whip cream. Fold in well drained pineapple and cottage cheese. Spread over red Jell-O layer. Chill. In another bowl prepare lime Jell-O as directed, using reserved pineapple juice as part of the water. Carefully pour green mixture over cream layer. Chill and serve.

This recipe comes from my dear sister-in-law, Helen. Her memory warms my heart at Christmas time and all through the year.

"Square" Jell-O

Ingredients:
1 (6oz.) pkg. Jell-O
2 cups HOT fruit juice or applesauce (Use fruits that will compliment the flavor of your Jell-O)
1 3/4 cup cold water
1 cup whipping cream
3 to 4 tbsp. sugar
1 (8oz.) carton flavored yogurt

Directions:
Lightly oil a 9 by 12 inch flat pan. In mixing bowl, combine dry Jell-O and hot fruit juice or applesauce. Stir to completely dissolve Jell-O. Stir in cold water. Pour into pan and chill until set. Cut into 1 1/2 inch squares.

In another bowl, whip cream, adding sugar to taste. Fold in yogurt and mix well. Carefully loosen Jell-O squares and fold into cream mixture. Serve in a pretty, clear bowl.

This is not only a tasty salad, but it is attractive, too. I like to serve it at Christmas time with a combination of red and green Jell-O squares.

Supper Smoke

Christmas 1988

Ah friends, the years change all our living,
And thrust our homes and lives apart.
But years don't change the golden twining
Of love that's woven in the heart
Love keeps a candle…ever lighted,
To glow and sparkle…warming each day;
Filling our hearts with glad thanksgiving,
Shedding it's light along our way.
And once again come Christmas greetings
And wishes…warm…across the years.
May God's great gift of love from heaven
Light up your candle as Christmas nears;
Spreading it's warming light of blessing;
Reaching to others, 'til all can know
The love of God shine soft around us,
Each day…all year…a Christmas glow.

                                              R.A.S.
                                              Christmas 1988

Chocolate Pizza

Ingredients:
1 (12oz.) pkg. semi-sweet chocolate chips
1 lb. white almond bark, divided
2 cups miniature marshmallows
1 cup crisp rice cereal
1 cup peanuts
1 (6oz.) jar red maraschino cherries, drained and cut in half
1/3 cup flaked coconut
1 tsp. oil

Directions:
In double boiler, melt chocolate chips and all but 2 oz. of the almond bark. In mixing bowl, combine marshmallows, cereal, and peanuts. Pour melted chocolate mixture over all and blend. Pour onto greased 12-inch pizza pan. Arrange cherries on top and sprinkle with coconut. Melt additional almond bark and oil and blend together. Drizzle over pizza. Chill until firm.

Add this to your Christmas goodie list.

Supper Smoke

Judy's Humdingers

Ingredients:
1/2 cup butter, or margarine
1 cup sugar
2 tbsp. corn syrup
1 tsp. vanilla
1/2 pound dates, chopped
3 cups Rice Krispies
2 cups chopped nuts
Powdered sugar

Directions:
In large saucepan, melt butter. Add sugar, syrup, vanilla, and dates. Cook, stirring constantly, until sugar is dissolved and dates are soft, not quite 10 minutes. Remove from heat and stir in Rice Krispies and nuts. Shape in small balls and roll in powdered sugar.

Judy is my cousin, and also a humdinger of a friend, excellent schoolteacher, and master gardener…oh, yes…a very good artist… and OH, MY YES…a gifted poet besides! HERE, HERE, Judy, have a humdinger…have TWO.

Christmas

Fruitcake Cookies

Ingredients:
2 cups sugar
1/2 cup butter or margarine
1/2 cup shortening
3 eggs
1/4 cup milk
1 tbsp. lemon extract
1 tbsp. vanilla
1 tsp. soda dissolved in 1 tbsp. water
3 1/4 cups sifted flour
1/4 tsp. cloves
1 heaping tsp. cinnamon
1 tsp. allspice
1 tsp. nutmeg
1 1/4 cups chopped pecans
2 1/4 cups chopped walnuts (I usually use just 2 cups walnuts)
1/2 lb. chopped dates
1 lb. raisins
1/4 lb. candied cherries
1/4 lb. candied pineapple (I just use 1/2 lb. fruitcake mix instead of candied cherries and pineapple)

Directions:
In large mixing bowl, cream together the sugar, butter, shortening and eggs. Add the next five ingredients. Sift together the flour and spices. Combine part of flour mixture with the nuts and fruit. Combine all together and bake on higher rack in oven at 350 degrees. Take out when BARELY browned.

Supper Smoke

Date Cookies

Ingredients:
1/2 cup butter or margarine
2 cups brown sugar
2 eggs
1 rounded tsp. soda, dissolved in water
1 tsp. baking powder
1 tsp. vanilla
4 cups flour
1 pkg. dates, chopped

Directions:
In mixing bowl, cream the butter and sugar. Blend in eggs. Add remaining ingredients in order given. Mold into small cookies and bake on greased baking sheets at 350 degrees for 7 to 10 minutes.

These were Christmas cookies back in North Dakota where my family originated. We needed all the help we could get on those howling prairies, so I'm glad there were dates in these; something to remind us of the tropics.

Christmas 1989

We wish for you a year that's blessed with all that makes you happiest.
A winter sunset in pearl-peach hues; The scrunch of snow beneath your shoes.
The smell of spring; green tinted hills; And ears to catch glad song bird trills.
A lazy summer day or two...A fishing hole...A joke or two!
The warm sweet smell of new-mown hay, upon a sun-splashed, bright blue day.
A love-lit smile across a room; The golden wash of a harvest moon.
The moan of the wind on a frosty night...A good book...An apple... A fire to light.
A song in your heart on a cheerless day; A letter from home to light the way.
A larder that's full enough to share, with friends and family from here and there.
A good, long talk with some dear friend; A cup of coffee, and hearts that blend.
A yearning to listen, to learn, to share; A heart that's brave enough to care.
But, above all these, throughout the year; Faith to guide you from doubt and fear.
A heart-felt prayer...A look above...The quiet touch of a Savior's love.
A candle of love in your heart, and mine; God's hand to light it, and make it shine.
A warm glow at Christmas, in all you do; God bless you and yours the whole year through.

R.A.S.
Christmas 1989

Supper Smoke

No-bake Fruitcake

Ingredients:
1 lb. graham crackers, crushed
1 lb. raisins
1 lb. candied fruit of choice
4 cups chopped nuts
3/4 cup milk
1 lb. marshmallows

Directions:
In large mixing bowl, combine graham crumbs, raisins, fruit, and nuts and blend well. Scald milk in double boiler and add marshmallows, cooking 'til smooth and stirring constantly. Pour over graham mixture and blend together with buttered hands. Line loaf pan with wax paper and press batter in pan until firm.

Christmas

Mom's Applesauce Cake

Ingredients:
2 cups flour
3 tbsp. cocoa
1 cup sugar
1/2 cup melted butter or margarine
1 egg, beaten
1 tsp. soda, dissolved in small amount of water
1/2 tsp. salt
1/2 tsp. nutmeg
1 tsp. cinnamon
1 cup applesauce
1 cup raisins
1 cup chopped walnuts
Candied fruit and/or maraschino cherries

Directions:
In large mixing bowl, combine all ingredients in order given. Pour batter into greased and floured loaf pan and bake at 350 degrees until toothpick comes out clean.

This is an old recipe from my mother. She often used this for a special Christmas cake. Mom's grocery budget was fairly meager; hence there wasn't a WHOLE lot of candied fruit and certainly not cherries TOO, but however she made it, we always thought it was delicious.

Christmas Pie #1

Ingredients:
1 baked pie shell
1/2 cup sugar
1/4 cup flour
1 envelope (1 tbsp.) unflavored gelatin
1/2 tsp. salt
1 3/4 cups milk
1 tsp. vanilla
1/4 tsp. almond flavoring
3 egg whites
1/4 tsp. cream of tartar
1/2 cup sugar
1/2 cup whipping cream
1 cup flaked coconut

Directions:
In saucepan, blend together the sugar, flour, gelatin, and salt. Gradually stir in milk. Cook over medium heat, stirring constantly until mixture boils. Boil one minute. Remove from heat and place over ice water. Cool until mixture begins to mound. Blend in the vanilla and almond flavorings. In another bowl, beat egg whites and cream of tartar until soft peaks form. Slowly beat in sugar, a little at a time, and beat until stiff peaks form. Carefully fold in the cooled gelatin mixture. In another bowl, whip the cream and fold in. Fold in coconut. Pour into baked pie shell. Garnish with more coconut, if desired. Chill several hours before serving.

Christmas Pie #2

Ingredients:
2 baked 8 inch pie shells
1 can sweetened condensed milk
1/3 cup lemon juice
1 (16oz.) can crushed pineapple, well drained
1/2 tsp. pineapple flavoring
1/3 cup coconut
1/2 cup chopped pecans
1 (12oz.) tub Cool Whip

Directions:
In large mixing bowl, combine all ingredients in order given, carefully folding in Cool whip last. Pour mixture into pie shells and chill at least one hour.

Peppermint Pie

Ingredients:
1 graham cracker crust
1/2 cup milk
2 tbsp. cornstarch
24 large marshmallows
1 tsp. vanilla
1/8 tsp. salt
Peppermint extract to taste
1 cup chilled whipping cream
3 tbsp. hard, peppermint candies, crushed
Red food coloring
Whipping cream, or Cool Whip

Directions:
In saucepan, combine milk and cornstarch. Add marshmallows and heat, stirring constantly, 'till thickened. Remove from heat and add vanilla, salt and peppermint extract. Refrigerate until it begins to thicken. Whip the cream and blend with peppermint mixture. Fold in red food coloring, (just enough to make it pink, NOT red, for goodness sake!) and 2 tbsp. candy. Pour into pie shell and chill. Garnish with whipped cream or Cool Whip and 1 tbsp. crushed candy.

This is a lovely pie, and the recipe comes from our nieces, Cheryl and Rhonda. They, at one time, developed a lucrative baking business in this county, delivering their luscious goods to a number of satisfied customers. They served up this pie during the Christmas season, when we were their guests, and then graciously served up the recipe also! Thanks gals!

Christmas Wishes 1995

Those near and far; the old, the young,
As weary travelers all,
We wend our way through darkening world
To Bethlehem's lowly stall.
What treasures we bring with us!
We hope they'll find a place,
Where we may lay them proudly,
And win His smiling face.
Our egos, and our money,
Our pens, our plans, our plots;
The deeds we've done for others,
Our prayers, our loving thoughts.
These treasures that we thought to bring
Seem paltry now, and poor.
We make a sorry heap of them
Beside the humble door.
We cast our eyes about the gloom.
How can we go inside?
We stand bereft; no gift to bring,
Our helplessness to hide.
Ah, then…a whisper…oh, so soft,
NO! NO!…It cannot be!
How can I give Him my own HEART?
For that is MINE. That's ME!
Yet, He is our creator;
No one could love us more.
Could we not trust Him with our heart?
Swing open wide the door!
Look up, and hear the angels!
Kneel down, and fears have flown.
Accept the warmest gift of love
This world has ever known!
Swing wide love's humble door and sing
Sweet carols, loud and clear.
Let love's warm glow light up the night,
For Christmas time is here!

                        R.A.S.
                        Christmas 1995

Divinity

Ingredients:
2 1/2 cups sugar
1/2 cup water
Dash of salt
1/2 cup light corn syrup
2 egg whites
1 tsp. vanilla
1 cup nuts

Directions:
In saucepan, combine sugar, water, salt and corn syrup. Place over heat and begin cooking. While mixture is cooking, beat egg whites until soft peaks form. Set aside. Watch divinity mixture closely, and when mixture first begins to form a thin thread when a little is poured from a spoon, then begin beating egg whites and slowly pouring a thin stream of candy mixture into egg whites. You have to guess here, but it should be only half the mixture, or less. Return the rest of mixture to heat and cook until a small amount dropped in COLD water crackles and turns glassy hard. Quickly remove from heat and continue slowly pouring hot mixture into egg whites, beating all the while until syrup is gone. Add vanilla and continue beating until mixture remains stiff when a small amount is dropped in greased pan. Quickly add nuts and pour into buttered pan.

It helps if you have someone to pour syrup for you when making this, but I hardly ever do, and it works after you get the hang of it. I've made more batches of this than you could shake a stick at. It seems to be a must at holiday time.

Holiday Divinity

Ingredients:
3 cups sugar
3/4 cup light corn syrup
3/4 cup water
2 egg whites, room temperature
1 (3oz.) pkg. flavored Jell-O
1 cup chopped nuts, optional
1/2 cup grated coconut, optional
1 tsp. vanilla

Directions:
In saucepan, combine sugar, corn syrup, and water, stirring over heat until sugar is dissolved. Cook to hardball stage, about 265 degrees.

Meanwhile, beat egg whites until fluffy. Gradually add Jell-O powder, beating until mixture holds peaks. Beat on high speed while pouring syrup into egg whites in thin stream. Beat constantly until candy holds shape and loses gloss. Beat in vanilla and fold in nuts and coconut, if desired. Pour quickly into buttered pan or drop by spoonfuls on waxed paper. If candy begins to set up too much, set over very hot water and stir.

**For any recipe that calls for egg whites only, and if you get a bit of yolk in by mistake, you'll have good luck getting it out if you use a piece of bread; the yolk will stick to it.

Supper Smoke

Chocolate Divinity

Ingredients:
3 tbsp. shortening
1/2 cup cocoa
2 1/2 cups sugar
1/4 tsp. salt
1/2 cup light corn syrup
1/3 cup water
2 egg whites
1 tsp. vanilla
1 cup chopped walnuts

Directions:
In small saucepan, melt shortening. Add cocoa and stir until smooth. Set saucepan in very warm water and set aside. In larger saucepan, combine sugar, salt, corn syrup, and water, blending well. Cook over medium heat until sugar is dissolved and mixture comes to a boil. Continue cooking without stirring until 246 degrees F. Now begin beating egg whites in a large bowl (not plastic,) until stiff peaks form. When syrup reaches 260 degrees F (or when small amount is dropped in cold water and forms hard ball,) remove from heat and immediately begin pouring syrup into beaten eggs in thin stream, beating at high speed with mixer. Add vanilla and continue beating until candy begins to hold it's shape. Quickly beat in the chocolate mixture and vanilla. Drop by spoonfuls onto waxed paper.

Christmas

Velvety Fudge

Ingredients:
4 cups sugar
3/4 cup cocoa
1/4 tsp. salt
4 tbsp. corn syrup
1 1/2 cups cream or whole milk
2 tbsp. butter or margarine
1 tbsp. vanilla
1 cup walnuts

Directions:
In large saucepan, combine the first five ingredients, blending well. Heat until sugars are melted, stirring constantly. Cover and cook until mixture comes to a boil. Uncover and cook 'til it forms firm ball when dropped in cold water.

Remove from heat and ad butter and vanilla. DON'T STIR. Let stand until partially cooled. Beat until creamy. Ad nuts and pour into buttered pan.

Supper Smoke

Seaman Fudge

I do not know when or where this recipe originated. It must have been before World War II because Richard remembers his brother begging for it, and their mother telling them, "I'll make it as soon as the war is over." They've been turning it out ever since!

Richard's family was very poor; yet there were a great many folks who passed through their door, and with a hearty welcome. Some stayed for months, and others only a day or two. They cheerfully entertained each other with a variety of activities, but when evening came, most of them were often found playing cards, drinking coffee, and eating fudge!

The recipe for this fudge was guarded with care, and even fledging young Seamans, launching out on their own, were dealt the recipe with caution.

However, now that I'm putting together this cookbook, it seems appropriate to share this fine recipe with mankind at last. I'll just check with Richard for permission, and then print it below.

Sorry folks, but as you can see, the secret remains with the Seaman clan!

Christmas

Penuche

Ingredients:
2 cups brown sugar, packed
1 cup white sugar
1/4 tsp. salt
1 cup cream, or canned milk
2 tbsp. light corn syrup
2 tbsp. butter or margarine
1 tsp. vanilla
1 cup chopped nuts

Directions:
In heavy saucepan, combine first five ingredients, blending well. Stir over heat until sugars are dissolved. Cover until mixture comes to a boil. Uncover and cook until mixture forms a firm ball when dropped in cold water. Remove from heat and add butter and vanilla. DON'T STIR. Let mixture sit until partially cooled. Beat with mixer until mixture loses gloss. Quickly add nuts and pour into buttered pan.

This is a holiday special at our house.

Chocolate Marshmallow Haystacks

Ingredients:
1 (3oz.) pkg. cream cheese, softened
2 tbsp. milk
2 cups sifted powdered sugar
2 (1oz.) squares unsweetened chocolate, melted
1/2 tsp. vanilla
Dash of salt
3 cups miniature marshmallows
Flaked coconut

Directions:
Combine softened cream cheese and milk, blending well. Gradually add sugar. Stir in chocolate, vanilla and salt. Fold in marshmallows. Drop by tsp. into coconut and toss til covered. Chill until firm.

Coconut Brittle

Ingredients:
2 cups sugar
1 cup white syrup
1/4 cup water
2 cups coconut
1 tsp. vanilla
3 tsp. soda

Directions:
In saucepan, combine sugar, syrup, and water. Heat to 225 degrees F. Add Coconut and cook to 300 degrees F. Remove from heat and add vanilla and soda. Pour onto sheets of buttered foil, or buttered shallow baking pan. When cool, break into pieces.

Christmas

Aunt Mary's Peanut Brittle

Ingredients:
2 cups sugar
1 cup light corn syrup
1 1/2 cups water
1 cup butter or margarine
2 cups raw Spanish peanuts
1 tsp. soda

Directions:
In large saucepan, combine sugar, syrup, and water. Cook and stir until sugar dissolves. When syrup boils, add butter and nuts. Stir frequently after it reaches syrup stage (230 degrees.) Cook until mixture reaches crack stage (300 degrees,) stirring constantly. Remove from heat and quickly stir in soda, mixing thoroughly. Pour onto two buttered cookie sheets. As candy begins to cool, stretch it out by lifting and pulling from edges with two forks, loosening from pan as soon as possible. Turn over and break into pieces.

We have been told that Aunt Mary became engaged to Uncle Hank in 1927, the same year Charles Lindberg made his famous Atlantic flight. When Mary broke her good news to her sister, she exclaimed "Oh, Mary, why couldn't it have been Lindy!"

Richard remembers one outstanding Christmas when Aunt Mary gave him the only roller skates he ever owned.

Supper Smoke

Peanut Butter Brittle

Ingredients:
1 (12oz.) pkg. peanut butter chips, divided
1 1/2 cups butter or margarine
1 3/4 cups sugar
3 tbsp. corn syrup
3 tbsp. water
1 1/2 cups chopped peanuts
1/2 cup semi-sweet chocolate mini-chips

Directions:
Butter a 9 by 13 inch pan and spread evenly with 1 cup of the peanut butter chips. Set aside.

In saucepan, melt butter. Add sugar, corn syrup and water and blend well. Cook, stirring constantly, to hard crack stage (300 degrees.) Remove from heat and stir in chopped peanuts. Pour into pan carefully, so as to not rearrange the peanut butter chips. Quickly spread the other 1 cup of peanut butter chips evenly over all and then the mini-chips. Cool and break in pieces to serve.

Glass Candy

Ingredients:
3 3/4 cups sugar
1 1/4 cups corn syrup
1 cup water
1 tsp. flavoring
Food coloring

Directions:
In large saucepan, combine sugar, corn syrup, and water. Mix well and bring to a boil and cook to 300 degrees, or hard crack stage. Quickly add flavoring and coloring to compliment the flavor you choose. Pour into pans, which have been dusted with powdered sugar. When hardened, break into pieces.

Christmas

Soda Cracker Crunch Candy

Ingredients:
1/2 cup butter or margarine, melted
1 cup evaporated milk
3 cups sugar
2/3 cup smooth peanut butter
1 cup flaked coconut
24 soda crackers, crumbled coarsely
1 tsp. vanilla

Directions:
In saucepan, combine butter, evaporated milk, and sugar, blending well. Cook over medium heat, stirring constantly and bring to a boil. Boil 4 minutes. Remove from heat and add peanut butter, coconut, crackers, and vanilla. Mix well and pour into buttered pan.

Bertha's Popcorn Balls

Ingredients:
2 1/4 cups brown sugar
1/2 cup butter or margarine
1 cup white syrup
1 can sweetened, condensed milk*
1 tsp. vanilla
12 quarts, or more, popped corn

Directions:
Combine first four ingredients in saucepan. Bring to a boil, stirring constantly, and cook to softball stage (234 degrees.) Remove from heat, add vanilla and pour over popcorn. Butter hands and form into balls.

*Homemade Sweetened Condensed Milk:
1 cup instant non-fat dry milk
1/3 cup boiling water
3 tbsp. butter or margarine, melted
2/3 cup sugar
1/8 tsp. salt
Combine all ingredients in blender and process until smooth. Equivalent to 14 oz. can

Supper Smoke

Caramel Corn

Ingredients:
1 gallon popped corn
1 cup brown sugar
1/2 cup butter or margarine
1/4 cup corn syrup
1/4 tsp. soda
1/4 tsp. salt

Directions:
In saucepan, combine sugar, butter, and syrup. Bring to a boil, stirring constantly, and cook for 3 or 4 minutes. Remove from heat and add soda and salt. Stir in quickly and pour over popped corn, mixing well. Spread out on well greased cookie sheet and bake for 1 hour at 200 degrees.

Lo-Fat Version:
Follow same procedure as above, but use this syrup recipe:
1 cup brown sugar
1/4 cup butter or margarine
1/4 cup corn syrup
1/4 cup molasses

**Popcorn pops better if dry kernels are stored in the refrigerator.

Rainbow Popcorn

Ingredients:
1 gallon popped corn
1/2 cup butter or margarine, melted
1/4 cup corn syrup
1 cup white sugar
1/8 tsp. cream of tartar
1/2 tsp. salt
1/2 tsp. soda
1/2 tsp. pure food flavoring (you can buy it in the drug stores in this area)
Food coloring

Directions:
In saucepan, combine butter, corn syrup and sugar, blending well. Bring to a boil, stirring constantly, and cook 6 minutes. While cooking, mix together the cream of tartar, salt and soda. Add these at end of cooking time. Remove from heat and add flavoring and color to compliment flavor you choose. Pour over popped corn and spread into well greased cooking sheet. Bake at 200 degrees for 1 hour.

For cinnamon flavor, add 1 (9oz.) pkg. Red Hots instead of food flavoring.

It's fun to make several flavors and combine for a party look.

Supper Smoke

Christmas 1998

I've been thinking of Mary, and of that awesome night.
What do you think she pondered, as the angels took their flight?
Did she feel her shoulders droop that night, within the lowly stall
And wonder how to raise a King—a promised one, for all?
Did she, while wrapping Jesus against the evenings chill,
Sense a lonely, winding path; a cross upon a hill?
I don't know, but as I ponder, I rather think that she
Just said a simple, heart-felt prayer, in words like you and me.
I think she told God, "It's so BIG…the world is cold tonight."
"I'll trust you, God of heaven, to give us warmth and light."
And then she kissed His downy head, so close to humble sod,
Crept to the arms of Joseph, and left it all with God.

We, too, look on a darkened world. We feel the pain and fear.
Ah…could we do like Mary (for angels linger near)
Could we but say a simple prayer, "It's BIG…the world is cold."
"I'll trust the God of heaven, just like in days of old."
Then lay our weary, aching hearts; within the King's own hands,
And creep into the arms of God, Who knows, and understands.

R.A.S.
Christmas 1998

Wassail

Ingredients:
1 orange
1 lemon
1 cup water
1 tsp. cloves
2 pieces cinnamon bark
2 quarts apple juice
1/2 cup brown sugar

Directions:
Squeeze the orange and the lemon, reserving the juice and rind. In saucepan, combine water and spices. Add the rinds. Place over heat and simmer for 45 minutes. Remove from heat and drain, reserving juice. In saucepan, combine apple juice, brown sugar, spice mixture, and reserved orange and lemon juices. Heat to boiling and serve.

The wassail bowl actually originated in Scandinavia, but was introduced in England in the 1400's. Wassail, in Old English wording, means be thou well.

So you can't go wrong on this one. It's warm and tasty and full of good wishes!

Supper Smoke

Old fashioned Egg Nog

Ingredients:
6 eggs, separated
1/2 cup sugar, divided
4 cups milk, divided
1/2 tsp. salt
1 pint whipping cream
2 tsp. vanilla
Nutmeg

Directions:
Beat egg yolks until light in color. Gradually add 1/4 of the sugar, beating well. Scald milk. Slowly stir in about 1 cup of the milk into egg yolk mixture. Return all of egg yolk mixture into the rest of the milk. Cook slowly over low heat, stirring constantly…not QUITE to a boil, and until mixture thickens somewhat. Remove from heat and chill.

Add salt to egg whites and beat until soft peaks form. Gradually add remaining 1/4 cup sugar, beating until mixture is stiff and glossy.

Whip cream until stiff. Fold egg white mixture into cooled custard. Add vanilla and carefully fold in whipped cream. Chill several hours. Just before serving, stir and add nutmeg to taste.

An entirely NICE noggin!

Christmas 2000

Christmas is coming! And the dear long-told story!
We bask in the blessings of that night filled with glory
And we think of that one who said" NO MORE ROOM."
What were his thoughts, staring out through the gloom?
Did he kick at the cat, and shout at his wife?
And say "IT'S NOT MY FAULT. I'VE NO TIME. THAT'S
JUST LIFE?"
Did he wake in the night, to toss on his bed?
And recall the tired maiden, and wish she were fed?
If only he'd listened, that dark lonely night,
And if only he'd looked, he'd have seen a warm light!
And stumbling, and falling, and leaving behind
All the mire of his thoughts, and the set of his mind—
He'd have swung wide the door, and knelt on the sod,
And found a new life, while he gazed at his God!

In all of our living, as ever before,
Let's take time to listen for that knock at our door.
Let's draw back the curtains that are shrouding our mind,
And search for the light that is humble, and kind.
Somewhere there is light for each dark, lonely road.
There's a spot on our knees where we're rid of our load.
There's a way of sweet peace for each step that we'll trod.
We can find a new life, as we gaze at our God!

R.A.S.
Christmas 2000

Supper Smoke

A Prayer

Lord, let me do my work this day.

If the darkened hours of despair overcome me, may I not forget the strength that comforted me in the desolation of other times.

May I remember the bright hours that found me walking over the silent hills of my childhood, or dreaming on the margin of a quiet river, when a light glowed within me and I promised my early God to have courage amid the tempest of the changing years. Spare me from bitterness and the sharp passions of unguarded moments.

May I not forget that poverty and riches are of the spirit. Though the world know me not, may my thoughts and actions be such as shall be friendly with myself. Lift my eyes from the earth, and let me not forget the meaning of the stars. Forbid that I should judge others, lest I condemn myself.

Let me not follow the clamor of the world, but walk calmly in thy path. Give me a few friends who will love me for what I am; and keep ever burning before my vagrant steps the kindly light of hope.

Though age and infirmity overcome me, and I come not within sight of the castle of my dreams, teach me to be thankful for life, and for time's golden memories that are good and sweet.

And may the evening's twilight find me gentle still.

-Author unknown

Table of Contents

Introduction ix

Dedication xiii

Appetizers and Beverages 1
    Ambrosia 11
    Berry Licuado 10
    Beverages 7
    Canned Tomato Juice 12
    Cappuccino Mix 13
    Citrus Punch 9
    Colorful Orangeade Punch 11
    Crab Dip 5
    Fireside Coffee 13
    Frothy Orange Drink 9
    Ham Ball 4
    Homemade Root Beer 8
    Honey Butter 6
    Mexican Mocha 7
    Olive Cream Cheese Dip 6
    Picante Bean Dip 5
    Razzy Lemonade 12
    Salinda's Easter Drink 7
    Snappy Oyster Crackers 6
    Spinach Dip 4
    Tango Mango Licuado 10
    Tea Brew 14
    Thumpin' Good Tea 15

A Sampler of Salads 21
    Apple Medley 27
    Apricot Pineapple Salad 47
    Bavarian Peach Mold 50
    BEST Cole Slaw Dressing 43

Broccoli Peanut Salad 38
Camella's Cherry Jell-O 48
Cherry Cola Salad 45
Citrus Crush Salad 48
College Salad 37
Creamy Orange Salad 49
Crunchy Crab Salad 36
Crunchy Pea Salad 39
Elaine's Creamy Cabbage 29
Five-Cup Fruit Salad 28
French Dressing 41
Frosted Lemon Jell-O 49
Graham Cracker Fluff 33
Hot Bean Salad 26
Ila's Potato Salad 25
Jo's Salad 39
Layered Lettuce Salad 34
Marjorie's Macaroni Salad 24
Martha Mae's Pineapple Delight 46
Michelle's Garden Salad 35
One More Cole Slaw! 30
Orange/Kiwi Delight 47
Phyllis's House Dressing 42
Pineapple Cream Salad 45
Potato or Macaroni Salad Dressing 44
Ranch Dressing 40
Red Mold Salad 50
Rippin' Good Rice 32
Simple Salad Dressing 40
South of the Border Dressing 44
Spring Rice Salad 31
The LAST Slaw Recipe! 30
Thousand Island Dressing 41
Twenty-four Hour Salad 28
Vickie's Seafood Pasta 23

Waldorf Coleslaw 29

Soups and Stews and Brothy Brews 53
   A Tad Tony Minestrone 68
   Big Old Brown Beef Stew 58
   Cauliflower Bacon Chowder 83
   Cheese 'N Chicken Chowder 69
   Chicken Barley Soup 70
   Chipper Chili 64
   Chompy Cheese Chowder 63
   Clam Chowder 59
   Cream of Broccoli Soup 81
   Cream of Cabbage Soup 82
   E.E.A.O.W.! Diet Vegetable Soup 85
   French Onion Beef Stew 57
   Hamburger Dumpling Soup 74
   Hamburger Stew 79
   Hissy Chicken Soup 72
   Humungous Hamburger Hullabaloo 76
   Lima Bean Stew 65
   Low Fat Bean/Rice Soup 86
   Meatball Stew 80
   Mexican Turkey Bean Soup 73
   North Idaho Moose Stew 56
   Pedacitos de Masa Stew 75
   Picante Tortilla Soup 78
   Pious Potato Soup 61
   Po' Boy Potato Soup 62
   Salmon Chowder 60
   Southern Chicken Gumbo 71
   Split Pea Soup 67
   Taco Soup 77
   Toothsome Tomato Soup 84
   Vegetable Bean Soup 66

What's For Supper? 91

Apricot-Onion Chicken 144
Baked Eggs 164
Barbeque Meatballs 104
Beef 'N Bean Tacos 120
Beef and Potato Nacho Casserole 128
Big Dinner Casserole 107
Biscuits: 140
Boneless Turkey Roast, Barbequed 148
Bread Pockets 94
Breakfast Sausage Casserole 160
Burrito Supreme 119
Café Con Leche 123
Cajun Red Beans and Rice 151
Carol's Chicken Casserole 135
Carole's Spaghetti Sauce 112
Chad's Grilled Chicken 143
Champion Cheesy Casserole 111
Chicken Biscuit Pie 140
Chicken Hash brown Casserole 141
Chicken or Pork Chop Coating 146
Chicken or Turkey Enchilada Casserole 139
Chicken Rice Casserole 136
Company Beans and Meatballs 105
Company Chicken Mushroom Casserole 134
Corn, Cheese and Wieners 155
Corned Beef 'N Cabbage 150
Corn Bread Pie 108
Crispy Baked Chicken 143
Deviled Tuna Bake 165
Easy Thanksgiving Day 147
Egg Salad Filling 167
Frankfurter Filling 167
Fried Chicken Casserole 137
Fry and Bake Chicken 144
Greek Chicken Roast 145

Haggis	153
Hamburger-Garden-Steamy-Creamy	109
Ham Barbeque Sandwiches	166
Ham or Bacon Quiche	162
Helen's Meat Loaf	95
Karen's Burritos	121
Karen's Stromboli	149
Laredo Casserole	127
Leftover Sunday	130
Little Quiche	161
Lo-Fat Gravy	168
Marjorie's Verenicka Casserole	156
Meatball Spaghetti Sauce	114
Meatball Stroganoff	99
Meat and Taters	106
Mediterranean Meal	138
Mexican Pizza	115
Mexican Rice	125
Mezetti	116
Mini-Meatloaves	96
Mountain Macaroni A fine recipe from the Swiss Alps	110
Mushroom Meatball Supreme	100
Oven Barbeque Chicken	142
Paco's Hamburgers	122
Pizza Burgers	117
Poor Man Steak	97
Pop-Over Pizza	118
Porky Pig Pie	152
Pork Adobo	133
Rice and Mushroom Casserole	99
Roast Beef Sandwich Spread	166
Round Steak Bake	132
Salsa Verde	123
Sausage Zucchini Bake	158
Seaman Supper Steak	98

Spaghetti Casserole	113
Spam Sham	157
Spicy Rice	124
Steak 'N Gravy	131
Stewed Chicken	141
Sunday Dinner Roast	129
Supper Sausage Casserole	159
Sweet & Sour Meatballs	103
Taco Quiche	163
Tamale Balls	102
The Enchilada Casserole	126
Turkey Meatballs	101
Vegetable pizza	117
Yummy Sandwich Filling	165

Bread and Beyond 173

Apple Streusel Coffee Cake	218
Banana Cream Muffins	209
Best Bran Muffins	216
BEST Whole Wheat Buns	188
Blueberry Muffins	214
Bonanza Bread Bowls	195
Boston Brown Bread	223
Breakfast Cake	222
Buttermilk Bran Muffins	211
Buttermilk Wheat Bread	180
Butter Dips	205
Cheese Crunchies	207
Cheesy Spud Buns	190
Chocolate Chip Banana Muffins	213
Cinnamon Rolls	198
Coffee Cake Muffins	208
Corn Meal Mountain Pancakes	224
Country Corn Bread	201
Crunchy Sweet Cornbread	201
Dandelion Jelly	227

Edith's Banana Bread	222
Farmhouse Biscuits	204
Favorite Oatmeal Rolls	189
Fiona's French Bread	184
French Bread Fillings	185
Fruit-filled Coffee Cake	221
Good Old Potato Buns	186
Grapefruit Jelly	227
Harvest Bread	181
Hearty Bran Muffins	215
Heavenly Waffles	224
Homemade Noodles	223
Honey Bun Cake	219
Hot Cross Buns #1	199
Hot Cross Buns #2	200
Italiano Cheese Twists	194
Italian Bread Sticks	193
Italian Parmesan Bread	182
Just Plain Good Coffee Cake	220
Lemon Poppy Seed Muffins	216
Light Baking Powder Biscuits	205
Mackie's Bundt Bread	183
Magnificent Muffins	217
Marlyn's Rolls	192
Mary's Brown Soda Bread	206
Mexican Corn Bread	202
Michelle's Biscuits	203
Momovers	218
Oatmeal Bread	179
Oaty-Apple Muffins	210
Overnight Pancakes	225
Pioneer Bread	176
Pluckets	187
Potato Bread	178
Quickie Cheese Biscuits	204

Ranch Rolls	191
Rose Petal Jelly	226
Saturday Sweet Rolls	197
Settler's Bread	177
The Great Pumpkin Muffin	212
Whole Wheat Bread Bowls	196

Vegetables	**231**
Baked Beans	241
Barbeque Green Beans	239
Cheddar Cheese Sauce	242
Grandma Amelia Amoth's Beet Pickles	244
Green Bean Supreme	239
Harvard Beets	237
Jazzy Carrots	238
Mom's Tomato Sauce	245
New Pan Potatoes	237
North Dakota Tomato Jam	243
Onion Bag Potatoes	235
Potato Cheese Casserole	236
Scalloped Potatoes	233
Shortcut Baked Beans	242
Tater Kryspies	234
Tex Mex Potatoes	232
Veggie Dip or Vegetables Incognito	240
Zippy Potatoes	232
Zucchini Relish	246

Just Desserts	**253**
Bread Pudding	262
Cherry Torte	266
Chocolate Date Dessert	264
Chocolate Marshmallow Dessert	263
Chocolate Peanut Supreme	258
Cranberry Apple Crisp	261
Éclair Torte	265

Fruit Pizza	260
Heavenly Raspberry Crunch	267
Huckleberries 'N Cream Supreme	268
Huckleberry Cake Dessert	256
Huckleberry Marshmallow Dessert	257
Marlyns's Fluted Cake Dessert	259
Norwegian Apple Pie	254
River Picnic Dessert	269
Strawberry Angel Food	255
"Let them eat cake!"	273
Absolutely Divine Devil's Food Cake	280
Angel Feather Icing	306
Angel Food Frosting	310
Applesauce Cupcakes	304
Blue Ribbon Banana Cake	298
Cake Mix Extender	305
Caramel Butter Sauce	312
Caramel Fudge Cake	275
Carrot Layer Cake	294
Chocolate Apple Cake	281
Chocolate Brownie Loaf	277
Chocolate Chip Fudge Frosting	308
Chocolate Date Dandy Cake	279
Chocolate Fudge Mallow	309
Chocolate Pumpkin Cupcakes	301
Cinnamon Bundt Cake	292
Cinnamon Sauce	311
Cocoa Fluff	311
Crystallized Flowers	313
Decorator Frosting	307
Double Lemon Cake	286
English Toffee Cake	299
Fudge Cream Frosting	308
Fudge Nut Cake	274
German Chocolate Frosting	310

Good Old Chocolate Cake 278
Graham Streusel Cake 290
Jo's Applesauce Cake 296
June's Chocolate Sour Cream Cake 276
Lazy Carrot Cake 295
Lemon Glazed Nectar Cake..293
Lemon Pineapple Cupcakes 303
Lemon Sauce.. 312
Lemon Streusel Cake 288
Maple Carrot Cupcakes 302
Moist Chocolate Cake 279
Pig-Lickin' Good Cake 285
Pineapple Torte 289
Pumpkin Cream Bundt Cake...291
Pumpkin Roll 297
Quick Fudge Frosting 309
Raspberry Cake... 284
Short Cake 305
Sour Cream Cake...283
Spring Dream Cake 287
Strawberry Cake..282
Surprise Cupcakes 300
Thrifty Frosting 307

Pie Baking...319
Banana Cream Pie...323
Beatlenut Pie 327
Cherry Pie Filling 337
Chocolate Pecan Pie 331
Cocoa Pie...320
Custard Mincemeat Pie...329
Fan's Pecan Pie...330
Foolproof Meringue 343
French Apple Pie 335
Fresh Berry Pie 339
Fruit Measures 340

Gloria's Pumpkin Pie 326
Green Tomato Mincemeat 332
Huckleberry Pie 336
Jell-O Fruit Pie 338
Lemon Meringue Pie 322
Light Pumpkin Pie 327
Lois's Rhubarb Pie 333
Magnolia Pie 331
Meringue 342
Michelle's Chocolate Pie 321
Oil Piecrust 341
Peanut Butter Cream Pie 323
Pineapple Cream Pie 325
Pineapple Mandarin Pie 334
Raisin Cream Pie 324
Raspberry Dream Pie 339
Rhubarb Custard Pie 334
Sour Cream Raisin Pie 324
Tiny Pecan Pies 328
Vinegar/Egg Pie Crust 342

The Old Cookie Jar 347
Amish Sugar Cookies 350
Aunt Florence's Tender Crisp Sugar Cookies 351
Brittle Cookies 380
Chocolate Caramel Pecan Bars 384
Chocolate Chip Meringues 357
Chocolate Crackles 355
Chocolate Cream Cheese Bars 378
Chocolate Oatmeal Bars 382
Chocolate Orange Brownies 377
Chocolate Peanut Clusters 356
Cinnamon Swirl Cookies 352
Cream Cheese Brownies 374
Crunchy Marshmallow Bars 381
Double Chocolate Oatmeal Cookies 369

Famous Candy Bars 383
Fudge Nuggets 354
Gingerbread Whoopie Pies 367
Golden Carrot Cookies 364
Gumdrop Cookies 365
Lacey Oatmeal Cookies 368
Lemon Snaps 352
Melting Moments 360
Meringue Cookies 358
Molasses Oatmeal Treats 373
Mom's Molasses Cookies 349
No-Bake Butterscotches 373
North Dakota Date Bars 374
Oatmeal Apple Bars 379
Oatmeal Cinnamon Cookies 370
Oatmeal Fruit Cookies 371
Oatmeal Peanut Cookies 370
Old Fashioned Cookies 348
Peanut-Butterscotch Bars 375
Peanut Butter Maple Cookies 362
Peanut Crunch Cookies 361
Raisin-Filled Cookies 363
Raisin Date Bars 376
Really Good Chocolate Chip Cookies 357
Sharon's Brownies 375
Snickerdoodles 359
Snow on the Mountain Cookies 353
Spicy Molasses Drops 372
Therapy Cookies 369
Whole-Wheat Snickerdoodles 360
Whoopie Pies 366

Christmas 389
    Aunt Mary's Peanut Brittle 415
    Bertha's Popcorn Balls 417
    Bunuelos 392

Caramel Corn 418
Chocolate Divinity 410
Chocolate Marshmallow Haystacks 413
Chocolate Pizza 397
Christmas Pie #1 404
Christmas Pie #2 405
Clam Chowder 393
Coconut Brittle 414
Date Cookies 400
Divinity 408
Fruitcake Cookies 399
Glass Candy 416
Holiday Divinity 409
Judy's Humdingers 398
Layered Christmas Salad 394
Mom's Applesauce Cake 403
No-bake Fruitcake 402
Norwegian Lefse 391
Old fashioned Egg Nog 422
Peanut Butter Brittle 416
Penuche 413
Peppermint Pie 406
Rainbow Popcorn 419
Seaman Fudge 412
Soda Cracker Crunch Candy 417
"Square" Jell-O 395
Velvety Fudge 411
Wassail 421

CPSIA information can be obtained at www.ICGtesting.com
Printed in the USA
LVOW041719210612

287115LV00006B/87/A